ESTRELLAS ERRANTES

Frederick Guttmann R.

WANDERING STARS, THE HISTORY OF THE UFO PHENOMENON

First edition. April 8, 2024.

Copyright © 2024 Frederick Guttmann.

ISBN: 979-8230661399

Written by Frederick Guttmann.

2011

1

Thanks to Aday Quintero, who helped me unconditionally with the review of my first works, and likewise a great appreciation to Abiam Palomares and for his collaboration in accompanying materials.

Thanks also to my father, my mother and my brothers.

I dedicate this book to those people who live in uncertainty or ignorance about extraterrestrial issues and the UFO phenomenon.

" You chased them in Your storm, You consumed them in Your whirlwind "
(Jasher 89:16)

In collaboration with:
Aday Quintero P.
Spelling, Grammar and Contexts

Frederick Guttmann Ramirez, 2011
Email: frederickguttmann@gmail.com
Web: www.frederickguttmann.com[1]
Revision:
Aday Quintero P.
296 pages
Original ISBN: 978-84-613-3062-1.
Registration No. 00/2008/4086
Legal Deposit: TF1562-2009

---

1.   http://www.frederickguttmann.com

CONTENT

INTRODUCTION

According *to a United Nations report, since 1947 more than 150 million people have witnessed sightings around the world. More than 20,000 of them have been documented landings."*
FastWalkers (SafeSpace - Disclosure Project)

MY INTEREST IN UFOS was born from reading several books in my teens about visits from other worlds, novels about life in nearby galaxies, and accounts of people who had been taken in spaceships to other planets. It was disheartening to think that this could not be true in such a large universe, being indoctrinated into the fact that in our galaxy alone there are millions of suns like ours and therefore the fact that there are systems like ours is quite plausible. If not, "how much wasted space". All this in a universe of so many possibilities makes it possible to conceive of life on other worlds, even analogous ones, such as Mars or Venus, in our own "neighborhood", or even below our surface. Even with everything, liking this genre or not, I had to verify that all these matters had reliability in the light of found artifacts, documents, filming, photographs, testimonies and other types of substantial evidence, which led to the next step in my life: full dedication to research.

I grew up in a very appropriate environment for these philosophies since the UFO issue in my family was neither a new subject nor a taboo subject, moreover, it was an area that was used to be touched on naturally and regularly. My father used to tell his friends about his striking UFO experience while working for the Colombian airline Avianca, as a flight captain. He describes his experience in those days, but not before talking about a case that caught the attention of the airline staff: «*In the 70s, the director of international pilots of one of the best-known Colombian aviation companies left above from the table of the Director of Flight Operations his letter of resignation, valid only if he did not return to continue his work in three days. With the frankness that the case warranted, this veteran aviator told his superior, who, like many other crew members in the country, knew about the extraterrestrial experiences of that pilot, that one of the following days he could be transported to another planet as a result of his constant contacts with these brothers of the galaxy. Unfortunately, that event did not happen due to the leak of the event that led to the presence of some people who apparently prevented that experience. A few years later that pilot, in good retirement, died of natural causes. In the year 1974, a couple of pilots from the same company on one of their flights suddenly found themselves with an artifact in front of them, in mid-flight, and seconds after observing it on their own initiative they made a couple of movements which were responded in the same way by that ship, 'undoubtedly not terrestrial', in the opinion of the then first officer. The experience lasted about seven to ten minutes, tops. The discoid-shaped device, with a matt silvery metallic appearance, surrounded by fast lights with splashing bright metallic tones, was suddenly seen on the co-pilot's side for about three minutes and in the same way disappeared to be seen on the commander's side by others. minutes when, after doing a maneuver that seemed like a greeting, he disappeared. A year later, the commander died with his crew and passengers in an accident when the plane crashed against a hill in the west of that country.*» (Felix G. Katchinsky)

In this unconventional youth and full of dedication to books -mainly archaeology, astronomy, mineralogy, mythology, theology and languages-, studying at the "Almirante Cristóbal Colón" Naval Academy in Colombia, I had the opportunity to hear testimonies from other people on flying saucers and marry abductions. However, the apparitions to my own family were always alive in our memories. For example, when we mentioned these topics, my mother told that on a couple of occasions she saw flying objects. At that time, she asked God, what were UFOs? Were they real? And what relationship did they have with the Holy Scriptures? Since my father maintained that the angels of antiquity were the aliens of the present and there were many discussions between them around these issues. One September afternoon in the late 1970s was the propitious moment for the sighting. My mother recounts: « *I was in Marseille (France) [...] even summer in Europe. I was on the 9th floor, at about 5 in the afternoon, when suddenly I saw a flying device in the shape of a hat in front of the building. It was like metallic [but] not shiny. I could see three oval windows like those in airplanes through which lights on inside the device could be seen. [...] As I was saying, you could see the hat on the side that was facing me, three oval windows illuminated inside, and below the hat, in the oval that would correspond to where the head would go, a glow of light as if it had a sun in there The hat-shaped device was flying at the same height as the 9th floor I was on, and it was so close that I could see its illuminated interior like an airplane. The speed with which it flew was like that of a helicopter, [however] it made no sound. And his flight was permanently horizontal. The people I was visiting at that time told me that it was a UFO, that they were used to seeing it and that they have their bases there in the sea. It was a local couple from the city, older people and quite educated. The device that I saw was similar to those that I have seen in some UFO photographs, with the difference that it had an intense glow from below in the form of a central sun that I have not seen in any of the photos. At that time I was an Avianca stewardess, which means that I was familiar with airplanes and it was easier for me to deduce what I was seeing in broad daylight and totally sober .»*

Flying Saucers or Collective Hysteria?

The notion of alien visitation is clearly not new to anyone. Some filmmakers such as George Lucas, James Cameron, Michael Bay or Steven Spielberg have given a transcendental approach to life outside of Earth and in relation to creatures from outer space, although many times they have done so with a somewhat exaggerated and fanciful approach. . This is part of the heritage of the so-called "science fiction", despite the fact that famous writers, great researchers, renowned soldiers and presidents -such as Ronald Reagan, Jimmy Carter and John F. Kennedy- have argued that such visits are part of the record. history of virtually every culture on Earth. Likewise, many people assume that they have been contacted by entities from other dimensions and other worlds for decades, even before the modern era of ufology, or let's say, official ufology, as they forcefully stated at the end of the first decade of the 21st century. the former Minister of Defense of Canada or the Prime Minister of Japan.

The UFO issue and its relationship with the appearance and development of man and existing life forms aroused more controversy than Darwin's Theory of Evolution itself, when it began to be aired in all the media in the 70s. Popularly to the People were impregnated with the idea of believing that the so-called UFOs were the result of a collective phenomenon born in the mid-40s, after the Second World War, when people still thought that an armed conflict or an air attack by some enemy nation and for this reason they were more curious with the visions in the sky. The truth is that reports of sightings of flying objects go back, not decades, but millions of years ago, which is clear when we look at the museum artifacts unearthed from the bowels of the Earth and the cave paintings of such alleged "cavemen". Likewise, the appearance of beings that are not from this planet are mentioned by great historians, chroniclers and scribes of the past, so we may be dealing with a topic that should be given some priority and annexed to history as it appears in the Royal Encyclopedia. British.

Entering into UFO matter is touching a subject of countless testimonies from all over the globe. In other words, " *the evidence is overwhelming and there is no doubt: flying saucers are real, many come from outside the planet Earth, although others do not...* " (Stanton Friedman, nuclear physicist and member of the Disclosure Project) And they have certainly been here since time immemorial, in fact, they have participated and taken a radical part in our affairs, mainly in hiding. The word UFO was born at radar stations and not on the streets, in the 1940s, when operators detected unusual artifacts that appeared in visors and did not respond to any flag, made impossible turns, did not follow any known flight pattern. , they violently broke the laws of gravity and potentially exceeded the sound barrier – at that time it was hardly a question of overcoming Match 1. It was proven that these vehicles were capable of entering the ocean and staying there indefinitely, they could move on the atmosphere at seemingly unlimited speeds – that is, they were able to maneuver around a space shuttle leaving Earth (they have been filmed shooting down some, potentially nuclear warheads that the US and Russia were carrying into space) and could exit the biosphere and get lost in infinity. Clarify that the fastest plane (Lockheed SR-71a "BlackBird") of the 90s barely exceeded Match 3 –made precisely to chase UFOs, but discontinued when it was seen that they cheated speed-, and this if we are not talking about vehicles US secrets like Aurora, or even a shuttle (Match 45. That is, about 44 times the speed of sound).

The birth of modern ufology

Despite the amount of information about the so-called UFOs (Unidentified Flying Objects), the military forces, under the protection of the governments, assumed all authority over the control of information in relation to said devices and their crews, as well as the study of its technology. None of this should, nor for the moment, should come to light officially, according to those who hold power, although groups such as the Vatican and some governments such as Brazil, the United Kingdom and France have already declared, in a certain way, that it was. there are ETs and visitors in their space vehicles, giving the public some reports they have on the "phenomenon".

UFOs were not really a national security issue until mass sightings between 1945 and 1948 shocked the world's population – not coincidentally after the US bombed the Japanese cities of Hiroshima and Nagasaki. At first, the American and Russian military forces believed that they were the Kugelblitze (also called by the Germans "Feuerbälle", that is: "Fireball"), Haunebu or Vril vehicles, secretly manufactured by the Luftwaffe during World War II. World War. This theory, however, was disproved when a discoidal ship crashed in Aztec, New Mexico, where the Armed Forces recovered bodies of beings that were not from this world along with mutilated human and animal bodies. The news alarmed then US President Dwight Eisenhower, who would have been General of the US Armed Forces in the attack against the Third Reich and the invasion of Berlin. Eisenhower mentioned the problem to his great friend Nelson Rockefeller, who took full control of it. This was added to a famous accident in Roswell, also in New Mexico, where an alien pilot was recovered alive, whom the renowned scientist Vannevar Bush nicknamed "EBE-1" (Extraterrestrial Biological Entity 1). I have to say that Vannevar Bush was already studying these ships before the war, but he did not make much progress, since President Franklin Delano Roosevelt told him that he would not receive any more money for the moment: "not now [we can give him *those funds*], *first we have to win the war*." (Statement by a senior White House official and adviser to Delano Roosevelt) On that occasion it was a ship that crashed on the ground before the US entered World War II.

Since then, until at least the 1990s, more than 40 artifacts have been captured and hidden by groups such as Alpha Team and Delta Force. These objects have been thoroughly studied and the survivors have been kept in captivity and under heavy interrogation and control measures. Keeping the public out of the truth was the most important purpose for which the CIA (Central Intelligence Agency) and important personalities were commissioned, so that anyone who spoke on the subject would be ridiculed, or if they had truthful information and trustworthy, he would be assassinated without delay. The UFO affair became almost as secret as the Manhattan Project.

A detailed study by the NSA (National Security Agency) discovered that the aforementioned UFOs were, for the most part, vehicles of extraterrestrial and extra-dimensional origin. For this reason the Navy called them VEDs (Extra-Dimensional Vehicles) and determined that they belonged to several different groups of civilizations. The military sources concluded that the vast majority were not hostile despite the fact that they classified 4 important groups that denoted an important confrontation between unions. Some of them would be identical to us and would come from places like: Vega in the Constellation of Lyra, Pleiades in the Constellation of Taurus, Arturo, Orion, Antares in the Constellation of Scorpio, the main moons of Jupiter, the moon Titan on Saturn, from Sirius and, according to others, from the planet Nibiru, cited by the sumerologist Zecharia Sitchin, among others.

Regressive war groups were also distinguished from these groups, with which important diplomatic relations were established, regardless of the media. The military who delved into the origin and motivation of these entities discovered that these organisms or Macrobes have been involved in the history of humanity and implicated in satanism, the occult and in relation to bankers, royalty and political leaders. This was terrifying and therefore has been cunningly kept hidden from the eyes of society. Now all this must see the light!

1.

PREHISTORIC VISITS

"In my Father's house there are many mansions; if it were not so, I would have told you; I go to prepare a place for you."
Jesus of Nazareth (Book of John 14:2, New Testament)

THE PRESENTER OF THE famous Coast to Coast radio station has recently said that he has never seen *"so many people stressed and doing absurd things.»* They are used to interviewing many people who talk about UFO testimonies and emphasize the change of humanity to receive a new century, but not before experiencing a series of upsetting events that are collapsing society. Many people say they have had some kind of experience with extraterrestrial beings and have received great knowledge from them. Much material is collected on this, letting us know, according to them, that in our world there are 250,000 extraterrestrial cultures working on all kinds of levels and dimensions. But those who have stood out the most in recent years are the Mayans, who say that at some point in 2015 the ETs will officially arrive in our world.

The Mayans themselves affirm that the changes for the new era have already begun since the late 90s, but we will go through a transcendental stage between the end of December 2012 and

February 2013. Although many who follow their prophecies believe that the world It will end between December 21 and 23, 2012, but the Mayans themselves have admitted that they already foresaw real changes since October 24, 2004 – when Comet Holmes was in our solar system, the largest body ever to enter our solar system. our celestial neighborhood- going through 7 or 8 years, making a kind of window of time that will take us to said new age, so quoted when talking about this mysterious town. But if this fact is so close, there will be more evidence, such as the Sumerian references that hint that we will soon meet our father, Sirius B, and our mother, Marduk –both are referred to as civilizations of giant beings. So, let's start the journey, because there is a lot to study.

ANCIENT ALIENS

The mention of extraterrestrial beings is as old as the history of the Earth itself. Contact Groups talk a lot about humans in prehistoric times, coming from the stars, but in archeology we see much clearer examples, such as paintings, writings, and artifacts. Who are they and where do they come from? To begin this section we must emphasize what an "alien" is. The word "alien" comes from the English language and means "foreigner". Aliens or visitors from the stars have always been portrayed in paintings, realistic figures have been made of them and they have even been venerated and dedicated to all kinds of rituals, considering them Masters, Spirits, Angels, Gods or Demons. We could say that the children of the stars, gods or the aliens of the ufological era, are an important section to take into account since they are the sovereign reason for the amazing social and technological progress of the human race since the Stone Age.

This chapter will be dedicated to the physical evidence that constitutes part of the E-2, or "Close Encounters in the Second

Phase" and that are a valuable treasure trove of solvent records in the knowledge and understanding of who are those who have been visiting us and what intentions have had. Furthermore, why have they not been openly disclosed? Archeology and paleontology have been arbitrarily censored as sources of information and science has presented only what has been convenient for them to support their popularly accepted paradigms and theories. Now let's see some of the reasons why. The alien presence has not only been part of the conspiracy under the imperial power of our world, but has appeared in the scientific and archaeological record so that we know of its existence.

The presence of some metals may be of extraterrestrial origin

As James Brenan, co-author of an important work on the primordial conditions of our planet, explains, *"the extreme temperature at which the Earth's core formed more than 4 billion years ago would have completely devastated any precious metal in the rocky crust. and would have deposited them in the core."* So the question for these scientists was why there are detectable concentrations of precious metals such as platinum and rhodium in the rocky part of the Earth: *"Our results indicate that these could not have ended up there by any known internal process and instead from this they must have been added as a "rain" of extraterrestrial debris, such as comets and meteorites»*, explains the researcher. Geologists have long speculated that 4.5 billion years ago Earth was a cold mass of rock mixed with iron metal that was melted by heat generated by the impact of planet-sized objects, allowing the iron to break apart. rock and form the Earth's core.

The scientists recreated the extreme pressure and temperatures of this process, subjected to a similar mix of temperatures above 2,000°C, and measured the composition of the resulting rock and iron. Because the rock is stripped of metal in the process, scientists speculate that the same thing would have happened when the

Earth formed and that some kind of external source, such as a shower of extraterrestrial material, contributed to the presence of some precious metals in the earth. the outer rock portion of Earth today: *« The notion of extraterrestrial rain could also explain another mystery, which is how the rock portion of Earth came to have hydrogen, carbon and phosphorus, the essential components of life, which they were probably lost during Earth's violent start,"* concludes Brenan.

The Harvard scientist, John A. Ball, reflecting on the subject said: *« ...Most evolutionists believe that it (life) was generated long ago, but perhaps it never was... Perhaps the Earth was infected from somewhere else...»* An interesting comment from the fascinating book "Mankind, Child of the Stars" (Mankind, Child of the Stars) can also be highlighted, where Max H. Flint and Otto O. Binder detail a very important anomaly: *«...molybdenum, a very rare metal plays an important role as a traceable element in the psychology of all creatures on Earth. It is surprising, therefore, that life so dependent on a rare metal arose in a world like ours, where molybdenum is so scarce...»* Which supports part of the Panspermia Theory, which would be aimed at thinking that life was brought here from other parts of the cosmos by superior intelligences.

Founders of ID (Intelligent Design), a new and bolder creationist branch, such as Michael J. Behe, a biochemist at the University of Pennsylvania, and other biologists, biochemists, chemists, physicists, philosophers, and historians wage war on Darwinism and assume that the creator of man could even be of extraterrestrial origin. If we allow for the idea that life had been brought here, we must reread the quotes from the Peruvian researcher and alleged contactee Sixto Paz Wells: *« Visitors came to our world from a planetary system in the constellation Cygnus, 6,000 light years away. of our Solar System. They planted spores in our world, about 3,000 million years ago, to change the acidity of the seas and make them alkaline, and thus modify the chemical conditions of the planet. This first humanity or extraterrestrial civilization is known as Antarctica or the Ancient Fathers.»* According to Sixto P. Wells, Pleiadian humans would bring patterns of life from Orion, which explains all the innumerable representations of this constellation in prehistory. Moreover, since 1990, Christopher Chyba, from the Institute for the Search for Extraterrestrial Intelligence, proposed that the water and gases in the Earth's atmosphere come from collisions with comets, meteorites, etc. that not only brought water and gases but also amino acids and other organic molecules. Evidence that this could have been the case is that the presence of kerogen, ethane and methane was detected in Halley's, Hale-Bopp and Hijakutake comets. Today this theory, called "panspermia" by the scientists who support it, points to the Orion nebula as the possible origin of the first molecules on Earth.

Alan Alford, one of many scientists who are open to the concept of extraterrestrial intervention, explains the anomalies surrounding the origin and supposed evolution of man: *«Homo sapiens has acquired a modern anatomy, language capacity and a sophisticated brain (much more beyond the necessities of their daily existence) apparently in defiance of the laws of Darwinism. There are a number of possible explanations for this anomaly. One is that humanity evolved in the sea, and that crucial fossil evidence is missing. Another is that Darwinian theory itself has a missing link. And a third explanation is that the genes of modern man were suddenly implanted by an intelligent extraterrestrial species that colonized the Earth."*

Master's Man

Although some of these references are documented in our work "Creation vs. Evolution", it is necessary to highlight them for the occasion, citing their relevance to understand that life led to this planet, not by chance, but deliberately. The human footprints, dubbed "Meister's Man," are a key point supporting the Prehistoric Astronaut Theory. We have already said that in 1968, William J. Meister – a collector of trilobites - discovered a stone that had the outline of a sandal, a shoe or a boot marked, and under the footprint there was a trilobite (see my book 'Creation vs. Evolution'). It is important to note that trilobites are believed to have disappeared more than 280 million years ago. The discovery occurred in a slate field near Antelope Spring (Utah, USA). The estimated date for its "printing" ranges from 590 to 505 million years. This suggests that "someone" was walking the Earth's surface at a time when the first forms of life were just appearing. Could it be precisely those who would have come to disseminate them?

The Tafilalet dwarf and other visitors

When we analyze the life that could have existed on our planet in the early days of its cooling -according to the official version-, based on the findings, we see a recognizable technology typical of intelligent beings. Moroccan professor Mohamed Zarouit discovered in July 2005, in the south of Morocco in the Tafilalet desert, a small skull measuring 6cm high by 3.9cm wide with its 32 corresponding teeth, belonging to the species Homo (modern man). The most surprising thing about this finding is not only its tiny size but the age of the aforementioned, which dates back to 360 million years. Let us bear in mind that 360 million years is older than that of the dinosaurs themselves, that is, this clarifies that they have always been able to be here. The Ica stones themselves speak of small beings living with dinosaurs, as it is referred to in cave paintings and affirm some assumptions Contacted with extraterrestrials, who even say that precisely people from other worlds, such as Mars, brought the dinosaurs a few hundred years ago. millions of years.

The same apparent Contactees say that the inhabitants of those times were dwarfs and giants, two typologies that later disappeared.

In places like the bed of the Paluxy River in Texas (USA) they found human footprints and dinosaur footprints, but those human footprints measured 38cm, which means that they belonged to a being of a stupendously tall size. Although we dealt with the evidence of giant human beings in the book The Sakla Rebellion, we can anticipate that the evidence of enormous human beings, in the era of the dinosaurs, coincides with the statements of the prestigious German scientist Her Horbigger that "*there were men in the Tertiary.*» So, if there were extraterrestrial civilizations on Earth billions of years ago, that explains the rhomboid, pyramidal, circular artifacts and unknown writing found in strata from 2.8 billion years old (spheres from the Klerksdrop Museum in South Africa) and up to 4,000 million years (Virtual Alien Museum of Grave Mountain, Kentucky – USA). Could all these artifacts be left behind by those who came to bring life, according to this theory?

The human civilizations of the age of the dinosaurs

Researcher Sixto Paz Wells, son of a high-ranking Peruvian military officer and who claims to have been advised by human beings from the Ganymede satellite on Jupiter, also cites some curious narratives of what would happen in prehistory. Sixto Paz says, for example, that a Pleiadian civilization was established in South America during the cooling of planet Earth, called Kayona, founded 100 million years ago. There are dozens of stories about aliens in prehistory and they are all interesting, mainly because of their parallelism. After studying many of them and checking if they have any archaeological support that supports them, I have discovered too many coincidences to call it a fable.

Another person who claims to have been contacted, if any, by people from Andromeda, Alex Collier, argues that many of the dinosaurs in our world were brought here from Mars and, for example, dolphins and whales would have been brought from

Sirius. According to this story, about 65 million years ago, some humans from the Pleiades stars, after "repairing" the depredation of the planet as a result of a great meteoric impact, settled on Earth with a large laboratory ship, a technological marvel of 50km in diameter that also functioned as a greenhouse on a now-defunct continent, «*the one that the English zoologist Philip R. Slater called Lemuria. This would be a land bridge between Africa and Madagascar...*». The researcher Drunvalo Melkisedek said that this continent was located near the Chilean Easter Island in the Pacific Ocean -where there are some huge stones in the shape of a human face whose origin is apparently unknown- (some Contactees say that they represent the Nephilim). In fact, Easter and Hawaii could be remnants of said civilization. Although all of these researchers seem to still be digressing on certain ideas, their contributions can serve as small pieces in the ancient puzzle. We are talking, then, that there could be more than one group of continent islands, one between Madagascar and Africa, another (Gondwana) to the southwest of Africa, another in the Pacific and another in the North Atlantic, which could be cradles of humanity. There is more evidence in favor of this supposition than against it and, in addition, we have a host of discoveries from those eras that mix advanced technology with caveman knowledge, but even so, much earlier than the age determined for said appearance according to the Theory of the Column. Geology proposed by the British Charles Darwin.

The Chinese Roswell

The general question of those who hear about this topic is that if those visitors were so sophisticated, why did they write in stone and in such an archaic way? The answer lies in Albert Einstein's statement: " *I don't know what the Third World War will be like, but the Fourth will be with sticks and stones .*" And it's even better glimpsed in the words of alternative historian, Michael Tsarion:

" *every evidence of the technology that brought this civilization to a violent end was incinerated in a nuclear exchange* ." (Interview on the Sci-Fi network) As we discussed in "Creation vs. Evolution", Peking University archeology professor Chi Pu Tei found tombs with buried skeletons, skulls and weak bones in a cave at Bayan Kara-Ula. On the walls it is said that they found figures alluding to these little men together with images of the solar system. Next to it, 716 disks were discovered that were charged with electricity, which is the conclusion some Russian scientists came to when studying them and studying their millimeter spiral graphs. According to a study in the 60s, it was concluded that the records reported an event that occurred 12,000 years ago, warning that the hosts came from heaven in a UFO that crashed in those mountains. Professor Nui, who translated this unknown script, was not taken seriously and left the country for Japan, but information about the extraterrestrial provenance of the record writers remains plausible in the results.

In the mountains of the area there are legends of tiny beings that came from heaven. According to the engravings on the discs, the Dropa tribe would have come from somewhere on the triple star Sirius. This issue has recently been studied by Matthew Hurley, author of "The Alien Chronicles." He highlights the figures of triangular-shaped flying objects found in stone carvings in Pashville, France, or astronauts carrying strange artifacts found in Valcamoni, Italy, which date back to 10,000 BC. We know that tens of thousands of disks similar to those have been found. dropa, called "Jade Bi", discovered throughout China for centuries. This is confirmed by Peter J. Lu of the Department of Physics at Harvard University. Also in China there are jars from 3,000 BC with beautiful spiral drawings. On that date the Egyptians also represented the hieroglyphics and among them the number 100 with the symbol of a spiral, although others believe that they are a representation of a galaxy. Likewise, what is now called the "Lalldoff Plate" from Nepal was discovered in the area, a piece from 4,000 years ago, which shows a disk-shaped UFO and an alien, similar to the gray ones described in various abduction cases. These discs are presumed to belong to the Dropa tribe.

Cheops had an alien friend

In 1987 the French Egyptologist Louis Caparat began negotiations with the Egyptian government with the intention of carrying out a series of excavations at the Great Pyramid which has been attributed to Cheops. The reason was that, according to Caparat, the most important rooms of the pyramid had not yet been discovered. Only he and his three helpers could dig there and access the hidden treasures. The Minister of Education and the French chancellor at the time demanded some kind of proof. Caparat brought to the stand a series of plans and manuscripts where it was stated -in a certain way- that among the sites discovered from the beginning of the century until the 1980s there were certain gray areas. These places could not be accessed by previous archaeologists. Likewise, Caparat presented a letter from an American company that made available a modern excavating machine, which would greatly help in the work. The Minister requested a week of recess in the talks and in the winter of the year 88, Caparat and his assistants were already digging in Cheops. He was granted a four-month term with the possibility of extending the time if any evidence was found. The work was precise and exhausted the archaeologist.

Before long, one of Caparat's helpers, named Ernest, began to have some discomfort in his chest. He couldn't eat any food. He vomited strangely, couldn't sleep, and whined when touched. A suggestive red mark around his neck. The archaeologist accompanied him to the nearest hospital. For their bad luck they must have interned him. Apparently he suffered from an unidentified virus that atrophied the internal passages of the lungs. The nostrils emanated a large quantity of phlegm of a reddish color. It is believed that it could be some kind of trap created and developed by the ancient Egyptians. The archaeologist faced a serious decision: either abandon the excavation for good, or continue on his own. The other helpers refused to render him services. They were afraid of catching it, but he did go ahead. In the height of the investigation, Caparat traversed long tunnels and survived any inconvenience both climatic and physical. It was common for the atmospheric pressure to be low, which prevented him from breathing properly. For this reason, he worked from 6 in the morning until 3 in the afternoon.

A week before the expiration of the period scheduled by the Egyptian government, Caparat found what appeared to be the beginning of an entrance. The earth was thick. He was not easily handled. Caparat discovered three hieroglyphics intertwined by what appeared to be an olive branch. It took about an hour to decode them. The signs referred to Pharaoh Cheops and his condescendants. The archaeologist, excited, contacted the French foreign minister. The excavation received direct support from the Egyptian government. He who was once a simple dreamer, was recognized as a talented researcher. Although there was still much to discover, Cheops would amaze the world again.

A hundred men and 61 days were enough to free the precious entrance from obstacles. The door lay in good order. It showed an interesting number of figures, represented in finely cut bas-reliefs. With the help of an external trailer, it was possible to knock down the obstacles that prevented it from being opened. The scientists covered their faces with masks as a precaution and carefully examined the site. It was completely dark. Caparat was the first to advance and, to his surprise, the chamber had two circles of about 20cm, located at both ends of the room through which it ventilated air. Caparat came across a gigantic tomb made of solid glass. He called his assistants - who had returned to their tasks after the good news - and asked them to illuminate the object as soon as possible. To the horror of many, a corpse lay inside the tomb and it did not appear to be human. The body was deposited in a special ambulance and was taken to a research center where various tests would be carried out. The tension grew when Caparat found an ancient papyrus between the being's legs. He left the place and retired to his rooms in a hotel. The Egyptian Foreign Minister was present at the dig along with the police force. He fenced the area and barred access.

Caparat transcribed the translation with grim care into his personal notebook, astonished at each new decoding. Hieroglyphs did not have the normal phonetic construction. The style varied by sign. Apparently, Pharaoh Cheops had signed a treaty with an alien from a distant star system. The being offered him complete protection during his life in exchange for shelter. Likewise, he explained the evolution of human history, the possibility of interplanetary travel, of exchanging people from world to world and similar things. Pharaoh, amazed, accepted the offer. They signed a pact where it was made explicit that the alien could reside in Egypt for as long as he wanted. The creature lived in peace for the rest of its long life. The tomb was built to a design he drew before he died. Caparat received a visit from the police at the hotel. His papyrus and notebooks were taken from him and he was forced to return to France.

reptilian catacombs

Although, not everything was peaceful when beings from space appeared. The sacred texts Vedas of India describe interplanetary wars and not only this, but they refer to the power of their flying devices, that is, the flying chariots of the gods, capable of leaving and entering the Earth, possessing atomic weapons and of rays.

Other similar events were recorded in the writings of Israelite prophets who observed chariots of fire, flying clouds, metal wheels with eyes (windows) and columns like whirlwinds that in some cases even abducted certain people such as the prophets Enoch, Elijah and the Jesus Christ himself. Some Islamic legends even argue that Muhamad (Mohammed) was taken to heaven alive in one of these chariots and one of the pieces of said ship was left on the ground —although others say it is a piece of an asteroid-, perhaps as a testimony. Around this "stone" would have been mounted the most important center for the Islamic world: Mecca.

If they weren't all benevolent beings with a human or semi-human appearance, would there also be amorphous beings like the ones Hollywood brings out? The truth is that the UFO records make few references to things like furry beings, strange animals, Michelin-like creatures, and the like. Rather, there are many cases of humans or androids being sent to inspect or collect samples. Even with everything, in the oldest narratives of the Earth there was always a common denominator: serpent gods. As for that, there is also physical evidence, including catacombs found in California, when Shufelt and his team introduced a probe on a sunny morning as a mechanical introspection to find wells and minerals. Now, the probe reached about 76 meters and by X-rays, and other search procedures, they captured large tunnels and strange objects. They were stunned when they realized that a strange vibration was surrounding the place, magnetism or abnormal waves that made them feel uncomfortable. The intuition of Shufelt, the mining engineer, led them to start digging with powerful drilling machines in a mythical area of Hollywood, near the famous Sunset Boulevard, Spring Street and North Broadway. As they advanced, it is said that they were finding treasures that have never been spoken of. Alien jewels, objects, statues, tunnels and 37 golden plates with non-human inscriptions were appearing.

The plates were photographed, but have been hidden from the public by the Illuminati. Shufelt had read legends and the Hopi Indians had told him that this city was created by some reptilian beings to escape catastrophes and fires some 5,000 years ago.

It is said that this civilization was very advanced and had hidden technology to dig tunnels with certain chemical substances and other procedures such as teleportation and levitation of rocks and objects from other dimensions. It is also said that the cities were home to about 1000 families. Subsequently almost all the data given to Shufelt were confirmed, but, of course, hidden. Some of the information was Shufelt's deductions from his radar and sonar, others were from actual excavations, but the authorities refused to do any further excavation and the matter was "buried." The information was then distorted to mislead and to appear as speculation, something that has always happened in Forbidden Archaeology. In any case, when progress was made towards the catacombs, the team came to stop and consult Dr. Shufelt what they should do, before communicating the finding to humanity, to the authorities. They reached more than 360 meters, coming across one tunnel after another, perfectly excavated in the stone with unknown technology and with a suspicious resemblance to the famous catacombs of Cappadocia, another enigma for archaeology.

It is claimed that Shufelt was following instructions from Hopi Indians who had told them about reptilian beings and the existence of this city. The Hopi Indians of Arizona, who also predicted cataclysms and an ice age, speak in their mythology of the Bakti, the fallen from heaven, who would become the Anunnaki of America. That is, those who appear in all the mythologies of the Earth. In Africa they are called Chitauris and in Asia and China, Jinns, jian-shi or dragons, and they are always associated with royalty, demonology and/or vampires. And this connection is not accidental, just as it is not by chance that cultural legends of vampire kings or aristocrats appear from time to time, such as Count Dracula or Vlad Tepes or Erzebet Bathory (the lesbian psychopathic countess who drinks Hungarian blood). These rituals have been secret and have always been done since Babylon by the elites or Illuminati and no longer seem to be simple myths. Moreover, the famous Saint George (Saint George), some believe that he defeated a reptilian dragon, who was precisely from Cappadocia (Turkey), a symbolic battle between good and evil, between the forces of light and darkness, as they believe some researchers, as Turkey was an important center of the Biblical Nephilim. But, let's not get ahead of ourselves yet, since this material will be better exposed in our work "The Rebellion of Sakla".

reptilian figures

Near the place where a huge bust carved from a rock hundreds of meters high was discovered, in the territory of Sierra Leone, Professor Pitoni was in charge of a diamond excavation. As he heard, a legend says that Allah was angry with some angels and put them in a stone and threw them to the Earth. The myth says that Allah also introduced the sky into a stone and threw it to the Earth, and introduced the stars and threw them to the Earth. Although, the old way of calling angels is that of "stars". Legends say that the sky can be seen in this stone, they call it "Sky Stones" (The Stones of Heaven), which were found in this area under the ground. Klaus Dona and Professor Pitoni investigated them in Vienna concluding that they are definitely artificial. It is not a natural stone, and although all the material could be found, it could not be concluded what type of color could have been used to achieve its true sky blue.

In these excavations, figurines of reptile men and giant men were also found, discovered at a depth of 20m and even 50m. Professor Pitoni always took some organic samples from the found place, and in this case, the dating of the antiquity of these stone artifacts ranges from about 2,500 years to the oldest, about 17,000 years. In another granite stone, popularly known as Nomoli - the stone has a spectacular carving - other fabulous things were discovered: it is black and has very strange representations, as well as a peculiar appearance. In another figure you can see a huge man on an elephant, as the legends of the giants all over Africa say. It is a very complicated work in stone and it is also very heavy. Other artifacts show human hybrids or men with the head of a reptile. One of many, shows a reptile-man with a kind of vessel in his hand to put something inside this vessel. At the top of several Nomolis there is a hole to put something inside, and most likely they were used for ceremonies.

Another artifact found shows a type of animal similar to a dinosaur. When Professor Pitoni discovered it, it made a strange noise, so he opened it. Inside he found a small black ball which was made of iron. When they studied it, the teacher called Klaus and said: " *Someone must have played a bad joke on me.*" The reason was because the research result said that it was chrome steel, but chrome steel was only discovered for the first time at the beginning of the 20th century in Austria. Consequently, this is impossible for a statue from 17,000 years ago. When called, Professor Pitoni was laughing and said: *"I am a geologist. If a statue makes a strange sound I not only open it up a considerable distance, but I also X-ray it."* So the professor looked inside and saw that the chrome steel ball already existed inside the closed statue.

representations or narratives of genetic manipulation are very frequent, which is why they are considered meaningless fables, or at most, allegorical figures of events that occurred or even dreams. The truth is that talking about genetic engineering is not talking about the discovery of the human genome in 2003 or about the experiments in Nazi Germany, but we have to go to Classical

Greece. Studying these events well, we see that what is told must have been a real event that permeated the Greeks, Egyptians and Mesopotamians, since both cultures, as well as other ancient civilizations, speak of beings that are half man and half animal, which, in many cases, were left as guardians of temples for being considered amulets, magical creatures, symbols of fear, talismans, sources of power or unique emblematic creatures. The first book of Enoch, whose antiquity goes back thousands of years, in its chapter 7:5 tells that some messengers and sons of Elohim came down to Earth and had children with humans and, in addition to this error, they had children who They were the gods of European and Middle Eastern mythology. Added to this, they made their children pose as gods and taught them all the secrets they had acquired, including the manipulation of genetics: "and they *began to [genetically] manipulate the birds, [acting] against [the nature of] the beasts, against [that of] the bug-insects and against [that of] the fish and devoured each other's flesh and drank the blood.* »

Could those serpent beings also have been a laboratory result? This would not seem absurd if it were not for the discovery of these fossilized, mummified beings or their clear representations in all kinds of pictograms. We see in the Egyptians beings half dog and half man, or half hawk and half man. We can also observe in distant Sumer creatures half eagle and half man, or the legends of the fish men, which are also mentioned by the Greeks (mermaids and mermen, for example), or by the Proto-Hebrew scribe Enoch himself. In museums in Japan, to avoid going into too much detail, mermaids and mermen can be seen today in a state very similar to mummification, and in Iran a satyr preserved in salt was found a couple of years ago. So, with the exception of benevolent beings and apparently draconic beings, are there extraterrestrial beings that don't seem to have a certain interest for or against humans?

A satyr in Iran

Adrienne Mayor of Stanford University, a folklorist, specializes in analyzing how fossil discoveries from prehistoric times may have contributed to legends such as the Titans of Greek mythology (reconstructed mammoth bones) or mystical water serpents in American legend. (fossilized crocodiles preserved in desert rock deposits). Since the era of the great Roman Emperor Constantine, who reigned from 312 to 337, cities had their own special attractions, Mayor explains. One of the earliest "Christian" writers, Jerome (said to be the patron saint of librarians in the Catholic Church, who died in 420), recounted that Constantine made a special journey from Constantinople (now Istanbul) to Antioch, on a time a great city of his empire, to see the exhibition of a "satyr" that had been preserved in salt.

In a book, The First Fossil Hunters: Paleontology in Greek and Roman Times, Mayor suggested that the "satyr" was likely a forgery, the patched-up bodies of a man and a goat. But now she thinks the recently discovered salt man in Iran may provide another explanation: " *Obviously, satyrs are mythical creatures,*" says Mayor, " *but the head of the man preserved in salt from 540-300 BC bears a striking resemblance. with ancient Greek [and] Roman paintings of satyrs,* " he adds. He also says that they are shown having similar hair and beards, a flat nose and prominent jaw: " *I think it highly probable that an ancient discovery of a man similarly preserved in salt, northwestern Iran, is the basis for St. Jerome's account." "of the satyr" preserved in salt and examined by the Emperor Constantine and other curious visitors in Antioquia* », concludes Mayor.

Expert opinions are mixed. Roman historian Andrew Merrills of the English University of Leicester commented in an email: "*Overall, sounds like a great 'maybe' to me. Interesting story, great idea, but I don't want to build too many arguments on it.*" However, archaeologist Bruce Hitchner of Tufts University in Massachusetts says the idea is credible. The 540 BC salt man from Iran more closely resembles a satyr figure commonly seen in Greek art, called a Silenus, Mayor says. Silenus was usually depicted with long golden hair, a beard, a curved forehead, a flat nose, and an open mouth. More suspicious that the first images of satyrs may have come from such discoveries, transformed into art (with the addition of the body of a goat) in the stories told by travelers from the ancient world: « When I saw the picture *of the salt man, I was impressed because it looked so much like a satyr,"* Mayor said: *"Satyrs were very popular in ancient times, so everyone knew what satyrs looked like. There's no reason to think that people back then wouldn't have made the same connection."* (Source: www.usatoday.com [1], as of July 22, 2007)

The Star Child's Skull

Another piece of information is that of the skull found in a cave in Chihuahua, Mexico. It dates from about 900 years old and according to several DNA tests commissioned by the Starchild Project, the mother would be human and the father's DNA is unknown so far. Obviously in this unknown case on Earth, it is synonymous with extraterrestrial. The locals say that beings from heaven who had children with their wives arrived and returned to look for them after a couple of years to take them away. This would be another irrefutable physical and irrefutable proof of many other cases of extraterrestrial contacts such as those so often cited by the American Indians. In another case, a photograph of a humanoid child being raised by a farm woman along with her legitimate children caused much controversy in decades past. The woman says that the child could express himself telepathically and also had other extrasensory faculties. They say that when he was a couple of years old his real parents came from heaven and took him away. Similar cases are those of the skeleton of a tiny being with a highly

---

1. http://www.usatoday.com

disproportionate head, found a few years ago in Venezuela, and the skull of a totally unknown being discovered in Bulgaria. Discoveries like these cannot be ignored and the archaeological record is littered with them. If someone does not believe it, we can observe the museums of Peru and the superhuman skulls located there, which, even giving an explanation to their extra bone volume, have differences in the rest of the bone structure (they do not have bone parts in the mandible that humans do have).

cuckold men

The horned skulls (a few of them were found) were found in Sayre (Bradford County), Pennsylvania in 1880. Anatomically the skeletons were absolutely normal except for the horns they possessed. The bodies were estimated to have been buried around 1,200 BC, a time when hybrid myths were rampant. The find was made by a group of highly reputable antique dealers, a historian and dignitary of the Presbyterian Church, and two professors from the American Museum of Research and the Phillips Academy in Andover, Massachusetts. The bones were sent to the American Research Museum in Philadelphia and mysteriously disappeared. What a coincidence, right? As always, any evidence that questions the accepted paradigm tends to be hidden. It is even rumored that some of them were on display in a British Museum, but they also disappeared.

The humanoid from the Mayan tomb

Photos show the detail of the drawing of the tomb of Pacal Votán, but the most interesting thing was inside. It is about a body found inside the tomb of Pacal Votán that has baffled archaeologists, why neither the proportions nor the physical characteristics match those of the ancient Maya. The skeleton shows a strong build and a large size that contrasts with the proportions of the natives. Another curious detail of the buried character is the mask that was with him, which shows rather non-indigenous features. Especially interesting is the nose bridge that extends to the forehead, something naturally from another planet.

The strange cases of elongated skulls

The elongated skulls found in archaeological sites are a reason for speculation, although the scientific answers are absurd, because they are the typical justifications to deny the facts. According to the official explanation, these skulls were artificially elongated, but what "official science" can no longer explain is how this was done, since they do not present any type of mark or indication that it was an induced elongation, such as a contusion. Therefore, if it was not something artificial, it is necessarily something genetic, inherited, or a manipulation of your DNA . Which brings us back to the Tiahuanaco relief, to the web-footed humanoid figure with an elongated skull. Wouldn't it be more logical to think that genetic interaction produced these elongated skulls? You have to think that in all the sacred texts of the Earth (including the Bible), there is talk of an interrelation between the gods come from heaven and humans, so this would be another physical proof of said genetic crossing.

The fact is not even isolated, these skulls have also been found in Russia, which were believed to be the work of South American tribes, although there are Egyptian figures that also represent them. Experts have affirmed that these skulls lack certain bones that Homo sapiens sapiens do have, that their bone density is greater than ours, and that furthermore, no prolongation of a skull by induction can increase its capacity by more than 50%. as seen in many of the cases.

Dwarves

The giant gibbon from China from about 10,000 years ago surprises the same as gigantophitecus, an almost 3m ape that does not fit with the hypothesis of human evolution. But in the same order of strange beings we find the hobbits, whom science calls "homo Floresensis" and whose bones were found in Indonesia. It is believed that these hobbits lived together with men until only 12,000 years ago. Ergo, it seems that the leprechauns were even older, because let's not forget that the Moroccan professor Mohamed Zarouit discovered a small skull of 360 million years.

An equally peculiar case is that of a skeleton found in Ladonia, Texas, which stunned discoverers and researchers. It is a humanoid with a rather incredible appearance, huge eye sockets reinforced with bone structure, four fingers and toes, extremely small and narrow jaw. He was found dressed in a kind of metallic suit, which can be seen in the detail of one of the photographs taken of said being.

the bones of the giants

Certainly the subject of the giants is a matter that I would like to fully cover in one of my next works - 'The Rebellion of Sakla' - but I will cite some interesting cases about these beings. In 1950 during the construction of a highway in Turkey, in the Euphrates valley, many tombs containing the remains of giants were discovered. The leg bones measured 1.2 m and thanks to this it is calculated that the height of the giant was about 4.2 m to about 4.8 m. Some can currently be seen on display at the Mont Blanc Fossil Musseum in Texas. Another skeleton was found in southeastern Saudi Arabia by the ARAMCO oil company. The government covered up the incident and confiscated all the evidence including 99.9% of the photographs. It was fought via the Internet through the dissemination of a series of false photos, to discredit the finding and it is believed that the same thing happened on the Indian border with the apparent discovery of a National Geographic group about a giant of more than 8m. If it was real, the discovery was quickly hushed up and mixed up with a Photoshop contest themed on unearthed giant humans.

A case similar to the previous one occurred in a cave in Atyueca (former Soviet Union), where skeletons of men measuring between 2.80 m and 3 m were found, they also presented, as in the Pentateuch (the Bible), 6 digits in hands and feet. Undeniably one of the most authentic photos of giants in circulation today, is of a fossilized giant that was discovered in 1895 by Mr. Dyer during a mining operation in County Antrim, Ireland. The measure of the giants was about 3.7 m in height and about 1.37 m in thoracic circumference. The owners and the giant disappeared (another added to the list). Other cases that we can name by quickly reviewing the archaeological annals are the tombs of Chenini, in Tunisia, where the remains of beings 3 m high rested; the Bradford tomb, in the United States, found in 1880, which contained skeletons more than 2 m high with strange horn-like prominences that protruded above the brow ridges; the Cretaceous tracks in Glen Rose, Texas, measuring 54.61 cm x 13.97 cm, and strikingly found next to the tracks of a brontosaurus; the young giants of Lixus, whose height at the average age of 11 was around 2.20 m; and the skeletal remains in Garós, in the Urbasa mountain system, in Castilla, Medinaceli, León, Cantabria and other places, all belonging to Spain.

Paintings

The common denominator in the cases of UFO sightings are the witnesses who represented the events inside caves since prehistoric times. The most interesting cave paintings about UFOs are, for example, those found in Tanzania. These are drawings found in the north of the island in 1951, where up to 186 locations appear with a total of more than 1,600 drawings. Following dating methods, the experts deduced that the "artists" had executed these paintings in a period ranging between 50,000 and 16,000 years ago. Many of them -perhaps the most interesting- dated back 29,000 years. Some of the most curious drawings are flying hats that shoot lightning bolts. Surprisingly, not far from there, on the neighboring island of Australia, amazing engravings were found on the wall of a cave. These petroglyphs are thousands of years old and in them you can see majestic and well-detailed modern ships of all kinds, which are identified, nothing more and nothing less, than ships that disappeared decades ago in the Bermuda Triangle. However, Australia has more incredible things like the Wandjina paintings or ancient representations of the Egyptian god Horus.

Other interesting figures are those of Utah (USA) in Barrier Canyon, made by the Ute Indians, and those also discovered in Arkansas. In them, humanoids with helmets and tight-fitting uniforms can be seen. Other similar drawings are exhibited in Death Valley, California, in which flying saucers in the form of hats are seen. In Spain we find the "Astronaut of Ciudad Rodrigo", which is a petroglyph that shows a strange being with a helmet and diving suit that is believed to date from 2000 BC. C. And in another part of Europe, in Valcamoni (Italy), there are drawings dating from 10,000 BC. C., where astronauts are seen carrying strange artifacts. These are drawings of men in space suits and dome-like helmets, with strange artifacts in their hands. Other paintings with flying objects shooting at each other can be found in France, and without a doubt, the most surprising are those in the Lussac-les-chateaux area. These represent people like us today, with modern hairstyles, hats, clothes that we wear today, drawings that identify something like men on horses and also dinosaurs. These Lussac-les-chateaux graffiti date back more than 40,000 years and were discovered by Colín Rivas in 1937. Did some prehistoric civilizations dress like this? Were they their clothes on their home planets? Or did they have future visions of our time?

Many of these drawings are very similar to those of Fergana and her main icon: The Man from Mars. The famous painting called "The Man from Mars" was discovered by the archaeologist

Guergui Chatski, in some caves in the region near the town of Fergana, near the Alai mountains, in Uzbekistan (former USSR), and it was not the only evidence found in this area, as well as having other Neolithic cave paintings. This 2m-tall, 10,000-year-old cave painting is "duplicated" and its copy is apparently currently on display at the Moscow Academy of Sciences. The famous ancient painting represents a man with a disc in his hand, similar to the dropa discs: full of writing similar to Braille or Ugaritic. Behind, a few meters away, a little man with a helmet equipped with antennas can be seen, with another disk in his hand and, above, a ship in the shape of a hat releasing smoke and taking off into the sky.

Some critics allude to the fact that the veracity of the painting was supposedly denied, however, the original sources are correct. What was said almost a decade ago about the Man from Mars, long after his discovery was in regards to an article in the French ufology magazine called: "Lumières Dans La Nuit" (Lights in the Night) No. 335 of February year 2000, where Mr. Didier Leroux tried to find the source of this image. This gentleman discovered that the popular image was recreated by a contemporary Russian artist to illustrate the cover of the 1967 edition of the Russian magazine "Sputnik", in which there was an article dedicated to the subject of visits by Ancient Astronauts for more than of 12,000 years. However, the painting had been inspired, among other things, by the original prehistoric depictions discovered in the Fergana caves by the archaeologist Guergui Chatski. In certain characteristics they were considered as an encounter, possibly, a millennial Encounter in the Third Kind. These paintings are real and some date back to 2000 BC, others to 7000 BC., and some even to 10,000 BC The real problem was that the original paintings, and in the case of the Man from Mars, were not used for Sputnik magazine, but the recreation of the Russian painter, which led to some misunderstandings, thinking it was a setup. In other words, instead of the real rock paintings, the fictional illustration was propagated as if it were the real one from Fergana.

The Russian artist, whether intentionally or to earn the "credits", signed the replica he sent to Sputnik magazine as his own, but Guergui Chatski did not receive any credit, knowing that he was the discoverer of the true cave paintings. There are other controversial paintings found by Gergui Chatski near the Alai Mountains depicting antediluvian astronauts. From a famous Internet article we highlight: « *In the upper part of the left, it is specified that the drawing illustrates an article by Dr. Viacheslav Zaitsev, a Russian philologist, whose name is related to the Dropa case.* » It's funny but the Fergana region is geographically not very far from Bayan Kara Ula, where the dropa ship fell – a topic I covered earlier.

In the list of petroglyphs, geoglyphs and hieroglyphs in this category, we see the Okinawan rosette stone, which shows men next to rockets and the typical spirals seen in many prehistoric drawings, which are also reminiscent of galaxies. Although there are many drawings and inscriptions of UFOs and aliens from ancient times, one that does not fail to impress is a Sumerian shield depicting various pharaohs and Egyptian gods under the power of a great goddess who controls a detailed disc-shaped spaceship. We can also see a huge flying saucer in the shape of a hat and with a dome on top, portrayed in a petroglyph found in Samaipata, Bolivia, with the archaeological complex of El Fuerte.

Other cave paintings and petroglyphs

In Ecuador, many quite peculiar ancient artifacts were found: in one of them you can see a petroglyph showing a man throwing rays through his eyes against a downcast people. He is sitting with a small pyramid in his hands as he attacks the other men. You can also see something like an antenna pointing towards the sky where there is a huge ovoid object throwing lights. In the same place, other carved stones were found showing spirals, pyramids, representations of the Orion Constellation and allusions to the coming of the "Son of the Creator". In another part of South America, you can see a stone engraving of the Mayan god of Antiquity, in the city of Tikal, in Guatemala. The image of this god is rather that of an astronaut similar to the representations of the Hindu god Ganesha. In both cases, a being can be seen with a diving suit, helmet, tubes, glasses, and devices all around his body, just like any modern astronaut. Other UFOs portrayed on walls can be seen on stones and pyramids in Peru, especially when talking about the Ica stones, studied by Professor Cabrera. There is too much evidence, but we will always try to abbreviate as much as possible and bring to light the highlights.

In the long history of ancient paintings with "flying discs", "astronauts", "dinosaurs", "non-human beings" and so on, we find the petroglyphs of Death Valley, California, the ancient stone engravings of unknown writing, the figures from Hoshin in Japan, from Valle del Cauca in Colombia, Navai in Uzbekistan, inexplicable figures engraved on the stones of Alice Spring in Australia, the tablets from Glozel, France, with more than 15,000 years, like the graffiti from Lussac-les-chateaux. In India there is also a place called Las Cuevas de Elora, where there are engravings in the stone of flying floats that take the princess from Earth and take them flying to heaven. The heads of shocked people are even portrayed, looking up at the sky.

A news item published on Friday, February 19, 2010 said that a group of anthropologists, who were doing some work in the district of Hoshangabad (State of Madhya Pradesh), just 70 km from the city of Raisen in India, made a surprising discovery: they found a complex network of cave paintings, in which contact with aliens and UFOs can be clearly seen. The cave paintings are hidden inside a dense jungle. You can see a being wearing what looks like an alien space suit, next to him a UFO, which can be said to be a classic flying saucer, and an object that emits light downwards, which could be clearly associated with the typical scenario of an abduction. We also observe a force field.

On the other hand, another object is also visible that seems to be prepared to enter a "wormhole", in a kind of communication tunnel with another dimension or another space. The ufological community has been surprised by these images that the Times Rajasthan newspaper has released, among them it is already commented that these images must have been made with the help of aliens. The local archaeologist, Mr. Wassim Khan, who has personally seen these cave paintings , comments that the objects and creatures he saw are abnormal, many of them representing scenes of daily acts they performed in that prehistoric time. Ufologists are already commenting that this only shows that human civilization was created with the help of extraterrestrial beings – called in ancient times "gods", which in Hebrew is said: Elohim – who came to our world.

the uluru

The Wandjinas or men of the cave figures found in the Kimberley in northwest Australia, are cited by the aborigines as beings from space. The paintings were discovered in the year 1838, but their dating date was only discovered in 1996 showing, like the indigenous legends regarding these beings, that they lived with giants up to 5m tall, which was corroborated by the discovery of hand axes, maces, knives and various tools weighing between 5 kg and 16 kg. As early as 1970, a human-shaped foot print 59 cm long by 18 cm wide had been discovered. The dating of the large tools discovered was set at about 100,000 years and the human fossil remains found are close to an age of 200,000 years.

According to Australian Aboriginal legend, in ancient times or "Dreamtime", a great battle was fought at Uluru, when a people called "the Venomous Serpent Men" attacked to destroy the peoples of the area, called "the Venomous Serpent Men". non-venomous snake"; but Bulari, the Mother Goddess of the Earth, defeated them by creating a cloud of lethal gases. The "venomous snake men" who managed to survive were locked up in a prison under Uluru - and according to legend, they still remain there today - the holiest point in all of aboriginal Australia. This is a huge hill of changing color granite, better known today as Ayer's Rock.

In the Dreamtime according to the legend, lived a race of giants that in some cases reached up to 5 m in height. In another sacred point of the aborigines of Australia, the so-called Moon City or "City of the Moon", another legend tells that there were also terrifying battles between the god of the Sun -who arrived from the sky in a ship- and the god of the Land. The remains of these struggles are reflected in the strange monoliths and shapes that are scattered throughout Australia, which according to scientists are naturally produced erosions, the aborigines denying this theory, assuring that they are the remains of the cities built by the "arientas", "yowies" and "luritchas": beings half man, half animal. Something similar had already been seen of this in other cultures, clear evidence of genetic manipulation of all kinds and by different races from one another, as well as in different times of the past.

Two researchers: Walsh and Roberts, traveled to the Kimberley in 1996 in search of more fossils on the cave paintings, finding two fossilized wasps' nests on a typical human-shaped painting or "wandjina". Prior to the analysis by Walsh and Roberts, archaeologists had estimated the age of these paintings at about 5,000 years. After the analysis, it was found that the wasps' nests were about 17,000 years old and, logically, the age of the paintings should go back even further, since they were made before the nests.

The dating of the "great" tools discovered was set at about 100,000 years and the human fossil remains found are close to an age of 200,000 years, thus contradicting what science said, that the first settlers of Australia had appeared at most a few years ago. 65,000 or 70,000 years.

Tassili, UNESCO heritage

The Sahara desert stretches from the Atlas Mountains in the north to the Sudan in the south, and from Egypt in the east to the Atlantic Ocean in the east. At 8 million km^2, this desert is a truly difficult place for any type of archaeological or scientific research. Even so, in 1933 a Meharian police officer, Lieutenant Brenans, was on police duty in the Tassili-n-Azyer Canyon area and came to a valley called Ighargharen. Brenans discovered between the rocky walls a whole huge group of improbable paintings (more than 5,000) made on the stone. Before his eyes were representations of giraffes, elephants with their trunks held high, hippos, gigantic animals, and humanoid figures, prominent among which were graphics of what appeared to be astronauts.

However, it was the explorer Henri Lhote who made this discovery of prehistoric art known to the whole world in 1957. Henry Lhote classified the large number of pictographs into twelve groups:

- Beings with round heads and small horns.
- Imps.
- Drawings of the middle period with men with round heads.
- Round-headed men evolved.
- Declining period of the round heads.
- Men with highly evolved round heads.
- Period of justices of the peace or terminal.
- Long-lined white men from the pre-Bovid period.
- Hunters with body paintings from the ancient Bovidense period.

- Bovidense style.

- Period of the chariots.

- Period of mounted horses or bitriangular men.

Of all the paintings, the most disconcerting is the one that shows a kind of diver in his full suit and diving suit with slits on the front that reflects having a clumsy movement giving the impression of levitating or flying tied to something by a cable. long. The main drawing, in which a man with a helmet is seen, which is 6m high, Henry Lhote called "the great Martian god". Another very interesting painting is the one that was dubbed "the striated woman" and represents a female figure (who appears to be floating) with long arms extended behind her, towing another being on her knees and hunched forward with an indifferent gesture to the scene. , while another humanoid appears coming out of a strange disk. Interestingly there are many "discs" made in different colors and they all seem to be floating. Tassili has been declared by UNESCO as a World Heritage Site and for some experts it is "The Sistine Chapel of the Paleolithic", with paintings that in some cases date back 10,000 years. Something quite similar was also discovered in the Caribbean some years ago.

deer hunting

There is a relief found in a labyrinth on Jotuo Island in Lake Toengt'ing (Japan), which was discovered after an expedition in 1957. The expedition was led by Professor Tsj'i Pen-Lai. They found several reliefs showing "human beings" in strange clothing which resembled astronaut suits (hose like objects attached to the clothing) and men hunting on flying saucers. They also found a painting that apparently resembled the Solar System. The third and fourth circles (planet) were connected with a line. There were also ten planets (except the sun as a planet). This, according to some, may coincide with the theories about Nibiru, planet X or Hercolumbus.

The controversial stones of Ica

Sadly, not only did the arrival of Spanish colonizers erase many of the pre-Columbian historical records, but relic thieves and antiquities dealers have looted, outraged, and sabotaged the history of the Americas. In the case of the Ica stones, something similar has happened. For quite some time it has been believed that Dr. Cabrera had forged a large number of stones, however, what he did, he did following the models already found for a long time, practically since the colony. It turns out that there are chronicles of priests from the old colony who already described these stones, demonstrating that they are not a recent phenomenon, that they exist and that fakes have been added to the real ones.

The real stones are currently on display at the Museum of Ica, in Peru, as they also exist in the possession of the family of the late Dr. Cabrera. The stones exhibited in the Museum were sent to a respectable mineralogy laboratory for analysis and they determined that the incisions made to make the figures are covered with rust that could only have formed, not in weeks or a hundred years, but in thousands of years. In addition, the people who were selling them illegally were ignorant who made believe that they were the ones who carved them so as not to go to jail for selling a nation's heritage. The people who were falsifying these stones, to manually carve a single and small size, according to the researchers, took approximately 5 months. That being the case, how could they carve 11,000 stones? It must be remembered that there are even larger stones also carved. In any case, the counterfeits did not have the same preciousness or perfection as the originals, and the usurers used any type of stone, despite the fact that the originals are andesite-type stones, which are one of the hardest, and which are not They are not found on the coast, but in the bowels of the Andes.

Among the most representative stones, you can see some that show the world map as it was in the Tertiary, with Gondwana and Pangea; others show open-heart and brain operations, as well as caesarean sections; others show the passage of a comet that was unknown until its crossing in the mid-1970s; others showed interrelationships between men and dinosaurs, men flying on certain species of "birds", and also the creation of a primitive human race by extraterrestrial entities using genetic engineering. Unordinary and scientifically recent concepts for an indigenous person to understand, except when the human genome was barely mapped in 2003 and it is not a subject that the Indians deal with in their schools.

The Children of Anu

Sumerian, Akkadian and Assyrian cultures are rich in stories and representations of rockets, astronauts and beings from the ends of our solar system. It is said that the stories portrayed in the Mesopotamian tablets tell that 12 sons of the supreme god ANU came to planet Earth in search of gold thousands of years ago. The sons of ANU would be based at various bases and space shuttles in Sinai and in Acadia, from where they had space communications centers in connection with orbiting shuttles. The oldest tablets may be over 5,800 years old, but the events they recount can be incredibly old. In fact, these proto-Sumerians, who came in their "shem" (rockets) or "mu", would have been the so-called "Anunnaki" who created one of the various human races that populated the Earth and would have revolutionized history and natural progress. of our civilization.

The Anunnaki (Those Who Came Down from Heaven, or "those who were deported to Earth") are credited with building the first Ziggurat (stepped pyramids) and the cultural advancement of cave-dwelling human civilization. This, although it is material from the last 30 years, approx. it was already aired among the followers of the Urantia Book, who claim to have been advised by divine-extraterrestrial beings in 1955. According to the version of the Urantia Book - long before the work of Zecharia Sitchin - they said that these beings would have told them what they were doing 200,000 there was a rebellion in the galaxy, led by the biblical Lucifer and followed on Earth by two of his henchmen: Caligastia and Daligastia, who would have come to Earth about 500,000 years ago. Although the Urantia Book is incongruous and untenable, it helps to visualize what life on other worlds might be like. Now, the Sumerian version says that there was a descent before the Anunnaki, by "reptilian beings", and then the Anunnaki descended around 475,000 years ago, although they are also considered reptilian. It is curious to see that the version of the myth of the descent of Caligastia and Daligastia resembles that of the arrival of EN.KI, EN.LI and the rest of the children of ANU. Likewise, there are many other striking parallels that may have their origin in the misinformation disseminated by the extraterrestrials themselves, according to some conspiracy theorists and former Illuminati. We already know today that all this gave rise to a vast number of the most famous and controversial mythologies in history.

The disappearance of the Tamil language

If there were extraterrestrial beings in the past, how much did they influence us? How much time did they stay? What language did they speak? Is it possible that we had learned it, or that it became the common language of the globe? Would this have been the mother tongue of all languages on Earth? That original language, if it existed, as everything indicates, it had to be the father of practically all the languages that are known today. It can be seen that the theories about human evolution do not fit with the discoveries made throughout history – this can be corroborated by the reader by reading our work "Creation vs. Evolution". It can also be clearly glimpsed that as the time of the caves progressed, technology decreased until the time of Adam, from where it began to develop again. Similarly, the evidence we see suggests that the world was once united, thousands of years ago, with great technology and high spiritual development that was crippled by wars involving new experimental weapons, drastic environmental changes, and other external effects, thus losing the corporate link and the global language: Tamil, also called "proto-Sanskrit". Since then, men began to live in caves and forgot who they were and where they came from, while at the same time they lost their notion of who were those beings from other worlds with whom they had lived and who had provided them with such knowledge that they no longer knew. could be considered primitive.

The Fuente Magna and the Pokotia monolith

In the 50s, in the town of Tiahuanaco, Bolivia, a farmer found a stone container that received the name of "Fuente Magna", which was released until the year 2000, and in 2002 a group of researchers discovered the so-called "Pokotia monolith". In both (Fuente Magna and the monolith) cuneiform inscriptions of possible Sumerian-Akkadian origin were found. Given the spectacular antiquity of these artifacts, it is not understood how they could have appeared in America, indeed, if they were from the region , how did a Mesopotamian language get there? It is curious, but ancient Aramaic writing was also found in California on the wall of a cave, which dates back to between 600 BC and 3,000 BC There are also ancient museums, many of them already almost forgotten or looted, with stones engraved with Aramaic and Akkadian script, whose antiquity predates the Conquest of America.

The prehistoric world map

A huge stone world map was found in 1984 in Ecuador while extracting gold from underground tunnels. In addition, another 350 artifacts that do not fit with any existing or known pre-Columbian culture were recovered. On this map there is a natural line of quartz that has an eye drawn at the height of what would be the Sinai or the northeast of Egypt, which may be related to the pyramid of Cheops (it is called that but it was not really built by Cheops). There is also a continent represented in the Pacific, which is usually called Lemuria or Mu, that is, this world map must be more than 10,000 or 12,000 years old, since Lemuria disappeared after the Flood or after the misnamed "Last Ice Age" -Drunvalo Melkizedek He says that until a few decades ago there were still times of the year when the tide allowed parts of the island to protrude up to a few meters below the surface of the sea. On the other side of the world map you can also see the famous Atlantean continent. A circle is also shown in the Bay of Guayaquil in Bolivia, that is, the place where the artifacts were found.

Another map, in this case by the Turkish vice-admiral Piri Reis, dated 1513, contains a complete detail of the globe, including America and Antarctica, which were not discovered until 1818. According to expert cartographers, it is only possible to create such a map with images. satellite. Who and how reproduced such a map? As in the case of the Nazca lines, it is seen that many ancient civilizations possessed the ability, already in antiquity, to observe the world from the air at extremely high altitudes.

aliens of mythology

In ufology, aliens are credited with the technological revolution and the "gnostic" improvement (gnosis = knowledge. Greek word) and the anatomical morphology of modern man. This is also true according to a group of alternative researchers and theorists, as well as scientists and senior military personnel from the Disclosure Project. Certain writers assume that the angels of antiquity are the so-called Pleiadian and Venusian extraterrestrials of ufology, and that such prehistoric gods were also human beings, mainly from the Pleiades, Nibiru, Sirius, Orion and the Dragon

Constellation. This would explain the great influences of the Mesopotamian gods, "Ilu" or "Annunaki", that of the first god-kings of antiquity in the Far East and Egypt, and likewise of the gods and titans of Greek mythology. Likewise, there are those who assume that despite the existence of positive extraterrestrial entities, they are not necessarily real angels, and they are behind the falsehoods in the UFO and Channeling religions. That is to say, some writers, researchers and lecturers maintain that there are two types of angels, the ethereal (ultraterrestrial) and the physical, where these latter would not be considered angels themselves but simply extraterrestrial collaborators and messengers, and rather would have been humans. who would misinterpret in the figure of these "angelic" beings.

The references to all these legendary events are countless, and despite the fact that many were lost after the destruction of the Library of Alexandria, many of them are still scattered everywhere, kept in the histories of the cultures of our globe, having even reached to the great inaccessible Library of the Vatican. Most of the information concerning the "gods" or extraterrestrials is after the so-called "Last Ice Age", which experts consider as the date of the sinking of the Atlantean and Lemurian continent. Detailed studies on the Masters of Heaven suggest that an Assembly of ancient Gods from outer space did indeed exist in the world, but could they be the gods of mythology? Or were they usurious aliens, who would have come later to take the place of the old gods who would have left Earth by then ?

I will cite the most representative events that imply the appearance of UFOs after this date and what has to do with all the extraterrestrial groups involved since then, according to UFO reports. Beginning we go to the sacred Hindu texts Vedas that speak about extraterrestrial gods: The Srimad Bhagavatam speaks of a race of demons which invaded three planetary systems, although the Mahabata and Ramayan detail flying chariots (vimanas or pushpakas). Then we find from the 15th century BC that Pharaoh Thutmose III the Great and his soldiers saw unidentified flying objects and even non-human beings. The appearance of UFOs and humanoid beings described in Egyptian hieroglyphics is quite regular. On the walls you can see insect men -like the one shown in an Egyptian hieroglyph from 2500 BC-, humans with disproportionately large heads, men with yellow, green and blue skin, as well as other amorphous creatures (there is a particular case that is not really an insectoid being but a bouquet with plants and flowers that from a certain optical perfection to some resemble an alien being).

In fact, there are inexplicably descriptions in Egypt of the 4 cataclysms of the last 600,000 years that have devastated our world. How can a civilization after 2500 BC know something like this if it is "assumed" that they did not live back then to tell or record it? The answer is simple: either human civilization lived several "eras" of which we no longer have information -as the Mayans and Aztecs say- or someone who did know told them: for example, their gods. Likewise, in Iraq, figurines of reptilian and demonic entities have been found, whose age is around 5,000 years old and which are reminiscent of the reptilian figures discovered a few years ago in Sierra Leone, Africa. Not surprisingly, references to reptilian beings, serpent-men or dragon-men are constant around the cultural record of ancient peoples. It even continues to be mentioned in modern ufology events, being the head of a hierarchy of negative physical entities in our galaxy, called homo saurus, draconians or reptilians.

In book VIII of the Aeneid, Virgil speaks of wheels that quickly transported the gods. This statement is very similar to those reported in the Mayan Aztec culture where the gods took princesses from their homes and took them to heaven in their thundering chariots. We can also see statements by the Hopi (Jopi) Indians about the masters of the sky who left in their impressive flying vehicles, with which they normally traveled above the oceans.

The Angkor Stegosaurus

More recently we found that the archaeological complex of Angkor Wat (Capital Temple), near the city of Siem Riep, and observable on one of the walls, the carved figure of an animal familiarly known by dinosaur fans as Stegosaurus. The set of constructions began at the beginning of the 12th century and it was not until well into the 16th century that Angkor Wat began to fall into complete oblivion. It is not understood how the ancient inhabitants of Angkor captured the image of an animal extinct millions of years ago that only the science of the 20th century has managed to recover.

The magnificent temples of the Cambodian jungle were built by the Khmer civilization, between the 8th and 14th centuries AD, one of the greatest builders of this empire was Jayavarman VII, crowned supreme king in 1181. Many of his constructions were rediscovered Centuries later and rehabilitated, others, on the other hand, as in the case of the Ta Prohm temple, one of the most picturesque, was left intact. In one of the corners at the entrance to the temple there is a column covered with decorative circles, in which you can see the shape of said "stegosaurus". Hundreds of decorative stone circles surround the complex with well-known animals such as monkeys, deer, water buffalo, parrots, etc. The strange thing about all this is that the carvers of these 10th century reliefs reproduced extinct stegosaurs more than 65 million years ago with the same precision as the monkeys, buffaloes, deer and other species present at the time. Who told you what these animals were like?

The origin of Angkor, which is located under the reign of Jayavarman II (810-850 AD), founder of the Khmer Empire, who began the cult of Hindu deities, not only shows a stegosaurus, in some of the representative figures on its walls They can appreciate a series of images such as a carnosaur and a stegosaurus-like sauropod, in addition to the mythical one. Keep in mind that dinosaurs were not known until 1922. The name was changed from Dragon to Dinosaur in 1822 by an English doctor named Gideon Mandell, who found gigantic buried bones (fossils) of what were evidently huge reptiles and due to to its size and to the immense teeth that some had, he called them "Dinosaur": Dino = Monstrous; Sauria = Reptile. From that moment on, what used to be known as dragons began to be called by their scientific name: Dinosaurs = Monstrous Reptiles.

2.

THE NANOTECHNOLOGY OF THE CAVEMEN

"Behold, I tell you a mystery: Not all of us will sleep; but we will all be transformed, in a moment, in the twinkling of an eye... the dead will be raised incorruptible, and we will be transformed. For this corruptible must put on incorruption, and this mortal must put on immortality."
Paul of Tarsus (1 Corinthians 15:51-53).

THE MAKER'S MAP

It was alleged that something about 5 feet deep, weighing one ton, was found in Ufa, Russia, which was given the name "Map of the Creator." It is a slab with the modest antiquity – experts say – 120 million years old, and it is an ancient topographical map, made by an unknown process, and was clearly the product of an advanced civilization. Some say that it is not that old, but rather that it is 25 million years old, but in any case, that date is very old. This made the story so unusual, it was a fact that it presented claims being made by the head of the Physics and Engineering Department of the well-known Russian University. The proponent of the claims, Aleksandr Nikolayevich Chuvyrov, had a Ph.D. in physics and mathematics, and had published many peer-reviewed articles in his field. When he gave his opinion on the manufacture of the stone, it was considered, by reading his Curriculum Vitae, such that it is known that he is an expert in that field. What was clear is that this could be a thousand-year-old piece with advanced technology that was clearly made by intelligent beings in full awakening from the age of the dinosaurs.

After the original article appeared and created a sensation, Chuvyrov participated in an online press conference in June 2002 where he responded to additional questions. Subsequent to this, really as far as the followers of the theme could see, not much else happened. When some researchers were preparing a web page in 2003 on the subject, interest in the "map" waned, so something strange must have happened. They tried to find an update or at least an interview given by Chuvyrov in 2004, in Italy, but apparently he was still on the faculty at the University of Bashkiria in Ufa, Russia. An American company, the History of Mapping Project in Wisconsin, according to the study of the Pravda slab, reported in 2004 that they had not seen the map even though they had been contacted by the professor. Would he have been threatened as usual in these cases?

A translation of his interview in Italian from 2004 is described as "Original story, Pravda, April 30, 2002," and it says: "A finding by Bashkir scientists contradicts traditional notions *of human history, it is It is a 120-million-year-old stone slab, covered with a relief map of the Ural Region. This seems to be impossible. Scientists from the Bashkir State University have indisputably found evidence of the existence of a highly developed ancient civilization.*" The issue revolves around a large plaque that was found in 1999, with the image of the region made according to unknown technology. This is a true relief map. Today the military makes almost similar maps. The map contains civil engineering works: a canal system with a length of about 12,000km, dams, powerful reservoirs. Not far from the canals, diamond-shaped motifs whose fate is unknown are displayed. The map also contains numerous inscriptions. At first, scientists thought that it was the ancient Chinese language, however, it turned out that the subscriptions were made in a hieroglyphic-syllabic language whose origin is unknown. Scientists say when reading it: " *The more I learn, the more I understand that I know nothing.*" Physician of physical sciences and mathematics, professor at the Bashkir State University, Alexander Chuvyrov admits this.

Starting in 1995, the professor and his postgraduate student from China, Huan Hun decided to study the hypothesis of the possible migration of the old Chinese population in the territory of Siberia and the Urals. On an expedition to Bashkiria, they found several engravings made in the old Chinese language. These findings confirm the hypothesis of Chinese migrants. The inscriptions were read, and it was seen that they mostly contain information about commercial offers, death and marriage records. However, during the searches, the notes of the 18th century were found in the archives of the Ufa Governor-General. About 200 unusual stone slabs were reported to be found not far from Chandar village, Nurimanov Region. Chuvyrov and his colleague ruled that the slabs could be related to Chinese migrants. An archive of notes also reported that in the 17th-18th centuries, expeditions of Russian scientists studying the Ural Region had analyzed 200 white plates with signs and patterns, while at the beginning of the 20th century, archaeologist A. Schmidt I had also seen some white plates in Bashkiria.

All this made the scientist start the search. So in 1998, having assembled a team from his students, Chuvyrov set to work. He asked for help from a helicopter, and the first flight expedition began and more around the area where the plates were supposed to be. Despite all efforts, the ancient slabs were not found. Chuvyrov was very upset and even thought that the thing about the slabs was just a beautiful legend. Luck was unexpected, since during one of Chuvyrov's trips to the village, the former chairman of the Local Council of Agriculture, Vladimir Krainov, came to him (by the way, in the house of Krainov's father, the archaeologist Schmidt met was left once) and said: «*"Are you looking for some stone plates? I have a strange slab in my patio". "At first, I didn't take that report seriously"* » - said Chuvyrov- « *Despite this, I decided to go to that yard to see it. I remember exactly today: July 21, 1999. Under the porch of the house, there was a table with some students lying on it. The stab was so heavy that I couldn't contain myself. So I went to the city of Ufa, to ask for help.*»

the black ball

A few years ago, the Russian magazine Aura-Z published an article by the Russian researcher Vladimir Rubtsov about a very strange finding: a mysterious artifact known only by the nickname "The Black Ball" and whose origin was supposedly extraterrestrial. The sphere had been submitted for consideration by highly regarded specialists from the Russian Academy of Sciences, the Moscow Institute of Physical Engineering, and the Soyuz Scientific and Industrial Association. The discovery of the device was the product of a lucky accident. In 1975, during routine excavations in a quarry in southern Ukraine, workers found the object at a depth of 8m. One of the workers was surprised by the almost perfect configuration of the object and extracted it, taking it home as a novelty for his son.

Over time, the layer of clay that covered the object began to crumble, revealing a sphere of obsidian-like consistency. A teacher took the strange formation to the county museum, where it remained for many years before coming into the hands of Boris Naumenko, an adjunct scholar at the Institute of Earth Sciences. Naumenko and his colleagues had heard accounts of the object's supposed "extraterrestrial" origin and its "psychic" powers, so they launched a scientific investigation of the object to find out its composition and origin. Initial tests on "the Black Ball" revealed that it weighed between 400g and 600g, had a diameter of 18 inches, and was covered in a yellowish layer of various deposits. It was not possible to determine its age, although the discovery had been made in a 10-million-year-old layer of clay, taking into account the possibility that the object may have been deposited there later. However, it was possible to estimate that the particles surrounding the object were several million years old.

Researcher Rubtsov goes on to say in his article that several x-rays were taken of the object and it was discovered that it had a nucleus whose density was less than zero. The glassy surface of the object bore no resemblance to any known glassy substance, and the object's age ruled out the possibility that it was manufactured by human civilizations. According to the researchers, the sphere was artificial, represented the technology of a non-human and possibly extra-planetary society. The negative mass of the object's nucleus led several scientists to believe that it was a container containing antimatter: part of the propulsion system of a possible spacecraft. Rubstov comments that the only way to determine the object's contents was to pierce it, with results that could well be catastrophic.

However, this sphere is not the only ancient mystery in a circular shape: In Shivapur, India, there is a mysterious sphere that becomes light and rises in the air when touched by various people chanting mantras like Qamar Ali Derbis. Another mystery occurs with the glazed ceramic technique of some discovered works of Persian art, which were not recovered until the times of the Industrial Revolution, or with the mythical flying carpets.

When there were no cranes

Things get more complicated for skeptics when they discover in Pépieux (France), on top of an isolated hill with steeply sloping slopes, the presence of a dolmen with a slab weighing more than 30 tons. How was it possible to get such a stone block up there? The naveta d'Es Tudons, in Menorca, or the Ibero-Roman wall of Tarragona (both in Spain), are two good examples of Cyclopean constructions. Obviously, it involved far fewer technical problems to erect a menhir than to build a dolmen. In any case, if we take into account that some of these menhirs far exceed 7m and their weight is close to 100 tons, we will have to recognize that the operation, at least in these cases, could not have been easy either, and that it was necessary to a sophisticated technique, as well as a considerable organization, to carry it out.

Most often, given the enormous difficulties that transporting the stone blocks must have represented, the megalithic monuments are found in places close to the material extraction site. However, this is not always the case and sometimes the monument is several kilometers away from the quarry. A slab from the false-domed dolmen of El Soto (Huelva, Spain) was transported more than 38km before being placed on the monument. Although the most spectacular case is that of the "blue stones" (Bluestones) of Stonehenge (England); these 24 stone blocks, with a total weight of more than 350 tons and constituting the second circle of the great monument, are said to have been extracted from the Prescelly Mountains, in the Country of Wales, and installed north of Salisbury, in a plain that is 280km from the place of origin. How is such a construction possible? The same question will be addressed to the enormous solid stone perfectly carved in a rectangular shape, found in Baal-Bek in Lebanon, which is impossible to move.

In the so-called "Happy Arabia" civilization (which flourished between the 2nd century BC and the 3rd century AD), and which currently lies buried under the sands of the Arabian desert, there was a very ancient, magical and sophisticated hydrological complex for irrigation, at least with regard to the Marib reservoir, which also lies buried. As investigated by American archaeologists Richard Le Baron Bowen and Frank P. Albright. Through the meticulous examination of the photographs taken in infrared, by various observation satellites. All the territory of the Kingdom of Hausan and the other kingdoms of Happy Arabia were located very close to the Red Sea and the Gulf of Aden, being governed by witch-priests, the Mukkarib. The existence of these kingdoms is rare in this region, as they had a written language with a Semitic alphabet, knew ceramics and metallurgy, as well as built huge channels of baked clay to prevent filtration and in conjunction with these, a system of wells. and major dams, particularly like the one at Marib which irrigated 4,000 acres of land. Their inscriptions tell us legends related to Rub el Jali, its Cyclopean cities and its vanished civilizations. Entire cities that once seen disappeared, some believed that they were transported entirely to heaven.

Currently, near the area of the sea in the Gulf of Aden there is something mysterious: It is said, due to the leak of confidential information, that several governments have ships cordoning off a specific area where serious investigations are being carried out on something that apparently is a " portal". The information is classified but reveals that that territory has never ceased to have a close link with those beings who settled in the region and left their knowledge before returning to heaven.

Excavation Machines

One of the ancient artifacts whose function has been reinterpreted by contemporary authors is a small figure that was classified as a toy jaguar when it was found in Panama in the 1920s. If we consider the suggestion that this figure is actually a bulldozer, like our current bulldozers, then the object takes on a different appearance. Despite the age of the model, the curious triangular appendages are now beginning to look like blades of mechanical arms. The sprockets that are mounted on the tail of the model look as if they are going to mesh with chains or belts. Also in this order, the excavating machine possessed by the Incas is impressive, and an alleged pre-Columbian dog-toy with wheels found in Veracruz, Mexico (and it is said that these cultures did not know the wheel).

In Lingjiatan, Hanshan county of Anhui province in China, archaeologists have discovered a primitive tribe, a site that was inhabited about 5,000 years ago. This town was remarkably advanced in drilling technology and the world's first stone drill bits were found at the site. Archeology professor Zhang Jingguo said there are still many mysteries in the Lingjiatan ruins waiting to be solved. The Lingjiatan Ruins is located in Lingjiatan Village of Tongzha Township of Hanshan County in Chaohu City, Anhui Province, covering about 1.5 million m^2. Archaeologists say that the 5,000-year-old city was probably a prosperous city developed with construction, ranching and crafts. Before the discovery of the Lingjiatan ruins, the oldest city in China was recognized by archaeologists in Dantu Village in Wulian County in Rizhao City, Shandong Province, which was built over 4,000 years ago.

In the fall of 1985, a Lingjiatan villager by the name of Wan Chuancang found jade rings, stone axes, and stone chisels when he was digging a grave for his mother. That was the beginning of the most important discovery of these ruins from the late Neolithic Age. From 1987 to 2000, archaeologists conducted 4 archaeological excavations at the site. They discovered more than 1,200 pieces of precious objects, including: an altar, 66 tombs, refined jade, stoneware, and pottery dating to the late Neolithic Age. Among them are the earliest Jade Dragon and the largest stone shovel discovered to date in China. Archaeologists believe that 5,000 years ago, the area was highly developed, supporting the theory that the Chaohu Lake basin was an important birthplace of Chinese culture. Listed among prehistoric ruins, Lingjiatan has the largest number of jade pieces. Professor Zhang Jingguo and his colleagues inspected these jade pieces with a binocular microscope for investigation of jade treatment with the technology of that day. With a magnification of less than 50 times, they found a small hole in the back of a jade statue. The hole diameter is only 0.15mm. This would have required a bit with a diameter slightly thicker than a strand of hair! At that time, before the use of metal for tools, the people in Lingjiatan, 5,000 years ago, already used this kind of advanced technology. The archaeologists also found a stone drill bit, wide at the top and narrow at the bottom, with drill holes at both ends. This perforation is screw-shaped, indicating that people in Lingjiatan knew about rotary power and centrifugal force. His knowledge of physics, mathematics, geometry, and mechanics seems to have been quite developed.

Many eminent archaeologists are surprised by how advanced the stone drill was. Archaeologists also discovered large stone relics with more than 10m (33ft) at Lingjiatan; built over 1,000 years before Stonehenge in Great Britain. 5,000 years ago, the Lingjiatan people have only been using stone and wood tools, it is not known how they cut and transported such huge and heavy stones. (Epoch Times Staff article from April 7, 2006)

Although most archaeological work deals with the trinkets and ruins left behind by ancient societies, from time to time objects appear that surpass all estimates hitherto made of the technical capacity of an ancient culture. During the 1970s, a team of archaeologists working on excavations in Bulgaria made a series of startling discoveries about the Neolithic culture of Karanovo, which flourished there around 4500 BC. The finds date from a time when man was thought to have he hardly knew metallurgy; however, the Karanovo tombs revealed an astonishing trove of beautifully crafted gold and copper weapons and jewelry.

Discoveries of this kind slowly but steadily force archaeologists to revise their ideas about ancient man's technical knowledge. Among these findings, a dagger from 3000 BC stands out.

vitrified walls

A perfectly preserved mummy found in China from 2,142 years ago shows that the Egyptians were the fathers of this body preservation system. How were all these civilizations related? The Mayans shared many things with the Egyptians, while they shared almost the entire language with the Asians. The science was very similar on both continents, and even other types of puzzling phenomena. In any case, not only the most legendary civilizations of the past keep almost unsolved mysteries. From Scotland to Hungary, from Norway to France, there are traces of vitrified enclosures. The age of these fortifications, most of the time partially vitrified, is estimated between 1800 BC and 200 BC To melt these granite walls, a temperature between 1,100° and 1,300°C is needed, combined with a slow combustion process. Several theories have been issued and some of them have even been tested -unsuccessfully so far. The most admissible emanates from the geologist Alain Ploquin when in 1988, he took out a "murrus gallicus" in the city of Affrique. It is about something that breaks the molds of our conception of the past; Either there were civilizations that came from other worlds and brought their technology, or in the past our ancestors had greater knowledge and scientific advances than we have today.

The Crystal Skulls

The famous crystal skulls, cut in the shape of a human skull, vary in shape, size and type of crystal, although some represent superhuman beings. It is said that some of them were carved by extraterrestrials, others believe that they were made by antediluvian civilizations; while others estimate that they were made by the Mayans and other cultures, while most of the skulls that we can see today are estimated to have been carved recently. The places where these objects have been found are generally located in Central America, especially in Aztec and Mayan ruins, although there have been news and rumors of possible finds in South America. In addition to astonishing us with the way they were carved, or the inability to determine how they were carved, there are claims that inexplicable and strange phenomena occur around them. The best known of these skulls, as well as the most mysterious, is the "Skull of Fate" or "Calavera del Destino" (Skull of Doom), discovered by Mitchell-Hedges, which has characteristics very similar to that of a true human skull. such as teeth and a moving jaw. Until now it has not been possible to determine the way in which it was carved, since it is a work impossible to carry out by the most talented sculptors of his time, and it is even an outstanding work to attempt today.

At the turn of the century, an English explorer and adventurer found a perfectly polished rock crystal skull among the ruins of a Mayan city. The origin of such a puzzling "sculpture" is still an enigma. The crystal skull, also called the "Skull of Destiny", was found by chance in an ancient Mayan city. In 1924, the versatile English explorer Frederick A. Mitchell-Hedges arrived in the tropical forests of Belize (British Honduras) in Central America, accompanied by his adoptive daughter Anna, his secretary Jane Houlson, the doctor and expert in Mayan culture Dr. Thomas Gann, the representative of the British Museum Captain Joyce and the financier of the Richmond Brown expedition. Frederick Mitchell-Hedges was quite a celebrity in the 1920s. An ambitious and intelligent adventurer, he spent years in different parts of North and South America, performing the most varied trades: from cowboy to professional gambler, going through revolutionary under Pancho's orders. Vila or archaeologist and frequenting the most contradictory environments, from explorers' clubs to millionaires' clubs.

It was Mitchell's adoptive daughter, little Anna, who produced the great discovery: " *For days we would see something between the stones receiving the reflections of the Sun,*" *Anna Mitchell-Hedges now recalls, "and we did not rest until we made that place accessible. It was me who rescued him because my hands were smaller than the others and I showed it to my father. He refused to believe in the discovery of that crystal skull...*», The Skull of Destiny was a life-size rock crystal skull, weighing 5kg sculpted in one piece. The absolute perfection of its carving and its unscathed polishing, the perfection of its details and its articulated jaw make it an exact replica of a human skull, but the origin of its manufacture, who knows how many centuries ago, is a true mystery.

But, despite the disinterest of the scientific establishment, this crystal skull existed, and with the passing of time it was attracting the curiosity of an increasing number of scholars free of academic prejudices. According to the aforementioned English archaeologist and adventurer, the Skull would have had a magical and ritual utility. This is how his daughter Anna explained it: « *The Mayans told us that they used it to cause death or to cure illnesses. For example, if a sorcerer was too old to perform ceremonies, he would choose a young man and they would both prostrate themselves at the (skull) altar. Then a priest would perform a ceremony and the old man's knowledge was passed on to the young man. From then on the old man could die in peace, since the young man became a wise man ...*" Those who have studied it say that this crystal skull has enormous powers, including prediction of future events.

Mitchell-Hedges himself said after the discovery of the enigmatic crystal skull: "*It they have embodied in it all the evils of the world*." Setting aside the debatable psychic ability of the Crystal Skull, the fundamental question remains unanswered: who built it?

It is known that the skills of art and pre-Columbian goldsmithing are surprising, but did they get that far? The elaborate pieces discovered in 1987 in northern Peru, belonging to the Sipán treasure, or the extraordinary jade mask of Mr. Pakal found in the Palenque temple are good examples of the technical precision of pre-Columbian goldsmiths, although it is not known who or who could pass that knowledge on to those ancient peoples. The perfection of the polish that the Calavera del Destino presents is far from the most worked pre-Columbian pieces.

The Skull of Destiny is carved on quartz crystal, which on the Mohs scale of mineral hardness reaches a value of 7 out of 10. With which only diamond is capable of cutting it with precision. So what is absolutely incomprehensible is that the "Skull of Destiny" is built in one piece (except for the movable jaw) and along and across its entire surface there is not a single mark or scratch from any tool. In 1970, the Hewlett-Packard company subjected the skull to a series of analyses, ruling that to obtain a product like the one examined, at least 300 years of coordinated manual labor were needed, acting on the stone by erosion of its surface. In short, it does not value the work of human action. Subsequently, it was the laboratory located in the basement of the prestigious British Museum that subjected this crystal skull to different analyses. However, the skull managed to evade all the evidence by keeping its secrets. Not a single clue allowed the British Museum's gemstone expert, Alan Jogins, to reveal the origin of the mysterious jewel: " *We have no positive evidence that any metal has been used - Jogins would explain - which does not mean that they have not. skillfully concealed. It is a dexterous and very sophisticated work. If it was made by primitive people it is amazing, because the level of hand carving is of the highest quality.*»

Experts place the time of manufacture of the crystal skull in the Aztec period, between 1300 BC and 1400 AD but, if so, what was an Aztec piece doing in a Mayan city located hundreds of kilometers further south? On the other hand, the indigenous people, direct descendants of the Maya, who worked with Mitchell-Hedges on his excavation of Lubaantun, told the intrepid archaeologist that the Skull of Destiny was more than 3,600 years old. Who was able to make this enigmatic object around the 1700s before Jesus Christ?

other skulls

The mystery deepens when it is discovered that the crystal skull found in Belize is not the only one. Already in 1889, a wealthy Mexican soldier discovered a similar skull in his country, with two differences from that of Mitchell-Hedges: First, the Mexican crystal skull is made of a quartz crystal of lesser purity, in one piece, with which the mandible is not mobile, but is attached to the rest of the skull. On the other hand, a large scratch on the upper part of the skull also differentiates it from the perfect "Skull of Doom". This crystal skull is preserved in the Museum of Humanity in London, who acquired it from the famous jeweler Tiffany's in New York. However, the well-known jewelry did not provide more information about the origin of this no less enigmatic archaeological piece. It is suspected that it could have been part of a booty obtained in Mexico by some anonymous mercenary dedicated to the illegal traffic of art and antique pieces. And as if all this were not enough, a third crystal skull, identical in style to the previous ones, is on display at the Musée de l'Homme in Paris. Museum experts say it was part of an Aztec "magic staff" from the 13th or 14th century AD and was used to ward off snakes and predict the future.

Of these three crystal skulls, only about "Skull of Doom" is the exact time and place of its discovery known. Its valuation is around 4 million dollars, and the unfathomable mysteries that surround it make it a star piece of world archaeology. Not surprisingly, the famous science fiction writer Arthur C. Clarke (author of "2001, A Space Odyssey") made it the emblem of his series "The Mysterious World of Arthur Clarke". But there are also other skulls. In general, the most prominent and considered authentic are:

SKULL OF DOOM · Discovered in 1927 by Mitchell-Hedges in the Mayan ruins of Lubaantum, Belize.

MAYA · Discovered in Guatemala in 1912.

LAZULI Carved in lapis lazuli. Discovered in 1995 in northern Peru by indigenous Incas.

JESUIT · There is news of it since 1534. San Ignacio de Loyola, founder of the Jesuits, had it in his possession.

SHUI TING ER · Carved in amazonite, discovered 130 years ago by the Chinese archaeologist Yeng Fo Huu in southwestern Mongolia.

OCEANÍA · Sculpted in quartz. It belonged to a Brazilian peasant who lives in a remote region of the Amazon. It is believed that it was discovered by indigenous nomads from this region.

ET · Discovered in 1906 in Guatemala. It's smoky quartz. It has certain air not humane. It is characterized by the pointed shape of the skull and pronounced jaw.

MAX · The largest known crystal skull.

BABY LUV · Rose quartz, discovered in the year 1700 by a monk from the Luov monastery (Ukraine). They had kept it for hundreds of years.

Nanotechnology in the Urals

Since 1991, gold prospectors, then scientific expeditions -commissioned by the Moscow Central Institute for Scientific Research in Geology and Prospecting for Precious and Nonferrous Metals- have discovered metallic objects, many in the form of spirals, the size of which varies from 3cm to larger up to 3/1000 of a millimeter in smaller ones. It is what is called "Nanotechnology in the Ice Age" in the Urals. Thousands of such artifacts have been found in many locations in the eastern part of the Ural Mountains, on the banks of various rivers in sedimentary layers dating to the Late Pleistocene, at various depths from 3m to 12m. These objects have been studied by the Russian Academy of Sciences in Syk ty vka, Moscow and Saint Petersburg, as well as by a scientific institute in Helsinki in Finland: The larger objects are made of copper, while the smaller ones are made of tungsten (melting point 3,410° C) or molybdenum (melting point 2,650° C).

Depending on the site and depth where they were found, the age of these objects is estimated to be between 20,000 and 31,800 years (take into account that the Pleistocene oscillates between 11,000 and 1.8 million years). The Moscow Institute published an expert report n° 18/485 of 11/29/96 which concluded: « *the data obtained allow us to think about the possibility of a technology of extraterrestrial origin.* »

Visitors from space or just from the Old World?

Now we are going exclusively to the ancient peoples and cultures, dusting off so many enigmas and things that are not normally counted. Thus we arrive at more answers as to why there are, for example, so many statues with features different from the indigenous Mayan culture in so many places in America, such as those discovered in Guatemala. Some examples are a statue made of lime, called "La Blanca", probably made of this material due to the color of the woman's skin, which shows traits between Orientals and Caucasians. Another is a wooden statue with a mustache, which is in a strange posture. It seems to manipulate a kind of large necklace. He has features that look oriental, reminiscent of the Mongols. Another figure of many is an Olmec, on this occasion apart from being able to perfectly distinguish the Negroid features of the figure, we can clearly see that she is wearing a fitted space suit with a helmet and the fine lines of its fabric can be distinguished on her face. It is reminiscent of the first layer of clothing in modern space suits. You can also clearly see the large gloves that he wears. He's handling some kind of unknown artifact. Other evidence is the case of a large human head discovered in the jungle of Guatemala (Monte Alto) in 1940, which has not been excessively publicized. Its enormous size stands out, as in the case of the Olmec heads and their evident Caucasian features.

About the visits of ancient astronauts Erich von Däniken has spoken a lot, but without a doubt, the expert in the Sumerian language, Zecharia Sitchin, had more elaborate theories. He pointed out that a space base located in the Sinai was destroyed 4,000 years ago and agrees with RA Boulay that it was replaced by another new site in Peru: Machu Pichu. The ancient buildings leave researchers speechless, the way in which these sites were built and the technology that these cultures had does not correspond to the idea we have of "primitive man". Let's travel again to these places to see more what science says, since thanks to the discoveries the possibility that prehistoric human civilization was closely linked to beings from space has been theorized. In fact, as Michael Tsarion states about the aliens that were here in the past: " *we are them.*"

Norway's mini tunnel

One of many fabulous discoveries corresponds to the discovery made by Buddy Broyt and Ole Gunnar Krovel while they were carrying out an excavation in Norway under the orders of the KA Aurstad Volda company for the construction of a Chiropractic Center. The excavation was carried out near a solid stone cliff. When they were several meters deep and when removing sediment soil, Krovel found a disconcerting hole in the shape of a seven-pointed star and about 6cm in diameter, as well as being very smooth and well polished. Surprised, Krovel removed 4m of rock to find out where the hole ended but, surprised, he observed that the strange hole entered the mountains of the northwestern fjords.

In the opinion of this expert excavator in his more than 30 years in the profession, he had never seen anything like it before.

Those responsible for the work could never explain the presence of the hole and other geologists in the region, such as Einar Anda, can only show their perplexity about the matter and what produced the enigmatic and tiny tunnel. So far, three possible explanations have been established, and none of them definitive:

Crystals: He argues that the hole was probably composed of a crystal that was dissolved by water over thousands of years and the hole formed by a spectacular coincidence of chance. Although it is already superficially ridiculous, we have against it that the hole goes straight into the mountain and then deviates to the right in an intentional way.

Artificial: The hole was produced in 1930 when the area was used as a quarry. Apparently there are pneumatic hammers that use 6 joined bit pieces that could be mounted horizontally thus forming the hole. In this way a drill that rotates and hammers with 6 points, can leave that shape. Against we have that the length of the hole is impossible for any tool of this type.

Civilization: This theory postulates that an ancient but advanced but vanished civilization created and was the maker of the hole. Against is a basic question: for what purpose did they do it?

Tiwanaku Ruins

Archaeologists and researchers discovered that about 4,000 years ago there was a huge impact in Argentina and the shock wave from this impact could have been the cause that destroyed many stone buildings in the Bolivian Altiplano. For example, from Puma Punku, a very strange place near Tiwanaku, in Bolivia. Here you see tons of perfectly built stone plates, destroyed. Perhaps this was the reaction to the big impact in Argentina, but we don't really know. The issue is that these stones, of such size and tonnage, could not be built except with modern machinery. Giancarlo Bonfanti, an Italian researcher, a friend of Klaus Dona, is seen in a photograph in the center of the well-known Puerta del Sol, in Tiwanaku, while inquiring into how this could be done. His studies and those of other analysts in this field say that there is no doubt: it was made by an advanced civilization.

Some researchers say that the figurines at the top of one side of the door show the Venusian calendar. On one of the large stone plaques at Puma Punku you can see the perfection with which this stone work was made. The question that always resounds and that the writer and researcher Colin Wilson left in the air in the documentary "La Atlántida" was: «Could *such work be carried out with simple tools?* » He and his companions studied Tiwanaku, coming to the conclusion that these constructions must have been contemporary with Atlantis, and in fact, the Atlantean knowledge would have wielded the science of the ancient world. When the Spanish conquistadores asked the Incas if they had built Tiwanaku they replied: «*No, we did not build it. It was done thousands of years before we lived.*" The same happened with the analysis of the Inca fortress of Sacsahuamán. The result: impossible to build without cranes, and impossible to move them with modern machinery. Something that shocked the archaeologist himself, Professor Neil Seede, when he analyzed the way in which the enormous Tiwanaku stones had been joined.

The Millennial Astronauts

The Spanish journalist and writer JJ Benítez, in his famous book "There was another Humanity" (Plaza y Janés, Barcelona, 1977), spoke of the discovery of two artificial hills that covered a pavement of engraved stones, in a place near Palpa (Peru) towards which nothing less than the Nazca lines seem to point. But spectacular photographs of what appear to be landing strips in Samaipata (Bolivia), and another 3,000 km south of Peru, among other similar discoveries, give rise to strong theories of possible "landings" of flight devices in millenary eras, don't sound so fictional after all.

After the list of unusual visits and legendary peoples more advanced than us today, we have the Nazca lines, in Peru, which can only be appreciated from the air at a considerable height, and extend for several kilometers in length and width. Among its interesting representations we find: spiders, monkeys, hummingbirds, other types of birds, unknown animals, fish from the prehistoric era, lizards, and other creatures that no longer exist, as well as landing strips and the enormous figure of an astronaut. Another example of visits from space is that of the Caral statuette, which represents a strange being of short stature and slanted eyes; It is not strange, these beings are seen throughout the Mesoamerican culture. Within this mysterious and fascinating region that is Peru, we have a large number of pyramids that could not be built without the help of sophisticated technology, as can be seen in areas such as Caral, Pantiacola and Sipán, for example, as is the case with the Mexican territory, where there are so many pyramids in addition to those already popularly known, and ancient ruins in the jungle, that, as in Mexico, the national budget for the study of heritage does not reach enough capital to study them and bring them to light.

The appearance of statuettes or other types of prehistoric representations of airplanes, rockets and astronauts have also left their discoverers and researchers who have analyzed them for decades speechless. In the Museum of Bogotá in Colombia, you can see small airplanes of all kinds that were discovered in indigenous tombs, and something similar occurs in Egypt where the model of an airplane was found in the temple of Saqqara. Although this is not the most surprising thing, rather it is the millenary figures of rockets discovered everywhere, such as those found in Turkey, Iraq, Peru or Mexico, or those of flying saucers represented in different ways and found in Tanzania, Morocco, Australia, Egypt, France, Peru, Ecuador, Bolivia, Russia, Japan, Nepal, Iraq, Syria, Israel or Mexico, among many others.

THE PALENQUE ASTRONAUT

A very special "heater" was found inside the Palenque complex, which is suspiciously similar to a modern nozzle, the same one used by space shuttles. But that is not the most incredible thing, but the well-known "Palenque Astronaut", which is an engraving 3.80m long, 2.20m wide, 25cm thick and weighing 5 tons. It is a relief image that was found in 1949 by the archaeologist Alberto Ruz de L'huiller in a temple in Mexico, inside a pyramid. The figure represents a man inside a rocket, pressing an accelerator. You can see the turbines, the levers and the entire internal system of the rocket.

Pyramids and unknown symbols in Bolivia

In a tunnel, found near the Bay of Guayaquil in Bolivia, some workers found the famous "Pyramid of the Eye", which is a well-shaped stone. The eye is an inlay. The stone is gray and white, and has 13 steps, and looks exactly like the Pyramid with the Glowing Eye on the US one dollar bill. If you put this pyramid under bright light, the eye glows brightly and looks really like an eye, but not really like a human eye but rather green in the eyeball and yellow in the iris. At the bottom of this pyramid, there is an inlay in small gold sheets showing the star constellation Orion, and there are also unknown writings. Professor Kurt Schildmann, who was President of the German Linguistic Association, and who was fluent in more than 40 languages, was able to translate this writing. He called it "pre-Sanskrit" since it is older than the oldest known script. And the translation of the four letters expressed is: "The Son of the Creator comes", and according to other scholars of ancient languages, it says: "The Son of 'The All' Comes". Something like the Son of God was on the way, although written thousands of years ago.

This information was taken from an interview by Byll Ryan to Klaus Dona, and it also states: «... *just as we have found the same writing on stones in certain countries such as Ecuador; Colombia; USA (specifically in Illinois); France (in Glozel); Malta, in the Mediterranean; Turkmenistan; Australia, and Italy, in southern Calabria, just a few years ago. There are always stones and ceramics, terracotta, with the same writing. That means that this script once existed all over the world, which means that there must have been a global civilization older than Sanskrit over 6,000 years old .*" Researcher Klaus Dona added: *"Professor Schildmann also told me that this script has a small similarity to the Hindu script and to the Easter Island script. As he said: 'this is older than Sanskrit'. He called this writing 'pre-Sanskrit'."* (Interview with Klaus Dona by Byll Ryan of Project Camelot and Project Avalon. February 20, 2010)

The world of the pyramids

In this order of technological advances and majestic buildings, impossible for a civilization that had just emerged from the caves and learned to use fire and stone tools, we find an endless number of pyramids spread all over the world: Cuba, Mexico, Peru, the Atlantic, Baigong (China), Egypt, Nepal, Bermuda, Australia, Canary Islands (Spain), Russia, and even many other places like the Moon and Mars, as astronomers and space probes have shown. Let us emphasize that in size, the largest pyramid on Earth has recently been discovered in the depths of the Atlantic Ocean, followed in size by those of Bosnia (Russia), and then those of Gize in Egypt, without forgetting that already in the distant Sumer there was talk of the construction of Ziggurats (stepped pyramids) of excessive sizes.

On the shore of one of the two Lakes of Lovers (one freshwater and the other saltwater), located at the foot of Mount Baigong and 40km southwest of the city of Delingha, stands a pyramid about 50m high. , connected by several metal tubes to the salt lake. At the front of the pyramid, there are 3 caves with triangular shaped entrances. Of the three entrances, the one in the middle is the largest and the only one accessible, since in the two on the sides the entrance holes are smaller and have collapsed. The central cave is approximately 6m deep and inside it is a tube of approx. 40cm in diameter that goes into the interior of the pyramid, with only the upper part of it visible. At the entrance to the cave there are a dozen tubes of different diameters (from 10cm to 40cm) that go into the interior of the mount. All tubes are brownish red, the same color as those of surrounding rocks. Approximately 80m from the caves, on the sand of the southern shore of the salt lake, there are a large number of oxidized metal remains, stones and remains of pipes of various diameters (from 2cm to 4.5cm) strangely distributed and Oriented in an east-west direction, there is even a tube as fine as a toothpick, and it is also strange that, after so much time next to the sand of the lake, none of them is clogged or clogged.

Stranger is that some of these tubes also enter the lake water from the shore, ignoring for now the depth reached by these and their purpose. According to Qin Jianwen, head of the publicity department of the Delingha government, samples were collected from the tubes for composition analysis. The result shows that the tubes are composed of 30% iron oxide, a high percentage of silicon dioxide as well as calcium oxide. But the most curious thing about this analysis carried out on the tubes is that 8% of the content could not be identified, that is, the tube is made of a material that does not exist on Earth. The fact that the tubes contain large amounts of silicon dioxide and calcium oxide is the result of a long interaction between the iron and the sand on the lake shore, so it follows that the tubes must be very old, Liu Shaolin said, the engineer who performed the analysis. Liu Shaolin dated the age of the tubes at about 5,000 years old, something exceptional if, as has been taught, man began working with metal alloys only 3,000 years ago.

The result of the analyses, the fact that the environment is inhospitable and deserted, there is no modern industry in the entire area and that the only people passing through the area are migratory herders from the north of the mountains, make this discovery even more mysterious. The area of the pyramid is located at an altitude of 2,200m, with fine and transparent air, ideal for astronomy. What's more, the Chinese Academy of Sciences built the Purple Mountain Observatory less than 70km from the area.

EGYPTIAN PYRAMIDS

When we take a look at Egypt we find that almost everything is still intact. The interior of the pyramid seems to be in the same state in which the Arabs found it in the year 820 AD. Although the red granite chest is its only decorative element, the absence of ornaments only enhances its interior. Nothing remains of everything that could have contained the King's, Queen's and Chaos Chambers. Uniting the three, there are tiny channels of unknown meaning, narrow passages that humiliate rather than dignify the man who walks through them. The Grand Gallery, impressive in size, dwarfs pride when one faces the solemn in utter solitude. 46 endless meters of walls, perfectly parallel, constitute the magnum opus of stone engineering. A whole framework that does not keep a single hieroglyph, not a single inscription, not the slightest relief made by the hand of the builders in any of the 2,800,000 stone blocks, in the almost 3,000,000 m 3 of ^{rock} , in the 7,000,000 tons of stone erected as an apparent homage to mysticism, science or madness.

However, Abd-al-Latif, a 13th-century Arab historian, said that a large number of inscriptions were engraved on the lining blocks, in unintelligible characters. Herodotus, who contemplated the pyramid around the year 440 BC, comments on the same signs, the interpretation of which was as unknown to him as to the guide who accompanied him. And it is strange that the meaning of the inscriptions was a mystery, since in the time of Herodotus hieroglyphics were still translated, as this historian was able to verify when he was introduced to the Isiac rites at the hands of the priests of Sais, who dominated the written characters. of ancient Egypt, as evidenced by the Rosetta stone, written in hieratic, demotic and Greek. Therefore, the writing that covered the facing blocks of the Great Pyramid was unknown to the Egyptians.

In Egypt there would be two types of pyramids, those before the pharaohs (usurped by the IV Dynasty) and those built by the Egyptians to try to emulate those built by the gods. Imhotep, King Djoser's architect , built the first "human" pyramid in Saqqara, being, like the other 100 that are distributed throughout Lower Egypt, a sloppy imitation of the first. It turns out that the architectural evolution to build pyramids does not explain that 50 years before building the pyramids of Gize the Egyptians did not know how to build perfect pyramids and that 20 years after the Fourth Dynasty they forgot, leaving the monuments of Gize as an anachronistic island technology within the pharaonic culture. In this regard, it is convenient to compare the pyramids of the III Dynasty with the pyramids of the V Dynasty, to verify that both have the same pattern of stepped pyramids, offering no engineering problem, and corresponding to the tools that we find from the Old Kingdom in the Museum. from Cairo. But what about the pyramids of Gize? There are no machines in museums that could cope with the magnitude of their construction. Who and how built them? Those mysteries can be best exposed in Ian Lawton and Chris Ogilvie-Herald's book, "Giza, The Truth".

The symbol pyramidal

In Klaus Dona's studies in South America, the fact that many finds deal with pyramids and the Orion constellation stands out. On a stone you can see two eyes at the tip, and then the right hand holding a pyramid and placing the left hand on top of the pyramid. That means, according to him, that he shows how to use this Pyramid with the Eye. Another artifact is a pyramidal stone also found in Ecuador. At the top you can see the pyramid with the eye, and below are various spirals and symbols. Klaus Dona says that they are very similar to Churchward's Naacal plates that he discovered in 1889 in India, and the translation talks about the sunken continent, Mu.

An equally intriguing carving can be seen on another stone: a man sitting on a stone, holding the pyramid exactly as shown in the previous artifact. Rays come out of his eyes and on the right side you can see two people leaning, where do the rays hit. On his head he has something like a small helmet and from this helmet he rises like an antenna to a strange object above him. That object looks like a flying ovoid sphere radiating a lot of light. A helmet was also discovered, « *we still cannot carry out a study on the metal or a review of the type of metal that was used but you can see that in the center of the helmet something is missing and that it may have been this type of antenna that is shown in the previous artifact .*» Dona says. It is believed that the helmets found are related to the image of the being that possesses the antenna. We can also appreciate a marble object with another spiral inlay that also sparkles very intensely under bright light; In the same way, another pyramid-shaped stone was found, with an inlay of an eye. Likewise, another larger one was found with the eye in the upper part of the pyramid and in the lower part of the stone the stellar constellation of Orion can be seen again, highlighting the three main stars of Orion: «Which can direct us *to the three pyramids of Egypt .*» (Interview with Klaus Dona by Byll Ryan of Project Camelot and Project Avalon. February 20, 2010)

The figures of South America

Based on the interview with Klaus Dona we can add: « *There is also a ceramic statue. She shows the style of sitting, which is not pre-Columbian but Asian, just like the character's eyes and nose. It seems to sit in the Asian Lotus style. A cap with some dots is visible on the head of the statue and it looks quite similar to many of the representations of the Buddha. The statue has closed eyes and it bites the tail of a snake or it is as if it were holding it with its tail and the snake looks suffering. This statue is not from any existing or known pre-Columbian culture. Another statue appears and looks just as seated and with a similar hat, although with the most prominent points, like tiny horns. The figure has an extremely prominent chin. In the center of the hat you can see the head or face of a frog. The frog is not only a very mystical animal from the ancient pre-Columbian cultures of South America but also from Africa and Asia .*» And Herr Klaus Dona continues: « *In another ceramic statue he is seen holding a kind of plate in his left hand, with slanted eyes and unpopular clothing. It does not seem to be from a pre-Columbian culture; We have another human figure. This is another very strange artifact holding a stick with a snake coiled around it .*"

The sad relationship that is usually made between the artifacts of ancient peoples with ceremonial and folklore pieces damages the true perspective of these figures. Dolls and statuettes of astronauts, rockets, and planes are seen throughout Central and South America, while the religious and uneducated believe they were ritual costumes. For example, an excavator possessed by the Incas, figurines showing women giving birth by caesarean section, brain and heart operations, toys with wheels (since the Mayans did not know this system), and the list goes on and on despite the so many cover ups

The strange artifacts of Colombia

Colombia's most famous industrial designer and architect, Professor Jaime Gutiérrez, who has been collecting rare artifacts from his country for several centuries, showed the highlights of his collection to Mr. Klaus Dona. Its most important piece is the so-called "Genetic Disc": " *a disc made entirely of lydite, a very hard stone. It is quite similar in strength to granite, but lydite has a sheet-like structure, so it would be virtually impossible to make the same disc today from the same material. The diameter of this disc is around 27cm. In it there are several things that are presented, which can only be seen with a microscope. For example, on the left side at around 11 o'clock, you can see a human egg without sperm and one with sperm. On the right side, at approximately one o'clock, you can see some sperm. And then there are various representations that we cannot explain .»*

«On the opposite side, at the top, there are several representations of fetuses of different sizes, different months, ending with what looks like a small child. Also at the end of the plate, at around six o'clock, a woman and a man are seen. And also on the right side around nine o'clock you can see the presentation of a man, woman and child. But the strange thing is how they present their heads, stretched to the sides, which seem human. You can also see a knife made of the same material, Lidita. At the top of the knife, on the handle, is the head of a mother, then there is the head of a child and the umbilical cord wrapped around the child's neck. So it means that this knife would have been used to cut the umbilical cord, to save the child's life. Another similar instrument could have been used to help deliver the child when there were complications. And it's also made of lydite. This

one seems to have a finger support, which would imply that it would not be used forcefully but rather to help with childbirth .»

Other small instruments that look like doctors and are perfect to hold in the hand have a point that would serve as a skewer. They are very similar to surgical instruments. In Vienna they determined that indeed they were entirely from Lydita. The experts said they did not know how they were made or who made them, the Vienna expert added: " *The only thing I can definitely tell you about the same material today is that we cannot make the same instruments .*" Dona said: " *We don't know how old they were, but since they were found in Colombia and don't fit with any existing pre-Columbian culture, we must consider these artifacts to be at least 6,000 years old. But we can't explain what kind of technology they used to create such instruments and such lydite tools . In another strange artifact we see a face similar to that of the Moai, the great stone statues of Easter Island. There is also a figurine that looks like a man sitting in a dentist's chair. This one is cute too. The question is, if they could make these figurines in Lydian, why don't they show natural human features, but instead have big round eyes and a small nose and mouth? »*

Another piece from lydite in Colombia shows a mother holding a baby and in the other hand something like a fish. In the back the man is seen as prepared for the hunt. Then in another piece of work in the stone we see a bird, but if viewed from the front side the two birds (one on each side of the stone) represent a human face. And between the wings of the birds the unknown scriptures are seen again. On another stone found in Colombia you can see an armadillo, and at the top you can see a very strange human face with long ears and two horns on top. In another figure, apparently made of the same type of stone as the armadillo, we can see a laughing face at the top. On the left side it has two triangles. On the right side there is an animal face as well, and with strange writings or unknown symbols. At the bottom of the object you can see something like a crocodile. Finally, another figure shows a mother with a very strange face holding a baby wrapped in something. This figure is of a jade type of material. In the case of another figurine of a different type of stone, and also found in Colombia, it can be seen that it is identical to the Moai statues of the Chilean Easter Island, despite its small size: 30cm high.

a colossal bust

In West Africa, specifically in Guinea, near the border with Mali, a huge granite mountain was found showing a female bust made of granite stone. The size of this statue from the top of the head to the middle of the torso is exactly 150m. Who was able to make such a granite statue 10,000 or 12,000 years ago? Well, the Italian geologist, Professor Pitoni, was at the location, took photos and examined the terrain at the top of the mountain, calculating that this statue would have been made some 10,000 to 12,000 years ago. « *Not even in our days could such a monument be built, not only because it is physically impossible but because it would be a million-dollar job, that is, it would cost so much that it would not be worth making. The experts considered that the face was not European or African, rather South American or Asian .*» clarifies Klaus Dona.

Bolivian and Ecuadorian artifacts

Among the objects studied by Klaus Dona, we have one that at the time could have been a very hard brown stone, changing color from the center of the stone to black, which generally does not occur in nature. And you can see, if you look very closely, a face with closed eyes, with a mouth, a nose, a long beard and long hair. On the left side, the face, and also the stone, are destroyed. On the opposite side of this stone you can see a spiral and a triangle. The center of the pyramid is very magnetic and also sparkles in bright light.

Another object is what on the one hand looks like a cobra. The cobra never existed in South America, but this one was found in the same place. On the other side of the cobra's head, there are 33 lines across, so 33 has also been a very mystical number for a long time. Dona adds: « *On the left and right side there are seven embedded points and perhaps these are the chakras. Likewise, the head of this cobra flashes very intensely if you expose it to bright light. Another thing found is a perfectly made dolphin head, and this artifact, too, sparkles in bright light. There is also a kind of stone helmet. You can put this granite stone helmet on your shoulders or you can put your head in the socket. And the embedded points you see on this helmet, some experts told me are exactly the acupuncture points on the human head* ."

« *A few months ago they found an unfinished stone helmet in the same place. So this means that some of these artifacts were also made directly in Ecuador, but many, many years ago. Also on the helmet from before the inlay on the object flashes in bright light. Another artifact is a fascinating jade snake. And also the inlaid dots sparkle under bright light. Another thing found there was an artifact that is perfectly carved on the back side so that means it may have been used to put this artifact on your forehead. The two embedded eyes can be seen. And on the opposite side is what is popularly known as the "third eye". Perhaps this artifact was used for some ceremonies or for meditation* ." Add Donut.

A jade plaque with a spiral inlay was also found, which also sparkles brightly under bright light. Others is an object with seven rings embedded in the jade plate and which also sparkle under bright light. « *Perhaps this could also be a representation of the seven chakras. One of the ceramics found there is a masterpiece, and the question is: "How can you make this artifact from a single piece of ceramic?" it shows a man standing on something like a sphinx or feline, and both have disproportionate skulls* .» Dona concludes.

Mexico, city of the gods

To know in detail the hidden and technological history of Central and South America, it is necessary to study what has happened in the last thousands of years, since the first gods, bearers of technology and wisdom, landed on Earth. The figures of Acambaro in Mexico, in a total of 33,500 pure ceramic objects, portray dinosaurs, extinct animals that are not known and various types of men, these date, according to the University of New Jersey by means of carbon 14, between 1110 BC and 4530 BC, although the University of Pennsylvania with thermoluminescence has dated them to 2500 BC. The same conclusion could be drawn from a very old sample of what looks like writing, described in the American Journal of Science in 1831. A block of marble quarried from the Earth at a minimum depth of 18m was cut into sheets. One of the cuts showed a 4cm by 1.5cm incision: it consisted of two "letters" similar to "i" and "u". The regularity of the letters gives the impression that they are two characters engraved by human hands and somehow preserved through millions of years (during which marble was formed), while all traces of the building in which they were engravings, or other additional engravings, would have disappeared.

3.

UFOs IN BIBLE HISTORY

"Ours is the age that is proud of thinking machines, and distrustful of trying men."
(H.M. Jones)

THE TREASURES OF KING Solomon

In King Solomon's Mines, the export of copper made this king very rich. According to the 1st Book of Kings, in chapters 9 and 10, Solomon sometimes sent Hiram with expeditionary groups to the mysterious country of Ophir (Hebrew: "city of flight"), whose ships were led by Hiram Abiff, king from Tire (Phoenicia), then returned laden with gold, ivory and exotic animals, with Sidonian and Israelite men, sometime between 1100 B.C. C. and 1000 a. C. When we see the 5th descendant after Shem (Noah's eldest son), we strikingly find the names of Ofir, Saba and Havila, which, as in many cases, are names of kingdoms, which according to some, are not on Earth or simply They no longer exist, and they are also associated with territories with gold, onyx, bdellium and borax mines. It is not possible to know with certainty if Ophir was a region on Earth or not, however, as far as the kingdom of Sheba is concerned, it has been said that Solomon visited it regularly. The distance between the kingdom of Sheba and Jerusalem was weeks away, but Solomon went back and forth from there and from Egypt in a matter of hours, which suggests that he traveled hundreds of times faster than a horse. In fact, an Arab myth says that Solomon had a son with the queen of Sheba and he stole one of the "flying discs" and left with much wealth.

It is said in Freemasonry that the architect Hiram -perhaps the same one who was King of Tyre, and a primary collaborator in the construction of the Temple of Jerusalem- was assassinated by his workers for not wanting to reveal the secret to the smelting of metals. This is the story of the MM.MM (Master Masons) about the birth of Freemasonry, although the historical reality is different. This same king would be the main collaborator of the son of David. Surely one of the most visited mines was located in Sfarad (today Spain), specifically in Toledo (from the Hebrew "toldot", which means: "generations") on the Iberian Peninsula (from the Hebrew "iberia", which means: "land of the Hebrews", which comes from "iberím" = "Hebrews"). The Spanish-German researcher Alberto Canosa has carried out extensive studies on many of the caves and underground galleries that would have been used for this work. These are called Cuevas de Hércules (Hercules caves) or Cuevas de Salomón (Solomon caves) and, according to him, they are full of secrets that the Spanish government does not want to be offered to the public. In fact, the Toledo mayor's office would be under pressure from the Spanish government not to reveal the secrets of these caves, but only show the public some areas of the caves that are completely uninteresting and, therefore, are empty. Canosa argues that he himself discovered part of the framework of the caves, discovering artifacts from some 3,000 years that were impossible for that time, highly advanced technology and evidence that he has not been able to openly offer the Spanish people. Some rumors maintain that in the caves there was a sophisticated computer-like machine that would have belonged to Solomon and even robots, some of which are still in operation.

Now, the current researchers, after scrutinizing various documents, finally found the remains of the port of Ezion-Geber, from where, according to the Bible, the ships left for the country of Ophir, but time went by and now all they had to do was find where that country was located, if it was on Earth. The passing of the years passed and the hypotheses varied from those that assured that it was in India, while another said that it was in Africa, while another in Yemen to the south of Arabia, and one assured that Ofir was in Rhodesia in what are the ruins of Zimbabwe. Later in the year 1968 an American explorer, Adam Renders arrived at the ruins in present-day Southern Rhodesia, the same ones to which he did not pay much attention until after 3 years when he saved the German geologist's life by falling into a ravine. Karl Gottlieb Maunch - who on December 5, 1871 found himself in front of the ruins of that city and discovered that the elliptical building was a copy of the Queen of Sheba's palace and that it had been built by the Phoenician architects and workers sent by the King Solomon. So everything was put on hold, until now.

The story of Solomon becomes even more controversial when studying the book of 1 Kings, chapter 6, where the shape of the Temple built by Solomon is explained: a launching platform for a rhomboid discoidal ship. This conclusion was first drawn by a NASA engineer alongside a mathematician, both of whom were stunned to finish their schematic: King Solomon had a flying saucer. On this point related to "extraterrestrial visits" they add a lot of information and the writers agree quite a lot: Zecharia Sitchin (The Twelfth Planet and The Lost Book of Enki), Erich von Däniken ('We are all Children of the Gods' and 'Chariots of the Gods'), William Bramley (Gods of Eden), Michael Tsarion (Atlantis, Alien Visitation and Genetic Manipulation) and RA Boulay (Serpents and Flying Dragons).

Today we know, through digital technology and carbon 14, that metallurgy existed in Israel in the 10th century BC, since it was believed since 1970 that it had not reached this kingdom until the 7th century BC, which makes the mines of copper actually correspond to the reign of Solomon, that is, one less myth to clarify. More detailed studies clarify that the such "Tajt-i-Suleiman" (Arabic: "Solomon's Temple") found throughout the Middle East, are precisely parking and tanking positions for oil -or some derivative of crude oil, as a means of fuel- King Solomon's "flying chariot".

But the idea of service stations from 3,000 years ago is not from a single person, although the Swiss writer and researcher Erich von Däniken was the greatest defender of this theory. The English archaeologist, Arthur Evans (1851 - 1941) began, at his own expense, enormous excavations in Crete at the beginning of this century. In Knossos he discovered the most important palace on the island, from the second millennium BC. In this place, among many other impossible things, he found oil containers, which pointed to being " *a prehistoric service station* ." This conclusion was also puzzled by Ralf Sonnenberg when he carried out a meticulous study of said storage vats, to such an extent that this was recorded in the ASS (Ancient Astronaut Society) publication. Some of those who studied this related the Cretans to the city of Saba and/or some of the territories near Gundam –mentioned in the Arabia Happy novels- due to many extremely disconcerting similarities.

the fiery rockets

It is not uncommon to see the history of religious movements accompanied by sightings of fantastic objects and strange beings. The history of the Persian prophet Zoroaster, of the Hindu prince Sidartha Gautama (the Buddha), of Muhamad (Mohammed), of the American Joseph Smith (founder of the Mormons) or of biblical characters, is strongly accompanied by these supernatural events and magnificent visions. In the Bible (ancient Greek: "compendium of books") one of the most prominent references to flying saucers appears in the book of Ezekiel – written after 5 years of the captivity of Judah by the Babylonians (581 BC approx.) - where we can read: «... *behold, a stormy wind came from the north, and a great 'anan' with an encircling fire, and around it a glow, and in the midst of the fire something that seemed like glowing bronze, and in the midst of it the figure of four 'nefesh chayah' .*» (Ezekiel 1:4-5) The word "anan" is usually translated as "cloud", despite the fact that it comes etymologically from something that "comes down" or that comes from "above". In fact, the main god of the Sumerians was called "AN" by the Sumerians, or "ANU" by the Akkadians, which would correspond to the god of heaven. For their part, the words "nefesh" (soul) and the word "chayah" (living) identify a creature that does have life, unlike those who, despite being physically alive, are dead in relation to the universe, spiritually talking. Emphasizing that they are living, contrary to how we are considered (dead or animals), because we are destitute of the glory of God.

The significance of the word "nefesh" does not refer to ancient Hebrew but to the Aramaic and Akkadian "NEF.ESH", which means: "fire that descends", although NEF or NAF is also often used to say "fall" or "fall". ". On the other hand, the word "chaiá" comes from "Chai" (life) which as a single letter, eighth in alphabetical order, represents "messianic purposes" or "plan of the Anointed" and used to be related to "mercy" in the hebrew culture. Therefore, we have there before the astonished eyes of the Israelite prophet, the appearance of some men and their vehicles descending from heaven like fire and representing eternal life and the purpose of the Messiah, more than 550 years before Jesus was born.

The word "ESH" translates as "fire" and it has been like this since ancient Akkadian, even the name of one of their "gods", SHAM.ASH derived from the Canaanite SHEM.ESH. Since the vowels are not written, we should note that "a" or "e" can be used, and that in the case of SHAM.ASH ("fire from there [above]" or "fire rocket") it was the star sun, as it is still called in Hebrew today: "shemesh". Another very significant thing that must be explained, as we previously mentioned about the Anunnaki, is that the word "SHEM" (as Noah called his eldest son), does not mean "name", as it is expressed by custom in modern Hebrew. Shem means "rocket" already in the Akkadian language, and from there "shemu" is derived, a word from "SHEM.MU" which is something like "space rocket" in the Sumerian language, also simplified as "MU", from where we see also the nickname of the legendary island continent of the Pacific. For that reason, Shem is used to define a "destination", to where something will be "thrown" or "projected" and, because of that, a person is given a "name" or "identification" of what it will be, of what identifies him or his projection: ISH.RA.EL (Israel: man who saw God), IERU.SHALA.IM (Jerusalem: Peace that will be given to many), IESHUA (Jesus: Salvation), ADAM (Adam: man), IACOF (Jacob: cheater or heel), AB.RAHA.M (Abraham: Father who will see multitudes), MOSHE (Moses: Messiah), SHLOMO (Solomon: the one of peace), SHMUEL (Samuel: God listen), etc. No names were ever given by chance.

An important connotation is the one we see in the book of Genesis 11:4, where it has been translated and is popularly believed that the Babylonians said "let us go and make a name so that it may reach heaven", being that it is from the original and, based *on* its Akkadian origin, would say: " *And they said: Come on, let us build ourselves a city and a tower, and its head-peak is in the heavens, and let us make [a] rocket in case we disperse from the surface of all the Arid.* " Clearly they, after proliferating after the Flood, wanted to "rebuild" the Sumerian city of Babili, the "Gate of Heaven" that the Anunnaki gods built and which had its great glory before the Flood. That Gate of Heaven, according to the Mesopotamian texts, was the ziggurat (stepped pyramid) from which the Shem/Mu of the gods "ascended to heaven", to connect with Nibiru (the Celestial Abode), their planet of origin. The Babylonians wanted to recreate this platform, just as a similar vestige is seen today: Teotihuacan (Mexico). This consisted of rebuilding the "City of Mu", in the likeness of Cape Canaveral in Florida today, followed by a gigantic launch pad at the top of a ziggurat or tower. Then they would put their built Shem there and whose "head" would be put into orbit to reach Nibiru, the "House of Anu", in the sky.

The visions of the prophets

Returning to the experience of the prophet, we see that, despite such a vision, in which the rest of the witnesses fled in terror, Jetzkiel (Hebrew name of the prophet, Ezekiel) kept observing: «*And this was their appearance: there was in them the likeness of man. Each had four faces and four wings. And their feet were straight, and the soles of their feet were like the soles of a calf's foot; and they sparkled like highly burnished bronze. Under their wings, on their four sides, they had the hands of a man; and their faces and their wings on all four sides. With their wings they joined each other. They did not turn as they went, but each walked straight ahead. And the appearance of their faces was the face of a man, and the face of a lion on the right side of the four, and the face of an ox on the left of the four; likewise there was an eagle's face on all four. That's how their faces were .*" (Ezekiel 1:5-11) Ezekiel is clear in identifying that it is about human beings, for which reason he continually reiterates it. However, he is aware that what these astronauts are "wearing" is incredibly peculiar to him. The witness observes the strangeness of the uniform of these men, their helmets with animal figures and their "jet-pack" equipment for movement with a system of 3 pairs of possibly synthetic wings –since at no time does he mention feathers.

Ezequiel advances in his description: « *And they had their wings extended above, each one two, which were joined; and the other two covered their bodies. And each one went straight ahead; where the wind moved them to go, they went; and when they went, they did not return. As for the likeness of the living souls, their appearance was like burning coals of fire, like a vision of burning torches that walked among the living beings; and the fire glowed, and lightning flashed from the fire. And the living souls ran and returned like lightning .*" (Ezekiel 1:11-14) The prophet highlights that the clothing of those men reflected a lot, more in broad daylight and with direct sunlight and emphasizes that their propellers only move them forward.

The astonished witness describes the metallic appearance of some discoidal objects that he analyzes still without coming out of his astonishment: « *While I was looking at the living souls, behold a wheel on the Earth next to the living souls, on all four sides. The appearance of the wheels and their work was similar to the color of chrysolite. And all four had the same likeness; his appearance and his work were like a wheel in the middle of a wheel. When they walked, they moved towards their four sides; they did not turn when they walked. And their hoops were tall and hideous, and full of eyes all around in all four.* » (Ezekiel 1:15-18) The clarification of the witness leaves no doubt that the objects were made of a translucent metal and had windows all around them. « *And when the living souls walked, the wheels walked with them; and when the living souls rose from the Earth, the wheels rose. Wherever the wind moved them to go, they went; Wherever the wind moved them, the wheels also rose up behind them; for the spirit of the living souls was in the wheels .*" (Ezekiel 1:19-20) After further describing how the ships were guided by the men in astronaut suits, Ezekiel describes the appearance of the helmets they were wearing and highlights the 4 main symbols of the God Jehovah: lion, calf -ox, man and eagle, mentioned in other parts of the Hebrew scripture.

Finally, in this first appearance of the astronauts to Ezequiel, he observes the glass of the helmets of those men and the domes of the discoidal metal ships: «And *on the heads of the living beings a 'rakiah' appeared as a marvelous crystal, spread out over their heads. And under the 'rakiah' their wings were straight, reaching out towards each other; and each one had two wings that covered its body. And I heard the sound of their wings as they moved, like the sound of many waters, like the voice of the Almighty, like the noise of a crowd, like the noise of an army. When they stood, they let down their wings. And when they stopped and lowered their wings, a voice was heard from above the expanse above their heads. And above the expanse that was above their heads was seen the figure of a throne that seemed to be made of sapphire stone; and on the figure of the throne there was a likeness that seemed to be of a man sitting on it. And I saw an appearance as of glowing bronze, as an appearance of fire within her all around, from the aspect of her loins upward; and from its loins downwards, I saw that it looked like fire, and that it had a glow around it. As the rainbow that is in the clouds appears on a rainy day, so was the appearance of the brightness around it. This was the vision of the likeness of the glory of Yehovah. And when I saw her, I fell on my face... "* (Ezekiel 1:22-28) This detailed experience was repeated in the life of the prophet later (see: Ezekiel 10:9-22). But, what was that "rakiah" that the prophet saw in the helmet of the astronauts? The word "rakiá" or "rakiyá" is erroneously translated in various biblical versions as "vault ", "expanse", "firmament" or "heaven", but it really emphasizes a "space" -like "outer space" - or "empty", from the Hebrew word: "rek" or "raki". That is to say, what the man saw in them was glass and through the glass the faces of these men but with peculiar helmets full of emblems.

OTHER INTERESTING TESTIMONIES of biblical characters

Another prophet before Ezekiel wrote: "... *the noise of kingdoms, of nations gathered together; Yehovah of armies reviews the troops for battle. Yehovah and the instruments of his wrath come from a distant land, from the end of the heavens, to destroy the whole earth .*" (Isaiah 13:4-5) And time later he would ask himself: « *Who are these that fly like clouds, and like doves to their dovecotes?* » (Isaiah 60:8) The words of Isaiah more than 2,600 years ago were clear: « *they come from a distant land* », whose location is in « *the end of the heavens* ». References to "kingdoms", "principalities", "governments", "worlds", "families" and "homes", beyond our world, are very frequent in the Bible, so there is still ground to be uncovered. Mixing religious issues with "Encounters in the Third Phase" leaves room for many doubts but also clarifies issues in the air that had not been explained before in our history, since the Bible has fallen into the hands of religious power and its lies since the fourth century.

Also the same messianic prophet, Isaiah, wrote in his book: «*... His arrows will be sharp and all his bows bent; the hooves of their horses will be like flint, and the wheels of their chariots like a whirlwind .*" (Isaiah 5:28) We see likewise here that he speaks of his "wheels" being like "Whirlwinds." It also appears written: "*For, behold, the Lord will come with fire and with his chariots like a whirlwind, to render his anger with fury and his rebuke with flames of fire .*" (Isaiah 66:15) The Hebrew concept does not necessarily have to be translated as a whirlwind but more as a storm, something loud that suddenly appears.

The history of Israel, since it was under Egyptian subjection, is peppered with UFO appearances. Huge objects were visible during the day as a column of cloud and at night as a tongue of fire, the same one that defended the Israelites from the hands of Pharaoh's army (some believe that it was in the days of Ahmosis I – the name "Ahmosis" means: "brother of Moses"-). For 40 years the appearance of said cloud from which Yehovah descended to speak with the prophet Moses was one of the longest and most widespread UFO events in post-Flood history. Just as it is narrated in the Greek novels, that the gods descended in flying clouds, likewise the appearance of the "malachim" (Hebrew: messenger-soldier) and the UFOs were important for a purpose of those beings with the offspring of the son of Terah and Amtelai, the famous Abraham.

The Mother Ship of Jesus Christ

We can highlight what the psalmist wrote in the time of the first kings of Israel in the Hebrew language: « *Chariots of the Gods [are counted in] scores of thousands, multitudes of the Lord come [from] Sinai in the 'kedesh'.* » (Psalm 68:17. Hebrew version, Torah.) The word "Kedesh" comes from "holy", "sacred" or "sanctuary" and, in this case, refers to the fact that Christ will return to our planet in an object or vehicle known as "El Sagrado", which may be a sacred ship. We are probably talking about the mother ship that is mentioned in the book of Revelation by John Zebedee, where it says: « *He who overcomes, I will make him a pillar in the temple of my God, and he will never go out from there again; and I will write on it the name of my God, and the name of the city of my God, the New Jerusalem, which comes down from heaven, from my God, and my new name.* " (Revelation 3:12) This is further emphasized when the end of the great War of Armageddon is quoted: " *And I John saw The Holy City, The New Jerusalem, coming down out of heaven, from [from] God, prepared as a wife decked out for her husband. And I heard a great voice from heaven saying: Behold the Tabernacle of God with men, and he will dwell with them; and they will be his people, and God himself will be with them as their God. God will wipe away every tear from their eyes; and there will be no more death, nor will there be more crying, nor clamor, nor pain; because the first things happened. And he that sat on the* throne said: *Behold, I make all things new. And he said to me: Write; for these words are faithful and true*." (Revelation 21:2-5)

Then, the Jewish missionary and envoy, John, beholds the mighty and magnificent ship-citadel: "*And he carried me on the wind to a great and high mountain, and showed me the great holy city of Jerusalem, coming down out of heaven from God.*", *having the glory of God. And its brilliance was similar to that of a most precious stone, like a jasper stone, clear as crystal. It had a great and high wall with twelve gates; and on the gates, twelve angels, and inscribed names, which are those of the twelve tribes of the children of Israel; to the east three doors; to the north three gates; to the south three gates; to the west three gates. And the wall of the city had twelve foundations, and on them the twelve names of the twelve apostles of the Lamb. The one who spoke to me had a golden measuring rod to measure the city, its gates and its wall. The city is established in square, and its length is equal to its width; and he measured the city with the reed, twelve thousand furlongs; the length, height and width of it are equal. And he measured its wall, one hundred and forty-four cubits, the measure of a man, which is that of an angel. The material of its wall was jasper; but the city was of pure gold, similar to clean glass; and the foundations of the city wall were adorned with all precious stones. The first foundation was jasper; the second, sapphire; the third, agate; the fourth, emerald; the fifth, onyx; the sixth, carnelian; the seventh, chrysolite; the eighth, beryl; the ninth, topaz; the tenth, chrysoprase; the eleventh, hyacinth; the twelfth, amethyst. The twelve gates were twelve pearls; each of the gates was a pearl. And the street of the city was pure gold, transparent as glass. And I saw no temple in it; for the Lord God Almighty is the temple of it, and the Lamb. The city does not need the sun or the moon to shine on it; for the glory of God illuminates it, and the Lamb is its light*." (Revelation 21:10-23)

Biblical abductions

Although, the ships are something phenomenal mentioned in the Holy Scriptures, as in the case of references to Leviathan and the Behemoth, a type of gigantic combat ships (cited by Enoch and Job), according to some scholars. But the most interesting appearances about superhuman beings and their "merkabot" (carriages) are cases prior to Ezekiel that drew a lot of attention, since they were Close Encounters in the Fourth Phase, that is: "Abduction". This is a synonym for "rapture", "estrangement" (Greek: "apostasy"), "ascension" or "rapture". The abduction in this case was not for strange experiments, but for a plan of that Hebrew God called Iehovah. The story of the three main witnesses of the so-called God's Plan (Enoch, Elijah and Jesus) is to astound any reader, so we will bring them to paper.

In the days of the kings of the nation of Israel, many decades after having arrived in the Promised Land - having crossed the desert from Egypt - and before being deported by the Assyrians, there lived an important prophet of whom it was written: " *When had passed, Elijah said to Elisha: Ask what you want me to do for you, before I am taken away from you. And Elisha said: I beg you that a double portion of your spirit be upon me. He said to him: A difficult thing you have asked. If you see me when I am taken from you, it will be done so to you; but if not, no. And it came to pass that as they went and spoke, behold, a chariot of fire and horses of fire separated the two; and Elijah went up in a storm from heaven. When Elisha saw him, he cried out: My father, my father, the chariot of Israel and its riders! And he never saw him again; and taking his clothes, he tore them in two parts* ." (2nd Kings 2:9-12) In this passage the translations are quite inaccurate, for that reason, over and over again, I often quote important parts of the Hebrew source. Here a whirlwind is regularly cited that lifts the prophet to heaven, however, the original source says that he is raised in a "saara" of the heavens, that is, something like a thunderous divine vehicle, for which the Hindus had two types of denominations: "Vimana" and "Pushpaka".

The same "divine noise", translated as "whirlwind" appeared to Jobab, a pious man from the offspring of Esau – the eldest son of Isaac, the beloved son of Abraham: «Then Jehovah answered Job out of a whirlwind, and said: *Who is that that obscures the advice with words without wisdom?* » (Job 38:1-2) A little later he returns and appears: « *Yehovah answered Job out of the whirlwind, and said, Gird up your loins now like a man; I will ask you, and you will answer me. Will you also invalidate my judgment? Will you condemn me, to justify yourself?* » (Job 40:6-8) In the same way we find that another prophet writes: « *Behold like clouds he will rise and storm is his light-light chariot, in the eagles are his riders. Woe to us, we destroy ourselves .*" (Jeremiah 4:13. Hebrew version, Torah)

Going far back in time, let's travel to the antediluvian era, when the world lived in the mythological age. There, Enoch, Noah's great-grandfather -nothing more and nothing less than the man who built the ark for the Flood- has several of the most fantastic experiences on record. We can read, before citing his texts, from the first book of the Bible about him: « *Jared lived 162 years, and begat Enoch. After he fathered Enoch, Jared lived 800 years, and fathered sons and daughters. Thus, all the days of Jared were 962, and he died. Enoch lived 65 years, and begat Methuselah. After he begat Methuselah, Enoch walked with God 300 years, and begat sons and daughters. Thus all the days of Enoch were 365 years. So Enoch walked with God, and disappeared, because God took him away .* » (Genesis 5:18-24) This is reiterated in the Brit ha-Hadasha (New Testament): « *By faith Enoch was translated so as not to see death, and was not found, because God had translated him; and before he was translated, he had testimony of having pleased God .*" (Hebrews 11:5) But Enoch was not only famous for being taken to heaven, or cosmos if we prefer to be more explicit, but he was the one who wrote the books of faith, culture and history that his progeny read until practically the year 100 AD.

Among his writings we can find a clear example of what it is like to be taken on a ship at such a speed that you see the stars pass all around you, backwards like contrails: «Behold, the clouds called me, the mist screamed at me and *the lightning and thunder urged me on and sent me off and in the vision the winds made me fly, lifted me up, carried me away and entered the heavens* . (1 Enoch 14:8) In that experience Enoch entered various places so immeasurable that he did not know how to describe them: " *Behold, I saw a door open before me and another house that was bigger than the previous one, built all with tongues of fire (incandescent). All of it was superior to the other in splendor, glory and majesty, so much so that I cannot describe to you its splendor and majesty. Its floor was of fire and its upper part of thunder and lightning and its roof of burning fire (fully lit). It was revealed to me and I saw in it a high throne whose appearance was that of crystal and whose outline was like the shining sun and I had a vision of a cherub. Above the throne came rivers of burning fire and I couldn't resist looking there. The Great Glory was seated on the throne and her dress was brighter than the sun and whiter than any snow* ." (1 Enoch 14:15-20)

The story is so long and detailed that it is better to take time to read it calmly, but we could not go on to identify another experience without citing his first encounter with non-human beings, when Janoj (Enoch) was called to ascend to heaven and leave our orb: « *In the first month, on the stipulated day of the first month, and on the first day, I Chanoj was alone in my house and I was resting in my bed and I fell asleep. And just as I fell asleep, great sadness rose to my heart, and cloudy -I sobbed- with my sleepy eyes, and I could not understand what this distress signal was, or what would happen to me. And two men (males) appeared to me, exceeding in size, in such a way that I never saw such on Earth; And their faces shone like the sun, their eyes were also like a burning torch, and fire came out of their lips [...] with their clothes and they sang [chants] of various kinds in purple appearance. His wings were brighter than gold, his hands whiter than snow. And they were standing at the head of my bed and they started calling my name. And I woke up from my sleep and clearly saw those two men standing in front of me, I greeted them and I was seized with fear and the appearance of my face (face) was changed from terror, and those men said to me: Have courage, Janoj, fear not; the Eternal God has sent us to you, and you must ascend with us today towards heaven, and you must tell your children and all your house everything that they must do without you on Earth in your house, and do not let anyone look for you until the Lord returns you to them ."* (2nd Enoch 1:2-9)

Enoch and Elijah are popular characters in Hebrew history for being the "Two Olive Trees" who are to return at the End Times –perhaps just before the start of World War III (Armageddon): «And I will command my two *witnesses (Enoch and Elijah) that they prophesy for 1,260 days, dressed in rough clothes (instability). These witnesses are the two olive trees and the two candlesticks that stand before the God of the Earth. If anyone wants to harm them, fire comes out of their mouths and devours their enemies; if anyone wants to harm them, they must die in the same way. These have power to close the sky so that it does not rain in the days of their prophecy; and they have power over the waters, to turn them into blood and to hurt the Earth with all plagues as many times as they want. When they have finished their testimony, The Beast who comes up from the abyss will make war against them, defeat them and kill them. Their corpses will be in the square of the Great City (Jerusalem) which in a spiritual sense is called Sodom and Egypt, where our Lord was also crucified. People of every town, tribe, language and nation will see their corpses for three and a half days and will not allow them to be buried. The inhabitants of the Earth will rejoice over them, they will be glad and they will send gifts to each other, because these two prophets had tormented the inhabitants of the Earth. But after three and a half days the spirit of life sent by God entered them, and they stood up on their feet, and great fear fell on those who saw them. Then they heard a loud voice from heaven saying to them: "Come up here!" And they went up to heaven in a cloud, and their enemies saw them. At that time there was a great earthquake and a tenth of the city collapsed. The earthquake killed 7,000 men. The others were terrified and gave glory to the God of heaven."* (Revelation 11:3-13)

Obviously everything related to Jesus of Nazareth is always a matter of controversy. Ergo, not many people question certain events that marked their history: « *They, having heard the king, left; And behold, <u>the star that they had seen in the east went before them</u>, until it came **and stopped** over where the child was."* (Matthew 2:9) Since when does a star that appears in one place guide someone for months to another place? If this were wonderful, a star that suddenly appears in the celestial vault implies a paranormal phenomenon since the stars are suns, and the suns do not move from their gravitational orbits, much less millions of light years will guide people in a tiny planet. What those wise Persians saw was not the size of a sun but the size of a star in proportion to the rest of the points (stars) seen in the sky, but it was not actually a star. No star "waits" for some wise men outside the city and "retraces the journey" to "stop" just above the place where Jesus was.

Jesus and the UFOs

Could Jesus have had the same fate as Enoch and Elijah? The Scripture repeats the case of the abduction that Jesus had, in the case of his Resurrection and ascension. 40 days after the Resurrection of Jesus of Nazareth, he was taken up while some messengers from heaven distracted the observers: « *Then those who had gathered asked him, saying: Lord, will you restore the kingdom to*

Israel at this time? And he said to them: It is not up to you to know the times or the seasons, which the Father put in his sole power; but you will receive power, when the Holy Spirit has come upon you, and you will be my witnesses in Jerusalem, in all Judea, in Samaria, and to the ends of the Earth. And having said these things, when they saw him, he was lifted up, and a cloud received him, which hid him from their eyes. And while they were with their eyes fixed on heaven, while he was leaving, behold, two men in white garments stood by them, who also said to them: Galilean men, why are you looking at heaven? This same Jesus, who has been taken from you into heaven, will come back just as you have seen him go into heaven." (Acts 1:6-11)

Jesus spoke of other worlds and other celestial mansions on a few occasions: « *In my Father's house there are many mansions; if it were not so, I would have told you; I go to prepare a place for you.* » (John 14:2) We also see in his conversation with the Roman procurator Pontius Pilate: « *Jesus answered:* **My kingdom is not of this world***; if my kingdom were of this world, my servants would fight so that I would not be handed over to the Jews; but my kingdom is not from here* .» (John 18:36) This is reiterated by his disciple John in his gospel a few chapters earlier: " *That true light, which enlightens every man, came into this world.*" (John 1:9) Perhaps the most important thing, also written by John, was when Jesus emphasized the place where he would go: «Again Jesus said to them: I am going away, and you will look for me, but *in your sin you will die; where I go, you cannot come. The Jews then said, Will he kill himself, who says, Where I am going, you cannot come? And he said to them:* **You are from below, I am from above; you are of this world, I am not of this world**." (John 8:21-23)

Apparently, Jesus left at that moment but he had addressed during those 40 days or shortly after leaving the Hebrew group of the Essenes who saw him come and go with the clouds several times while he was preaching to them: «And then *the Full moon between the torn clouds and engulfed Jesus in its glow. Sparkles rose from his hair, and he stood among them in the moonlight, as if he floated on air. And no one moved, and no one's voice was heard. And no one knew how much time had passed, because time seemed to have stopped. Then Jesus stretched out his hands towards them and said: "Peace be with you." And so, he departed like the breeze that sways the leaves of the trees."* (Essene Gospel of Peace 6:6-10).

One of the most shocking cases happened on a mountain: « *Six days later, Jesus took Peter, James and John his brother, and led them up a high mountain by themselves; and he was transfigured before them, and his face shone like the sun, and **his clothes became white as light**. [...] While he was still speaking, <u>a cloud of light covered them</u>; and behold a voice from the cloud, which said: This is my beloved Son, in whom I am well pleased; listen to him."* (Matthew 17:1-5) John Mark collected the same testimony, saying in his words: « *Then there came a cloud that overshadowed them, and from the cloud a voice that said: This is my beloved Son; hear him. And then, when they looked, they no longer saw anyone with them, except Jesus alone."* (Mark 9:7-8) The event of that "transformation" (Greek: "metemorfosi") seems to have occurred in daylight and even with all that that covered them it was "of light" and Jesus himself made it *look* different. That also happened with Moses, who, being in a cloud for a while, in a similar situation, shone to the degree that no one could see him face to face. What was that cloud of light that first shaded them and then lit up? Many cases of UFOs inside clouds or with a cloud camouflage system have been recorded for centuries and, in this case, it was from where those two men that Peter believed were Elijah and Moses came down and went up.

Moreover, after Jesus, his apostles were taken from one place to another by the work of a non-human technology: « *When they came up out of the water, <u>the Spirit of the Lord snatched Philip</u>*

*away ; and the eunuch saw him no more, and went on his way rejoicing. **But Philip found himself at Azotus ; And passing by, he preached the gospel in all the cities, until he came to Caesarea**.*" (Acts 8:39-40) Felipe was moved tens of kilometers, from one place to another, in an instant, by that "Ruaj Yehova", which means: "Wind of Jehovah". On another occasion, at least 500 years before, the prophet Daniel was put in a den of lions by order of the Babylonian king Nebuchadnezzar, but *"the prophet Habakkuk was in Judea "* and yet, *" the angel of the Lord said to Habakkuk:" Take the food you have and give it to Daniel where he is, [in the den of] lions in Babylon. But Habakkuk said, "Lord, I have never seen Babylon, and I don't know anything about the den." Then the angel of the Lord <u>took him by the crown of his head and led him by his hair, **with the speed of the wind** put him in Babylon </u>, right into the den. [...] Then Daniel got up and ate. And the angel of God <u>returned Habakkuk **immediately** to his own place</u>."* (Daniel 13:33-39 or Apocryphon of Bel 1:33-39)

This matter is hardly understood by Biblical scholars, first because they view the Bible with religious eyes, and second, because Rome diligently took Greek and Hebrew words from the sources and turned them into Latin in Bible translations, in order to distort their actual meaning. This occurs with the Hebrew word "ruach" ("wind" or "force"), which was translated into Greek as "pneuma" ("air" or "wind", from which comes "tire" or "pneumonia") and Catholicism. it passed to the Latin concept of "spirítu" ("[something] lofty non-human" or "[something] subtle"). For this reason, when it is said that *" Jesus was led by the Spirit into the desert to be tempted by the devil "* (Matthew 4:1), there is already a clear misrepresentation and confusion. The correct thing is to translate that *" Jesus was carried away by the wind "* to such a "desert", which is not defined. That wind brought him before the "accuser" (Latin: "diabolos". Known in Hebrew as "shatan", that is: "adversary") who took him to the "pinnacle *of the temple*" to tempt him . The point is that the Temple did not have a pinnacle, because it was rectangular. The sanctuaries, mosques and temples of the whole world have the shape of a dome and a cone pointing to the sky, alluding to prehistoric rockets, but the Temple of Jerusalem did not have that shape and, in addition, John Mark and Matthew Levi say that "the devil took it. *" to a very high mountain, and showed him all the kingdoms of the world and their glory ...*" (Matthew 4:8)

What kingdoms? Rome? And from where did he show it all? From Everest? Common sense implies that no matter how good eyesight Jesus had, from no mountain you can see the entire Earth, first because it is round and second because human sight cannot see 100 km away from any point on Earth by the agglomeration of particles in the air. It is obvious that they were being displaced by advanced artifacts and using non-human technology. The religious perspective already fell under its own weight and we must discard it, just like the case of the prophet Jonah and the supposed whale, an obvious case of an OSNI (Unidentified Underwater Object). If the UFO cases of Israel in the Sinai desert are not enough to understand that aliens have been a constant fact in our history, then we continue with a veil over our eyes: «And Aaron speaking to all the congregation *of the children of Israel They looked toward the desert, and, behold, the glory of the Lord appeared in the cloud*.>> (Exodus 16:10)

mass abduction

The most significant event itself for modern Christianity is part of the so-called "abduction phenomenon." We can read the details of a massive "rapture" where thousands - if not millions - of human beings will literally be taken from Earth in a matter of minutes, or maybe hours, before the reign of the so-called Antichrist begins: «Then the sign *will appear of the Son of Man in heaven; and then all the tribes of the Earth will lament, and they* *will see the Son of Man **coming on the clouds of heaven**, with power and great glory. And he will send his angels with a loud trumpet call, and they will gather his elect from the four winds, from one end of heaven to the other. Learn the parable from the fig tree: When its branch is tender and its leaves sprout, you know that summer is near. So also you, when you see all these things, know that it is near, at the gates. Truly I tell you, this generation will not pass away until all this happens. Heaven and Earth will pass away, but my words will not pass away. But of the day and hour no one knows, not even the angels of heaven, but only my Father. But as in the days of Noah, so will be the coming of the Son of Man. For as in the days before the flood they were eating and drinking, marrying and giving in marriage, until the day that Noah entered the ark, and they did not understand until the flood came and took them all away, so will the coming of the Son of Man. <u>Then there will be two in the field; the one will be taken, and the other will be left</u>. **Two women will be grinding in a mill; the one will be taken, and the other will be left**. Watch therefore, for you do not know what hour your Lord is coming.* » (Matthew 24:30-41)

For this event it is emphatically assured, over and over again, that no one, only the Creator Father himself, knows when it will happen: « *Therefore, you also be prepared; for the Son of Man will come at an hour you do not expect.*" (Matthew 24:44) Believers in Christ are also rebuked to strive to earn that place in the aforementioned event, instead of going through the Great Tribulation for not having borne fruit: "Watch therefore, always praying that you may *be counted worthy to escape all these things that will come to pass, and to stand before the Son of Man.*" (Luke 21:36)

In the same book of Luke we can read: «*Asked by the Pharisees, when the kingdom of God was to come, he answered them and said: The kingdom of God will not come with warning, nor will they say: Behold it here, or behold there; for behold, the kingdom of God is within you. And he said to his disciples: The time will come when you* *will desire to see one of the days of the Son of Man, and you will not see him. And they will tell you: Here it is, or here it is. You do not go, you do not follow him. For **as lightning flashes from one end of heaven to the other, so will the Son of Man be in his day**. But first it is necessary that he suffer much, and be rejected by this generation. As it was in the days of Noah, so it will also be in the days of the Son of Man. They ate, they drank, they married and they were given in marriage, until the day that Noah entered the ark, and the flood came and destroyed them all. Likewise as it happened in the days of Lot; they ate, drank, bought, sold, planted, built; but on the day that Lot left Sodom, it rained fire and brimstone from heaven, and destroyed them all. This is how it will be on the day the Son of Man is revealed. <u>On that day, let him who is on the roof, and his goods in the house, not come down to take them; and whoever is in the field, likewise does not turn back.</u> Remember Lot's wife. Everyone who tries to save his life will lose it; and everyone who loses it will save it. I tell you that on that night there will be two in one bed; the one will be taken, and the other will be left."* (Luke 17:20-34)

By saying that if someone is on the roof *" do not go down "* to take anything that has been left, he explains that they must be in sight in clear or high places for the moment of abduction. So all this religion suggests that Christ will return, but for all those who call themselves Christians and later they will go to heaven where they will stay forever in clouds and playing the harp, but it is not like that in reality. What he explains is that he will come for some "chosen ones" to take them for 3 and a half years to a place outside this planet and then they will return to Earth to take control of it: «But regarding the coming *of our Lord Jesus Christ, and our meeting with him, we beg you, brothers, not to be easily moved from your way of thinking, nor be disturbed, neither by spirit, nor by word, nor by letter as if it were ours, in the sense that the day of the Lord is near. Let no one deceive you in any way; because <u>it will</u>*

not come without the Distancing first coming, and the man of sin, the son of perdition, who opposes and rises up against everything that is called God or is the object of worship; so much so that he sits in the temple of God as God, posing as God." (2 Thessalonians 2:1-4) That "estrangement," from the Greek word "apostasy," is the same as "rapture" (the name by which many Christian believers call the event), or the "rapture" (name more prevalent in English-speaking believers), which are synonymous with the word "abduction".

Paul had already written about this, saying: «For the Lord himself *will descend from heaven with a shout, with the voice of the archangel, and with the trumpet of God; and the dead in Christ will rise first. Then we who are alive, who are left, **will be caught up together with them in the clouds, to receive the Lord in the air,** and thus we will always be with the Lord."* (1 Thessalonians 4:16-17) The question is, where will they be taken? In the book of the Revelation of the missionary John it is clarified: «*Then one of the elders spoke, saying to me: These who are dressed in white clothes, who are they, and where did they come from? I told him: Lord, you know it. And he said to me: These are the ones who have come out of great tribulation, and have washed their robes, and have made them white in the blood of the Lamb. For this reason they are before the throne of God, and serve him day and night in his temple; and he who sits on the throne will spread his tabernacle over them. They will no longer hunger or thirst, and the sun will no longer fall on them, nor any heat; for the Lamb that is in the midst of the throne will shepherd them, and will guide them to springs of water of life; and God will wipe away every tear from their eyes."* (Revelation 7:13-17) A little later John exposes this in a symbolic way saying that those chosen ones will be kept safe away from Earth, while the danger passes: «And the two wings of the great were *given to the woman. eagle, so that it might fly from before the serpent into the wilderness, to its* *place, where it is sustained for a time, and times, and half a time."* (Revelation 12:14)

Help from the divine chariots

We can also find circumstances where the prophets or missionaries are taken from one place to another in divine vehicles. As I have quoted just before, at the beginning of Jesus' ministry, the doctor Luke recounts that: «*Jesus, full of the Holy Spirit, returned from the Jordan, and was carried away by the wind into the desert for 40 days, tempted by the devil.*» (Luke 4:1-2) Another revealing case occurred several years later with one of his disciples: "*... And answering, he said: I believe that Jesus Christ is the Son of God. And he ordered the car to stop; and they both went down into the water, Philip and the eunuch, and he baptized him. When they came up out of the water, the Spirit of the Lord snatched Philip away; and the eunuch saw him no more, and went on his way rejoicing. But Philip found himself at Azotus; And passing by, he announced the gospel in all the cities ...*» (Acts 8:37-40) Although, Philip was taken in a matter of moments to a place that was more than 40 km from the place where he baptized the eunuch. However, Moses and his brother Aaron were also helped to pass from the Hebrew camp to Pharaoh's chambers without the guard seeing them. But how did they do it? Based on the precedent, the logical thing is that they also took them and placed them in front of Pharaoh, over and over again, since he had threatened Moses with death, even so he could never touch him.

The protection of divine vehicles was frequent among the children of Israel: "*And Yehovah went before them, by day in a pillar of cloud to guide them on the way and by night in a pillar of fire to give them light."* (Exodus 13:21-22) And we can also read: « *The angel of Yehovah, who marched in front of the army of Israel, stood up and stood behind them. The column of cloud also rose from before them and stood behind them, thus interspersing itself between the camp of the Egyptians and the camp of the Israelites. It was cloud and darkness (on the one hand), and (on the other) it illuminated the night, so that those could not approach them all night*." (Exodus 14:19-20). The fabulous light that projected that strange portent is recorded in another book of Hebrew history: *"... [I Yehovah] provided light for you [through] a pillar of fire, and I did great wonders among you*." (4th Ezra 1:14)

Moses' own life, in his last 40 years, was dotted with visits from men of God and he rubbed shoulders with them day by day: « *Moses went up on the mountain, and the cloud covered the mountain. The glory of Yahweh rested on Mount Sinai and the cloud covered it for six days. On the seventh day, Jehovah called Moses out of the midst of the cloud. The glory of Yahweh appeared in the sight of the children of Israel like devouring fire on the top of the mountain. Moses entered the cloud and went up the mountain. And Moses remained on the mountain 40 days and 40 nights.* (Exodus 24:15-18) These cases are repeated over and over again throughout the history of the Israelites.

Jehovah's Technology

But UFO phenomena not only implied lights in the sky, strange clouds or flying floats but the application of highly advanced technology. It is strange to imagine an ethereal god using technical devices like the ones we use today. The holograms and projections occurred in many cases like the burning bush that Moses saw and that was never consumed. But among the most singular we can name the case of the warning of the birth of Samson: « *And Manoah took a kid and an offering, and offered them on a rock to Yehovah; and the angel performed a miracle before the eyes of Manoah and his wife. For it came to pass that as the flame ascended from the altar toward heaven, the angel of Jehovah ascended in the flame of the altar before the eyes of Manoah and his wife, and they prostrated themselves on the ground. And the angel of Yehovah did not appear again to Manoah or to his wife. Then Manoah knew that it was the angel of Yehovah [...] And the woman gave birth to a son, and she named him Samson."* (Judges 13:19-24) We cannot ignore the fact that in the vast majority of cases the witnesses did not realize that those men from heaven were indeed messengers of God, given their similarity to humans. In fact, how are they different?

In addition to all these spectacular apparitions, these angels send information and power through powerful aces of light, very typical of futuristic movies: « *And suddenly there came from heaven a noise as of a mighty rushing wind, which filled the whole house where they were sitting; and **divided tongues appeared to them, as of fire**, <u>settling on each one of them</u>. And they were all filled with the Holy Spirit, and **began to speak in other languages,** as the Spirit gave them to speak. At that time there were dwelling in Jerusalem Jews, devout men, from every nation under heaven. And when this noise was made, the crowd gathered; and they were confused, because each one heard them speak in his own language. And they were astonished and amazed, saying, Behold, are not all these that speak Galileans? How, then, do we each hear them speak in our language in which we were born? Parthians, Medes, Elamites, and those of us who inhabit Mesopotamia, in Judea, in Cappadocia, in Pontus and in Asia, in Phrygia and Pamphylia, in Egypt and in the regions of Africa beyond Cyrene, and Roman residents here, both Jews as proselytes, Cretans and Arabs, we hear them speak in our languages the wonders of God."* (Acts 2:2-11)

Beyond this fact, we can also appreciate the technical ability of these men to appear and disappear as they please. The invisibility system has potentially been studied for decades by military forces with great results, but it is not admitted that someone developed it 3,000 years ago. In the story of the prophet Elisha, one can read an astonishing case of the sudden appearance of said "knights" and of the teleportation of Elisha and those who were with him into the city of Samaria: «And he rose early in the morning and went out the one *who I served the man of God, and behold the army that had the city besieged, with horsemen and chariots. Then his servant said to him: Ah, my lord! What will we do? He said to him: Do not be afraid, because more are those who are with us than those who are with them. And Elisha prayed, and said, I beseech you, O Lord, open his eyes that he may see. Then Yahweh opened the eyes of the servant, and he looked; and, behold,* **the mountain was full of people on horseback, and with chariots of fire around Elisha.** *And after the Syrians came down to him, Elisha prayed to Jehovah, and said, I beg you, strike these people with blindness. And <u>he struck them with blindness, according to Elisha's request.</u> Then Elisha said to them: This is not the way, nor is this the city; follow me, and I will guide you to the man you seek. And he led them to Samaria. And when they came to Samaria, Elisha said: O Lord, open their eyes, that they may see. And* **Jehovah opened their eyes, and they looked, and they were in the midst of Samaria.**" (2nd Kings 6:15-20)

God's collaboration in Israel's wars was more than notorious, as much as the case in which Moses had to hold his rod high for the nation to win the battle. What was it about that rod that God himself had "touched" it and that it had previously turned into a serpent in the eyes of Pharaoh in Egypt? But more striking is the fact of the war against the Amorites to enter the Promised Land that was full of giants: « *Then Joshua spoke to Yehovah on the day that Yehovah delivered the Amorites before the children of Israel, and said in the presence of the Israelites: Sun, stop at Gibeon; And you, Luna, in the valley of Ajalón. And <u>the sun stood still and the moon stood still,</u> until the people had taken revenge on their enemies. Isn't this written in the book of Jasher? And* **the sun stood still in the midst of heaven, and did not hasten to set nearly a whole day.** *And there was no day like that, neither before nor after it, having* *listened to the voice of a man; for Yahweh fought for Israel."* (Joshua 10:12-14) Whether God stopped the sun or it was a gigantic object that replaced it while it was making its natural decline, in any case the miracle was portentous and powerfully reminiscent of the so-called "Miracle of Fatima."

Some time after the ascension of Jesus, he manifested himself to the Benjaminite Shaulo (Paul), in the style of Steven Spielberg's movies, in which the viewer was blinded for several days because of such a powerful light that appeared to him: « *Saul, still breathing threats and death against the disciples of the Lord, came to the high priest, and asked him for letters to the synagogues of Damascus, so that if he found any men or women of this Way, he would bring them prisoners to Jerusalem. But as he was going along the road, it happened that when he was near Damascus,* **suddenly a flash of light from heaven surrounded him;** *and falling to the ground, he heard a voice saying to him: Saulo, Saulo, why are you persecuting me? He said: Who are you, Lord? And he said to him: I am Jesus, whom you persecute; it is hard for you to kick against the pricks. He, trembling and fearful, said: Lord, what do you want me to do? And the Lord said to him: Get up and go into the city, and you will be told what you must do. And the men who went with Saul stood amazed, hearing the voice indeed, but seeing no one. Then Saul got up from the ground, and opening his eyes, he saw no one; so, leading him by the hand, they brought him into Damascus, where he remained three days without seeing, and did not eat or drink .*" (Book of the Acts of Apostles 9:1-9)

But this would not be his first and only UFO experience: «...*[Pablo] looked up and saw how [the twelve] greeted him. Then the Holy [Spirit], who was conversing with him,* **caught him up** *to the Third Heaven. Then he passed to the Room [Heaven]. The [Holy] Spirit addressed him saying: Look and see your likeness on Earth.* <u>*He [looked] down and saw the things that were on the Earth* ...</u>"

(Revelation of Paul 1:19. Nag Hammadi Library, Egypt) And this he reiterated later speaking of himself in the third person: "I *know a man in Christ, who fourteen years ago (if in the body, I don't know; if out of the body, I don't know; God knows)* **was caught up to the Third Heaven** *. And I know of such a man (whether in the body or out of the body, I do not know; God knows), who was caught up in Paradise, where he heard ineffable words that man is not allowed to express.* " (2nd Corinthians 12:2-4) The concept of the Third Heaven was understood as the stellar universe itself.

We can also read in the Holy Hebrew Scriptures: " *And David built there an altar to Jehovah, on which he offered burnt offerings and peace offerings, and called upon Jehovah, who answered* **him by fire from heaven** *on the altar of burnt offering* ." (1 Chronicles 21:26) And also: « *When Solomon had finished praying, fire came down from heaven, and consumed the holocaust and the victims; and the glory of Jehovah filled the house* ." (2nd Chronicles 7:1) We can think that everything is a product of his imagination, despite the fact that the most logical thing is to deduce that a man in ancient times would have no other way of explaining a sighting than by describing it with the things of which he is aware. : its environment. We cannot think that 2,600 years ago someone could speak of the Earth as a sphere in the universe, but even here we are surprised: « **He is seated on the circle of the Earth** *, whose inhabitants are like locusts; <u>he stretches out the heavens like a curtain</u> , unfolds them like a tent to dwell in*." (Isaiah 40:22) Isaiah said this about Jehovah, and it is not strange, since Enoch, in pre-Flood times, already spoke of the circumference of the Earth, of the planets of our solar system and of other "celestial circles".

The intercession of the angels and their fabulous celestial chariots, as well as a great spectacle, was notably seen in the destruction of Egypt and Pharaoh's army, when he pursued the people to destroy them at the moment they left Egypt in search of the Promised Land: « *The Egyptians followed them with all the cavalry and chariots of Pharaoh, his horsemen and all his army; They overtook them where they were encamped by the sea, near Pi-hahirot, opposite Baal-zephon. When Pharaoh had come near, the children of Israel raised their eyes and saw that the Egyptians were coming after them, so the children of Israel cried out to Yahweh full of fear [...] Moses answered the people:—Do not* fear *; stand firm and see the salvation that Yehovah will give you today, because the Egyptians that you have seen today, you will never see again. Yehovah will fight for you, and you will be calm. Then Yehovah said to Moshe:—Why do you cry out to me? Tell the children of Israel to march. And you, lift up your rod, stretch out your hand over the sea and divide it, so that the children of Israel pass through the middle of the sea on dry land. I will harden the hearts of the Egyptians, so that they follow them; then I will glorify myself in Pharaoh and in all his army, in his chariots and in his cavalry. And the Egyptians will know that I am Jehovah, when I glorify myself in Pharaoh, in his chariots, and in his horsemen. The angel of God, who went before the camp of Israel, withdrew and stood behind them; likewise the Pillar of Cloud that went before them withdrew and stood behind their backs, and went between the camp of the Egyptians and the camp of Israel; For those it was a dark cloud, but it gave light to Israel at night; for this reason, in all that night they never approached each other .»* (Exodus 14:13-20)

God and weapons of mass destruction

Yehovah's angels, always identified as male, once appeared to Abraham, before his nephew Lot was led out of Sodom and Gomorrah. These men had to intervene technologically so as not to be raped by the citizens of these towns. Those men from heaven were the day before in the morning at Abraham's house "eating" with him and resting: " *Yehovah appeared to Abraham in the oak grove of Mamre, while he was sitting at the door of his tent, at the hour of more heat. He looked up and saw three men standing next to him. Seeing them, he ran out of the door of his tent to meet them, prostrated himself on the ground and said: - Lord, if I have found grace in your eyes, I beg you, do not pass by your servant. Now I will have a little water brought so that you can wash your feet, and then you will lie down under a tree. I will also bring a morsel of bread so that you can restore your strength before continuing, for that is why you have passed near your servant. They said:—Do as you have said.* (Genesis 18:1-5)

After having even eaten food that is not in accordance with the rudiments of the laws given by God to the people (kosher), they rested and later left for Sodom: « *The men left there and went towards Sodom; but Abraham remained before Yehovah... the angels went to Sodom but, before they lay down, the men of the city, the men of Sodom, surrounded the house, all the people, from the youngest to the oldest. And they called to Lot, shouting:—Where are the men who came to you tonight?* **Bring them out, so that we may know them,** *then Lot went out to them at the door, closed the door behind him and said:—I beg you, my brothers, do not do such wickedness. Look, I have two daughters who have not known a man; I will bring them to you and you can do with them what you see fit; only do not do anything to these men, since they have come under the shelter of my roof... But the guests reached out their hands, brought Lot into the house with them, and closed the door. And the men who were at the door of the house were struck with blindness, from the youngest to the greatest, so that they exhausted themselves looking for the door. Then the guests said to Lot: Do you have any more here? Take your sons-in-law, sons, and daughters, and all that you have in the city, out of this place, for we are going to destroy this place, because the outcry against the people of this city has grown louder before Jehovah. Therefore, Jehovah has sent us to destroy it.*" (Genesis 19:4-13). Not even the angels themselves knew how many people lived in Lot's house, slept, tired, ate, drank and, therefore, would make their bowel movements. In addition, they came to procreate with humans (Genesis 6).

It is written: "*Then **Jehovah rained sulfur on Sodom and Gomorrah, and fire** from Jehovah <u>out of heaven</u>. And <u>I destroy those cities, and all the plain with all the inhabitants of the cities</u>, even the plants of the ground. But Lot's wife looked back and **turned into a pillar of salt**. Abraham got up early in the morning and went to the place where he had been standing before the LORD. He looked toward Sodom and Gomorrah, and toward the whole region of the plain, and saw that **smoke was rising from that Land, like smoke from a furnace**.*" (Genesis 19:24-28) The case of Lot's wife has a profound parallelism with the victims of Armero (Colombia), Vesuvius or the story of Pliny the Elder. In fact, I had the opportunity to visit this territory in the Galilee desert in the year 2000. Between the Dead Sea and the Sea of Tiberias there used to be a river, but it disappeared due to something of great magnitude. What's more, the Red Sea was not called that, but after what happened in that region it was totally dead and salty, which is why it received the name it has until today: Iam ha-Melaj (Sea of Salt). Whatever destroyed Sodom and Gomorrah must have been very powerful, as the region is the deepest depression on the globe: 400m below sea level. It is only followed by a depression of about 100m in the Caspian.

Walking through the area, in the middle of the desert, I collected sea shells and fossilized starfish, as well as pieces of quartz the size of my hand. Throughout the territory there is a terrible dryness. There is no life in the salt sea either, nor in the desert. The Israeli government carried out tests in the lake (what they call the Salt Sea or Dead Sea) placing eggs at different levels of depth with a rope -since a massive body cannot sink given the density of the water- verifying that the deeper the egg descends more than cooked

The region has a certain amount of radiation and more below the surface, Israel installed a nuclear reactor underground in the area.

Let us not forget that Yehovah rained fire on Egypt when Pharaoh did not want to let his people go free: « *Then Pharaoh sent to call Moses and Aaron, and said to them: I have sinned this time; Yehovah is righteous, and I and my people wicked. Pray to Jehovah that **the thunders of God and the hail cease,** and I will let you go, and you will stay no more.*" (Exodus 9:27-28) What kind of bombardment was falling on Egypt to the point that Pharaoh had to humble himself before the God of the Hebrews? Those same thunders are reminiscent of the "thunders of Zeus", with which everything was destroyed; we see that such "hail" fell like missiles against the kingdom of Egypt, which destroyed everything.

a particular whale

The prophet Jonah was mysteriously swallowed by an apparent fish. But what kind of fish can keep a person in its belly for three days? What person can survive three days inside a fish? What breathes? It is a reptile thing to swallow something and digest it in a matter of days, but not a fish, but what about the gastric juices? Of the few marine animals gigantic enough to be able to swallow a person whole -counting that against their nature they did not digest it- there could be: a blue whale or a whale shark, but these animals only eat plankton and phytoplankton (microorganisms). Common sense leads us to think of some kind of submarine, otherwise, said fish would have choked, suffocated, drowned, would have died when ingesting a man: « *And they took Jonah, and threw him into the sea [...] But Yehovah **had prepared a great fish** to swallow Jonah; and Jonas was in the belly of the fish three days and three nights. Then Jonah prayed to Jehovah his God from the belly of the fish [...] And Jehovah commanded the fish, and **it vomited Jonah on the ground.***" (Jonah 1:15 to 2:9) Did a whale of this magnitude come ashore to vomit you up?

ANGELS OR ALIENS?

Plato and Socrates in their day presented an idea of what in their opinion would be angels; his own criteria inspired by his mythologies, personal studies and analysis. These ideas were embodied in Hellenic, Catholic, Christian and Islamic society: winged and incorporeal beings, who inhabit the clouds and play harps day and night. Although it is true, the Persians, Arabs, Hebrews, Assyrians and Babylonians already believed in these creatures from much earlier times, this vision of angels was associated with the Greek ideas of these philosophers. The name "angel" comes from the Greek and means: "messenger". In the time of the Greek gods, the "aggelous" or "angels" were the messengers between the gods, and in the lower category were the "daimones" or "demons", who were intercessors between men and the gods. But who taught that angels were immaterial beings? The Roman Catholic Apostolic Church.

The Hebrew culture brings to mind a large number of experiences with these men whose morphological affinity is exactly the same as ours, what is more, in the vast majority of cases the witnesses do not recognize them until they identify themselves as "messengers from on high". as Prince Gabriel himself has done on a few occasions: " *And I heard a man's voice between the banks of the Ulai, who cried out and said: 'Gabriel, teach this one the vision.' "He then came near where I was. And as he came, I was frightened and fell on my face. But he said to me, 'Understand, son of man, that the vision is for the time of the end.'" While he was talking to me I fell asleep on the ground on my face. He touched me and made me stand up. And he said: "I will teach you what is to come at the end of the wrath; because that is for the time of the end ".* » (Daniel 8:16-19)

Gabriel is presented as an ordinary man, as highlighted by the historical descriptions. In no case is there talk of a being with abnormal or report characteristics, nor of someone incorporeal or that differs from human likeness. The same prophet Daniel writes of his experience later: « *I was still speaking, praying and confessing my sin and the sin of my people Israel, and I poured out my prayer before Jehovah, my God, for the holy mountain of my God; I was still speaking in prayer, when the man Gabriel, whom I had seen in the vision, at first, flying swiftly, came to me about the time of the evening sacrifice. He made me understand, and spoke to me saying: "Daniel, now I have come out to give you wisdom and understanding. At the beginning of your prayers the order was given, and I have come to teach it to you, because you are very loved. Understand, then, the order, and understands the vision.»* (Daniel 9:20-23)

The feasibility that the angels could fly by means of natural wings is doubtful because the scribe Enoch recounted: « *Behold, in those days I saw how long ropes were given to those angels and they* **put on wings** *and flew north.* » (1 Enoch 61:1) For this reason it is not spoken but on one occasion of wings with feathers. Rather, an artificial short-range flight element is described, which is placed in order to move more comfortably: « *Then an angel of the Lord appeared to him, standing to the right of the incense altar. Seeing him, Zacarias was disturbed and fear seized him. But the angel said to him: - Zacharias, do not fear, because your prayer has been heard and your wife Elizabeth will give birth to a son, and you will name him Juan. Zacarías asked the angel:—In what will I know this?, because I am old and my wife is of advanced age. Answering the angel, he said to him: - I am Gabriel, who stands before God, and I have been sent to speak to you and give you this good news* ." (Luke 1:11-19) Here the birth of the last prophet and herald of the coming of the Messiah –John the Baptist- is announced. In any case, it is always Gabriel who presents himself personally to identify a transcendental event or order on the part of God.

After this, Gabriel himself appears to announce to Mary the birth of her firstborn Jesus: « *In the sixth month, the angel Gabriel was sent by God to a city of Galilee called Natzeret, to a virgin betrothed to a man named Yosef, of the house of David; and the virgin's name was Myriam. Entering the angel where she was, he said:—Hail, highly favored! The Lord is with you; blessed are you among women. But she, when she saw him, was troubled by his words, and wondered what salutation this would be. Then the angel said to her:—Myriam, do not fear, because you have found grace before God. You will conceive in your womb and give birth to a son, and you will call his name Yeshua. This one will be great, and will be called the Son of the Most High. The Lord God will give him the throne of David his father; He will reign over the house of Jacob forever, and his Kingdom will have no end* ." (Luke 1:26-33). The appearance of Gabriel is notable in many cases because according to the biblical texts he is a prince who works in relation to the Ministry of Salvation, followed by the prophet Elijah and later John the Baptist. Undoubtedly, in all cases in which a delegate comes to give crucial information, the greatest dignitary appears in person, in his case he is sometimes associated as the "Greater Light", which is described at the beginning of the book of Genesis.

Another transcendental character within the framework of the events that formed Israel and in which superhuman characters intervened, is the archangel Michael. Said the angel Gabriel to Daniel: «... *Because of your words I have come. But the prince of the kingdom of Persia opposed me for twenty-one days; but Michael, one of the chief princes, came to help me, and I stayed there with the kings of Persia. I have come to let you know what will happen to your people in the last days, because the vision is for those days.*" (Daniel 10:12-15) It is irrelevant to think that if these angels are incorporeal beings they can be retained in a conflict against kingdoms like the Persian – if we consider that it is terrestrial Persia and not an extraterrestrial kingdom that also has that name.

And Gabriel said again to the prophet Daniel: " *But I will declare to you what is written in the book of truth: no one helps me against them, except Michael your prince.*" (Daniel 10:21). And again he highlights the events of the future where Michael will intervene: « *At that time Michael will rise, the great prince who is on the side of the sons of your people." It will be a time of anguish, such as never was since there were people until then; At that time your people will be released, all those who are inscribed in the book. Many of those who sleep in the dust of the Earth will be awakened: some to eternal life, others to shame and perpetual confusion.* " (Daniel 12:1-2)

It is written in the New Covenant: " *But when Michael the archangel wrestled with the devil over the body of Moses, he dared not pronounce a curse on him, but said, 'The Lord rebuke you.'* " (Jude 1:9). It is known that, according to some theorists, the Devil had intentions of taking possession of the corpse of Moses to use his DNA knowing who Moses represented for the nation of Israel, because if Lucifer had gotten away with it, he would have easily deceived all the nation cloning Moses. Although it seems more science-fiction than theory, for those connoisseurs in the matter, this would have been a very ambitious project of said "evil forces", if we visualize that they are no longer talking about fantastic beings but about extraterrestrials with regressive purposes; although it obviously sounds like archetypal creatures.

The Jewish apostle John writes in reference to Michael about the End Times: « *Then there was a war in heaven: Michael and his angels fought against the dragon. The dragon and his angels fought, but they did not prevail, nor was a place found for them in heaven. And the great dragon was cast out, the old serpent, called the Devil and Satan, who deceives the whole world. He was cast down to Earth and his angels were cast down with him."* (Revelation 12:7-9) Here John's clarification reveals that the "Dragon" and/or the "Ancient Serpent" is not in a fictitious Hell but in heaven (outer space) and in that near future it will be defeated in that war cornering him before so that in his flight he lashes out at planet Earth to devastate it.

Evidently the appearance of Michael on the biblical scene is linked to war events and wars against different kingdoms, since he is the general of the military forces, as assumed by those learned in the Scriptures, Jewish traditions and the apocrypha. Some believe that his appointment appears in the book of Genesis, where he is called: "Minor Light", and is the arch-strategist who directs the final operation of the Apocalypse in the military field. Many other angels or messengers have also manifested but little is written about them, or their intercessions are recounted in books that do not appear in the compendium of the 66 books that today make up the so-called "Bible". Some of these messengers are: "Pelí" who appeared to Manoa to reveal the birth of Samson; Rafael the healer, who helped Tobias when his father was sick; Uriel who in the books of the scribe Enoch plays an important role, since he is in charge of Hades, and of taking Enoch through the heavens in the flying clouds; there are also Sakiel, Rauel and Remeiel who make up, together with Gabriel, Uriel, Miguel and Rafael, the so-called "seven spirits of God", who guard the Earth. According to the theologians, they are the 7 delegated princes of the administration of the Earth and who carry out the projects of the Elohim. In this regard it is good to see the works of the Master of the Holy Scriptures and messianic rabbi Felix G. Katchinsky.

The so-called "angels" are hailed in Hebrew and Aramaic under the pseudonym "malachim", which translates as "messenger-soldier". This term is used for the first time in the book of Genesis, being one of those individuals who speaks with Hagar, the servant of Sarai, Abraham's wife, giving her the promise that her offspring by her son Ishamel – from where she is born Islam - would be numerous on Earth. This appearance of the angel happens twice to Hagar to ratify God's promise to her lineage. The angels or "men of God" mixed with the people and interceded at all times in events, including in the life of Jacob son of Isaac, the second son of Abraham.

Among his experiences with extraterrestrials, Jacob had a special one just like Gideon in the time of the Judges: « *This is how Iacof was left alone; and a man wrestled with him until daybreak. When the man saw that he could not with him, he touched the place of the socket of his thigh, and Iacof's thigh was dislocated while he fought with him. And he said:—Leave me, because the dawn is breaking. Iacof answered him:—I will not leave you, if you do not bless me.—What's your name? the man asked.—Iacof—he answered. Then the man said:—You will no longer be called Iacof, but Israel, because you have struggled with God and with men, and you have won.—Tell me now your name—asked Iacof.—Why do you ask me by my name?—replied the man. And blessed him right there. Iacof called that place Peniel, because he said: "I saw God face to face, and my soul was delivered."* » (Genesis 32:24-30). The fact that a man defeats an angel borders on the absurd. He was forced to dislocate Jacob's thigh to let him go, if they were incorporeal or ethereal beings, why didn't he dematerialize? How could a being that is not made of flesh fight with one that is?

It is curious that the same angel, being a superior being, did not know the name of Jacob. To all this, he leaves for granted the fact that the angel was not an immaterial being, but rather quite human, so much so that he was forced to have to evade Jacob by disengaging his muscle. Let us keep in mind at all times that the Bible is not a tale of wonderful fables or mythologies as many still believe today. Before becoming a religious symbol shortly after

AD 100 and losing the true message on which it focused, after the Council of Nicaea in AD 325, these scriptures were clearly and purely the "Homeland History" of the nation of Israel. : its foundation, its most important characters, its kings, its prophets, its judges, its victories, its defeats, its exiles, its invasions, its laws and the life in general of the people who marked history, added to incredible phenomena, the work of alien and extraterrestrial beings.

Historical data have provided historians and scientists in all areas when it comes to knowing the past, ancient cultures, peoples and languages of that time, evidence that corroborates the facts narrated in the Bible and the legends of yesteryear, as already we have exposed in the libor "Reality or Religion". Everything comes to light more and more with archaeological discoveries and in no case has it had to do with mythology or religion.

The kings of Israel: Saul, David, Solomon and those who came after also saw the men from above. In many cases they were helped and in others the transgressions of the people or the king caused them to be corrected: « *Then Yahweh sent the plague on Israel, from that morning until the appointed time, and 70,000 men of the people died from Dan to Beersheba. And when the angel extended his hand over Jerusalem to destroy it, Yehovah repented of that evil, and said to the angel that exterminated the people: "Enough already; stay your hand." The angel of Yehovah was by the threshing floor of Araunah, the Jebusite. When David saw the angel punishing the people, he said to Jehovah:—I sinned, I did evil; what did these sheep do? I beg you, turn your hand against me and against my father's house."* (2 Samuel 24:15-17).

A supernatural apparition in Babylon astonished the prophet Daniel and made him write: « *On the 24th day of the first month, while I was on the bank of the great river, the tiger, I lifted up my eyes and looked, and saw a man dressed in white linen and girded the loins of gold of Ufaz. His body was like chrysolite, his face was like lightning, his eyes were like fiery torches, his arms and feet shone like burnished bronze, and the sound of his words was like the roar of a great crowd.* (Daniel 10:4-6)

There is also an aside that points out that there are not only men in this divine delegation but there are also many women working together at the service of the beneficent entity of our race: «I then raised my eyes and saw a vision: two women appeared who *had wings like those of stork; the wind impelled their wings, and they raised the ephah between the Earth and the heavens. I asked the angel who was talking to me:—Where do they take the efa? He answered me:—They are going to build him a house in the land of Shinar; and when it is ready, they will put it on its base.*» (Zechariah 5:9-11). The surprising aspects of the intercession of "Positive Forces" are accompanied by a control of Travel in Time which allows them to know the future, as it is revealed in the Torah or Pentateuch, where by means of numerical codes they have been codified in the Hebrew language all the events of the last 4,000 years and those that still await us.

Gods or aliens?

In earlier times, "angels" of this type -because there are others who are not extraterrestrials but extraterrestrials and intraterrestrials- would have descended to Earth and would have caused great evils. Such was the case that many epic novels, legends and myths about them were written and narrated from generation to generation. Apparently, there were at least five descents in ancient times, where "angels" -many of them- posed as gods. Those false gods, really extraterrestrial beings, would have abused their technology and knowledge to dominate and subjugate the human races in many regions and at many times.

According to Enoch, there was a descent in the days of Adam and Eve where those beings deserted the heavenly host and settled on Earth. Later another group would have come in the days of Jared, the father of Noah and, together with the previous group, they would have hindered the development of human civilization. It is said that they taught humanity to make swords, machetes, chain mail, helmets, shields, breastplates and all kinds of weapons for war, while the earthlings did not know this. Also back then they would have taught magic and sorcery, along with instructions on astrology and astronomy. They are also credited with professing unknown laws and doctrines that revolutionized society. Among his other feats is making vanity known to women, paints and the use of accessories to beautify themselves, in addition to making their own terrestrial wives great experimenters of the genetic code, which resulted in the creation of all kinds of of hybrid beings that today we call "mythological beings", when they had access to the laboratories. Also aliens would have given us the gift of agriculture by teaching us about seeds, but this is a factor that only a group of researchers defends.

The birth of the novels about Zeus, Poseidon and Hades, the wars recounted in the sacred Vedas such as the Mahabarata or Ramayan, the Australian aboriginal novels about the wandjinas, the Nordic narrations and other descriptions, added to the Egyptian ones, are clear evidence of said "intercession" that changed our history definitively and radically. Aparts like these plague the ancient scriptures: « *He who puts the clouds for his chariot, He who walks on the wings of the wind; He who makes the winds his messengers, and the flames of fire his ministers.*" (Psalms 104:3-4) Or we find: " *Behold, Yehovah rides on a light cloud, and will enter Egypt ...*" (Isaiah 19:1) And we can also see: " *Yehovah walks in the storm and the whirlwind, and the clouds are the dust of his feet.*" (Nahum 1:3)

The B-Code

Some 3,500 years ago Moses was on Mount Sinai, between Egypt and Israel, when Yehovah gave him the Pentateuch (Greek: "Five Blocks", that is, the Torah). No one would imagine that behind the symbols written on the scrolls there would be a secret code. Michael Drosnin, an American researcher and journalist, published several versions of a conference in Jerusalem, about a study by the Jewish mathematician Eliyahu Rips, which would become a best seller: "The Secret Code of the Bible", based on a historical fact: « *On September 1, 1994, I flew to Israel to meet the poet Chaim Gun, a close friend of Prime Minister Itzhak Rabin, in Jerusalem. "An Israeli mathematician has discovered a hidden code in the Bible that seems to reveal events that occurred thousands of years after it was written," my letter to Rabin read. If I have allowed myself to write to you, it is because the only time that his full name -Itzhak Rabin- appears encoded in the Bible, the words 'assassin who will assassinate' intersect it. This should not be taken lightly, since the assassinations of Anwar al-Sadat and John and Robert Kennedy are also encoded in the Bible; in the case of Sadat, with the full name of the murderer, the date and place of the attack, and the manner in which it was perpetrated. I believe that you are in grave danger, but also that the danger can be avoided.* »

On November 4, 1995, the terrible confirmation came. A man who thought he was sent by God had just shot Rabin in the back. For 3,000 years, the attack had remained hidden in the secret code of the Bible. Rabin's death dramatically confirmed that the Biblical code, the hidden text in the Old Testament that predicts the future, was an undeniable reality. The code was discovered by Dr. Eliyahu Rips, one of the world's leading experts in group theory, the mathematical model on which quantum physics is based. It has been corroborated by renowned mathematicians from Harvard, Yale and the Hebrew University. It has been verified by a decryption expert from the United States Department of Defense.

It has passed three levels of review by a leading scientific publication.

Rabin's assassination is not the only modern event reported in the code. In addition to the attacks against Sadat or the Kennedy brothers, hundreds of crucial events for the world are encoded in the Bible, from World War II and the Nazi Holocaust, to the Watergate scandal, the Hiroshima bomb, the arrival of Apollo XI to the Moon, the impact of a comet on Jupiter, the attack on the World Trade Center and the invasion of Iraq. Nor was Rabin's assassination the only event announced in advance. The exact day that the aforementioned comet would collide with Jupiter was decoded before it happened, and the same happened with the dates of the last Persian Gulf war.

None of this seems to conform to the rules of our pragmatic world, and since its writer was a non-believer, and would be one of the first to dismiss it as a millennial fever, it is even more spectacular. But after having been involved in it for 5 years and having spent many weeks with Dr. Rips, its discoverer, everything has changed. He said: " *I have learned Hebrew and checked the code day after day on my personal computer.*" Michael Drosnin spoke with the US Defense official who personally confirmed the existence of the code in the Bible. He then traveled to Harvard, Yale, and the Hebrew University to interview three of the world's most eminent mathematicians. All of them have coincided in affirming that there is a code in the Bible and that it predicts the future.

Eliyahu Rips stated: *"I, on the other hand, have always been reticent. Until Rabin was assassinated. Although I myself had found in the code the clear warning that Rabin would be assassinated during the Jewish year beginning at the end of 1995, I never believed it could happen. When Rabin died when and as the prediction said, the first thing I thought was: 'My God, this is serious.' It couldn't be a coincidence. The words 'murderer who will murder' intersect the name 'Itzhak Rabin' the only time it appears in its entirety in the Old Testament. According to the Bible code, Rabin would die in the Jewish year beginning in September 1995. On November 4, 1995, the world learned the tragic news of his death. Chaim Guri, Rabin's friend, confessed to me that he thought the same thing when he found out about the attack. "It was like a knife was pierced through my heart," Guri said. I called the chief of the General Staff, General Barak, and told him: 'The American journalist knew this for a year; I warned the prime minister. It was in the Bible.' »*

The attack on the World Trade Center was not only predicted by the Jew Michael Nostradamus and by the secret code of the Bible, but it also appears portrayed in Egyptian hieroglyphics. It can clearly be seen in the images that warn of the End of the World, a plane going through a skyscraper that is taller than other buildings. Which then leads to the invasion of the attacked town to another town on the other side of the ocean. Somehow someone also told this to Moses to write it down or they gave it to him "themselves" from "on high", and well, by that rule, Moses would not have been the only one to whom they made known the future between lines of written scrolls.

The Assumption of the Ark of the Covenant

Many discuss and inquire to this day what happened to the Ark of the Covenant. Some believe that it was taken to Ethiopia, others that it is still hidden among the secret passages that are under Jerusalem, others that it was hidden by the priests, and others that it was taken with the captives in the Babylonian invasion of King Nebuchadnezzar. The truth is that although there are many speculations, the writing has recorded the event in two versions. One of them affirms that the Ark was taken from Earth and the "angels" themselves (those who in ufology are called "Pleiadian-Venusian extraterrestrials"), destined for this purpose, destroyed what was inside the Temple when Jerusalem was invaded.

by the Babylonians: « *And behold, suddenly a strong wind took me, carried me up [and put me] on top of the wall of Jerusalem. And I saw, and behold! four angels standing at the four corners of the city, each of them holding a flaming torch in his hands. And another angel began to descend from heaven. And he said to them: "Enhance your lights, but they do not come on until I say. For first [the Lord] sent me to speak a word to the Earth, and to the place where the Lord Most High has sent me. " And I saw him descend into the Holy of Holies, and from there take the veil, and the holy ark, mercy, and plazas, and the two tables [of the Law], and the holy garment of the priests, and the altar of incense, and forty-eight precious stones, with which the priest was adorned, and all the sacred vessels of the tabernacle."* (2nd Baruk 6:3-7) And he goes on to say: " *And after these things I heard [this] angel say to the [other] angels who had the lights: 'Destroy, therefore, their wall and overthrow its foundations, lest the enemy should boast and say, "We have broken down the wall of Zion, And burned the place of God's power." And take advantage of the place before which I had been standing. Now the angels did as he had commanded them, and when they had broken the corners of the walls, a voice was heard from within the temple, after the fall of [the] wall had said: come in, enemies, And come the adversaries; Because the one who maintains the house has abandoned it."* (2nd Baruk 7:1 to 8:1)

The apocalypse

We could not end the references to the conventional Bible without naming the most controversial of its books: Revelation. The word "apocalypse" means in Greek: "revelation", because it reveals what was manifested to John, one of Jesus' disciples, on the Greek island of Patmos, while he had been exiled there. Many suggest —without any type of proof- that Juan invented everything he wrote in his book, however, the realization and fulfillment of each one of his predictions has changed that idea. But how did he know what would happen? John himself says it, he was put on a ship where he was shown the future: «*After this I looked, and behold, a door was open in heaven; and the first voice that I heard, as of a trumpet, speaking with me, said: Come up here, and I will show you the things that will happen after these. And instantly I was in the wind; and, behold, a throne was established in heaven, and on the throne, one seated* ." (Revelation 4:1-2) I have to clarify that the Hebrew word "ruaj" and Greek "pneuma" have been biasedly translated subjectively as "wind" or "spirit" depending on their convenience. However, before referring to something ethereal or of the spirit, the Hebrew word "RUAH" means "wind"; Likewise, the Greek word "pneuma" is where it derives from: "pneumatic" or "pneumonia", which are related to air and breathing.

After this, Juan sees a huge screen on the floor inside the great nave, which projected scenes of things that are difficult to describe: « And *in front of the throne there was like a sea of glass similar to crystal...*» (Revelation 4:6) So, everything that John prophesied was revealed to him by superior entities and not by ecstasy, drug effects or hallucinations.

UFOs and the Book of Mormon

We can also find sightings and close encounters in the controversial book of The Church of Jesus Christ of Latter-day Saints (Mormon), specifically about its founder: "...a column of light exactly over my head, above the bright light *of the Sun, which gradually descended until it fell on top of me. Nothing more when this appeared than I felt freed from the enemy that kept me tied up. As the light stopped above me, I saw two personages, whose brilliance and glory defied all description, suspended in the air above me. One of them spoke within me, calling me by name and saying, pointing to the other: 'This is my beloved son. Listen to it'.*» (Josef Smith 2:16-17) Later he wrote another nocturnal apparition: " *I discovered a light appearing in my room which increased in intensity until the room was brighter than noon, when suddenly a figure appeared by my side, suspended in the air, because his feet did not touch the ground. He had a warm cloak of the most exquisite whiteness, beyond anything I had seen on Earth; I could not believe that there was a terrestrial thing that was made of such excessive whiteness and brilliance.»* (Joseph Smith 2:30-31)

Another important case happened right after: «... *I saw how the light in the room began to diminish immediately around the character who had been speaking to me, and continued like this until the room was again dark, except around him; when instantly I saw a direct open conduit in the sky through which it ascended until it completely disappeared ...*" (Joseph Smith 2:43) In his well-known book William Bramley he highlights: " *The Mormon doctrine revealed by Smith establishes that there are many inhabited planets in the Universe. This was quite a bold idea for an ignorant 19th century man. Smith added, that a God inhabited a body of flesh and blood, (see for example: Doctrines and Commitments 130:22) and that God lives near a star called Kolob (Abraham 3:1–3). In other words, "they" are human aliens living on other planets."* (William Bramley, Gods of Eden)

Likewise, the use of nuclear weapons is described -as in the case of the destruction of Sodom and Gomorrah in the Bible-, but this time in the Americas some 2,000 years ago: The Book of Mormon reports that this cataclysm was extraordinary. It truly describes a nuclear cataclysm: "*... in the third and fourth year, in the first month, on the fourth day of the month, there arose a great storm, such as we had never known on Earth. And there was also a great and terrible storm (violent winds); and there were terrible thunderclaps, besides this making the whole Earth shake as if it were going to split into pieces. And there was intense and excessive lightning, such as has never been known on Earth. And also the city of Zarahemla caught fire. And the city of Moroni sank into the depths of the sea, and all its inhabitants were swept away with it. And the Earth collapsed on the* city of Moronihah that in the place of the city a great mountain was formed. And there was a terrible and great destruction in the lands towards the South. But behold, there was a greater and more terrible destruction in the lands to the North, for behold, the face of the Earth was totally changed, for because of the tempest and the whirlwind and the thunders, and the lightnings, and the enormous number of earthquakes all over the Earth, the roads were broken and the level crossings were damaged and many peaceful and level places became abrupt. And many of the great and notorious cities were sunk and many were burned, and many were shaken until the buildings fell to the ground; and the inhabitants of these died and the places were left desolate. And there were some cities that resisted, but the damage in them was too great and there were many of them that perished."

And he goes on to describe the event like this: « *And there were some cities that resisted, but the damage in them was too great and there were many of them that perished. And there were some that were carried away by the wind and carried to a condition unknown to man, except that they realized they were being carried away. And so the face of the entire Earth was deformed as a consequence of the storm and the thunder and lightning and the movements of the Earth. And behold, the rocks were torn in pieces; they were broken all over the face of the Earth, to such a degree that they were found in broken fragments and in cracks all over the face of the Earth. And all this happened, when the explosions and lightning, the storm and the seismic movements ended; because they lasted for three hours; and some said that the time was greater; nevertheless, all those great and terrible things were done in the space of three hours and some said that the time was longer; nevertheless, all those great and terrible things were done in the space of three hours and then, behold, a darkness appeared over the whole face of the Earth. And it came to pass that there was a thick darkness over the whole face of the Earth to such a degree that the inhabitants of it who had not died felt the vapor in the darkness. And there was no light there because of the darkness, no candles, no torches, nor could there be a fire lit with plenty of good dry wood, so there could be no light at all. And there was no light to life, neither fire, nor dim light, nor the Sun, nor the Moon, nor the stars, because the mist of darkness was so great, which was on the face of the Earth. And it came to pass that this ended for the space of three days that had not seen light; and there was a dawn and howling and weeping among all the people continually; yea, great was the groaning of the people because of the darkness and the great destruction that had befallen them.* (3 Nephi 8:5-23)

A case of Adam that was never told

As in any published work, be it a book or a movie, there are scenes that do not appear in the official edition. The same is the case with the Bible. We can read in some texts found in the Israeli territory of Qumran, near the so-called Dead Sea in 1947: « *This is the story of Adam and Eve after they had left Paradise. And Adam met his wife Eve and* **went up** *to the sun and he lived there for 18 years and 2 months. And Eve [was] naked and conceived two sons; Adiaphotos, who is called Cain and Amilabes who is called Abel. And after this, Adam and Eve went to each other.* » (Revelation of Moses 1:1 to 2:1) So Adam was with the "aliens" for a while? As other apocryphal writings (Greek: "kept", "hidden") say about him, and equally about Abraham, Zephaniah, Baruch, Noah, Enoch, Peter and Paul, among many others, he was walking outside this globe.

4.

LIGHTS AND SHIELDS IN THE SKY

"When a madman seems completely sane, it's time to put him in a straitjacket."
Edgar Allan Poe (1809-1849)

THE STRANGE FLYING objects in modern history

Not only ancient sculptures, engravings and mythologies allude to the fabulous flying saucers, but also contemporary history records the appearance of such exceptional vehicles. History records that in the 4th century BC Alexander the Great and Timoleon saw certain unidentified flying objects, but specifically in the year 498 BC Aulio Postumius saw his battle against Tarquin and Ocatavio Manilio supported by Lake Regilo, due to the sudden presence of two strange horsemen of greater than human stature, who took the lead of the troops of Aulio Postumio and turned the battle, in favor of Postumio.

More than a century and a half later, in 322 BC, Alexander the Great was aided by several flying shields in a triangular formation that led to the assault and capture of the city of Tyre. Decades later, approx. In the year 216 BC during the battle of Cannae, between the Romans and the Carthaginians, they observed some round objects and others in the shape of a ship, a phenomenon that lasted all night. The writer Julius Obsequens reproduces in his book "Prodigorium Liber", the following account of said year: « *Things similar to ships were seen in the sky over Italy... In Arpi (Italy) a round shield was seen in the sky... In Capua, the sky was all fire, and one saw ship-like figures ...*"

In 205 BC at Fregallae (near Rome), night became like day and at Setie a bright light was seen flying from east to west in the sky. Ergo, the most interesting thing about those times happened in the year 173 BC when Postomio Paulo and P. Mario Scaevola were Consuls. In broad daylight, with clear weather and clear skies, a thing like an arch was seen in the sky over the Roman Forum and over the Temple of Saturn. At that time, the Maccabees in Judea were also helped by non-human forces that supported them in combat against the Hellenes.

During the year 99 BC, when C. Murio and L. Velario were Consuls, in Turquinia, towards sunset, a round object like a globe, round or circular shield, crossed the sky from west to east. Later, in 90 BC in Aenarie, while Livio Torso was promulgating the laws at the beginning of the Italic wars, at dawn a tremendous sound came from the sky and a ball of golden fire fell to the ground spinning. It increased in size, and was seen rising from the ground and flying across the sky, darkening the solar disk with its brilliance.

Records say that in the 1st century BC Gaius Julius Caesar and Pompey saw flying objects in the sky. On January 1, 49 BC, Cayo Suetonius reports that Julius Caesar ran into a superhuman figure next to the Rubicon River. Caesar's life is dotted with appearances of superhuman appearances, among which stands out the igneous object that fell from the sky to rush into the camp of his adversary Pompey, in the year 48 BC, to finally decide the victory in favor of Caesar.

Years later, in 42 BC, in Italy, something like a projectile rose from the Earth with a great noise and flew into the sky. Tito Livio informs for his part: « *Ghost ships have been seen shining in the sky... While in the district of Amitermo, "men" with flashing dresses appeared in many places, from afar and without approaching anyone.* » In the "Book of Wonders", the historian Julio Obsequens collects original texts by Cicero, Tito Livio, Seneca and others. We can read there: « *When Gaius Mario and Lucio Valerio were consuls, an object that resembled a burning torch that suddenly fell from the sky could be seen in various places in Tarquinia. Towards evening a circular flying object was seen, similar in shape to a flaming clypeus (round shield used by the Romans), crossing the sky from west to east." In the same book it is said: " ... in In the territory of Spoleto, in Umbria, a sphere of fire, of a golden color, fell to earth, spinning, then seemed to increase in size, rose from the ground and ascended towards the sky, where it obscured the disk of the Sun with its blinding clarity. Then it disappeared in the direction of the eastern quadrant of the sky.*

In another passage of said book it is mentioned: «*In March of the year 2, under the reign of Emperor Tian yu, one night a "star" emerged from the vault of heaven. It was five times the size of a celemi and was flying in a northwesterly direction. It descended to 30m from the ground. Its upper part released red-orange fire lights. Its lights reached more than 5m. It moved like a snake, surrounded by numerous small "stars" and disappeared in the blink of an eye. A kind of vapor was seen rising very high into the sky.*» Pliny also speaks of unidentified flying objects in Book II of his "Natural History".

Events after Jesus Christ

In the first century AD, the famed Roman statesman Cicero comments on a night during which a sun accompanied by loud noises was repeatedly seen in the night sky. The sky seemed to open up heartbreakingly and reveal strange "spheres". Around the same century in Bethlehem (Israel) let us remember that a wandering star was seen that brought 3 wise men from Persia to witness the birth of Jesus of Nazareth, stopping just above the place where the child was staying with his mother. It is noteworthy the considerable appearance of flying objects and semi-human beings in the story of Jesus, which took place in that first century. In fact, Flavio Josefo tells us that at that time a flying sword was seen over Jerusalem, which remained fixed for a whole year.

In the "New Book of the Tang", chapter XXII, it says: « *the year 2 under the reign of Emperor Quian-fu, two "stars", one red and the other white, measuring about twice the head of a man , they headed side by side to the southeast. Once standing on the ground, they slowly increased in size and released violent lights. The following year, a moving "star" shone by day like a great torch, the size of a head. Arriving from the northeast, it gently flew over the region, finally disappearing in a northwesterly direction.* »

The historian Zhang Zuo, author of the "History of Power and Opposition", writes that: « *on May 29 of the year 2 under the reign of Emperor Kai Yuan, during the night, a large moving "star" appeared, from the the size of a vat, flying in the northern sky, accompanied by other smaller "stars"; This lasted until dawn.*" Much later, in the year 312 AD, Constantine the Great and his entire army saw a luminous cross in the sky. On another occasion, Constantine was victorious over Maxentius, after a huge unidentified sword-shaped flying object appeared above his troops. Remarkably in the 3rd century, already around our age, Constantine saw this type of flying objects and testified to having had supernatural experiences that led him to a religious "conversion".

Gregory relates that just before the Plague invaded the Auvergne region of France in AD 567, three or four bright lights appeared around the sun and the sky seemed alight. This may have been a natural effect called "dog sun"; however, another strange celestial phenomenon had also been seen in the area. Another historian recounted a similar event in AD 590 in another part of France: at Avignon. Strange visions were reported in the sky, and the Earth was sometimes as brightly lit at night as it was during the day. Shortly thereafter, a disastrous outbreak of the plague occurred there. Gregory reported a vision in Rome consisting of a huge "dragon" floating around the city and descending into the sea, followed by a severe outbreak of the Plague just after this.

In AD 577 a thing like a spear crossed the sky of France, from north to west. Then Bede, in his "Ecclesiastical History", affirms that in the year 664 a luminous flying sheet appeared on the heads of the nuns of a monastery in Parking, next to the Thames. Later in 774, while Charlemagne broke into Italy, the Saxons besieged Sigisburg, until two reddish flying shields appeared in the air, causing them to flee hastily and then submit to Charlemagne. In 919 a thing like a flaming torch was seen in the sky and bright balls like stars drifted in the air over Hungary. UFOs became so disruptive in the eighth and ninth centuries that Emperor Charlemagne of France issued an edict prohibiting them from disturbing the air and causing storms. In one episode, some of Charlemagne's subjects were taken up in an air "ship," pointing out wonders to them, then returning them to Earth where an angry mob killed them. Those troublesome ships were also accused of destroying crops.

The most significant events of the previous millennium

In Chihuahua, Mexico, they found a cave with a skull that does not correspond to human patterns and that are not malformations. It is over 1,000 years old and there are legends of visits from outer space in the area. In the year 1094, in England, a fiery arrow was seen flying in the sky from south to west, at 7 pm on August 1. Later this episode was recorded: « *In the year 1117, in January, a comet passed like an army on fire from the North to the East; the Moon was covered by a reddish-blue cloud as in an eclipse; a year later a light brighter than the Sun appeared. This was followed by great cold, famine and plague, which was said to have caused the death of a third of humanity.* »

Year 1118: In France, a cross and a moon shining white appeared in the sky and it was believed that the end of the world was imminent. Years later, in 1150, a cross appeared in the sky at noon in England, when King Richard the Lionheart and Philip of France were preparing to do battle against Saladin, Emperor of the Saracens.

July 24, 1239: In France, being twilight, a great star made its appearance, it was like a torch, it emerged from the south and flew to both sides emitting a powerful light in the sky. He changed direction to the north, without haste, without any speed, but exactly as if he wanted to ascend to a place in the sky. But when it apparently reached the middle of the sky, in our northern hemisphere, it left behind smoke and sparks.

January 1, 1254: At midnight, in the clear and serene sky and with the Moon of 8 days, suddenly appeared in the sky a kind of large ship, elegantly designed, well equipped and of various wonderful colors. Certain monks in the Abbey of St. Albans in Hertfordshire (England) saw it for a long time, as if it were painted and made of plates; but eventually it began to fade.

December 6, 1269: At twilight, something rare and bright, in the shape of a cross, gave light from a place high in the sky and illuminated the city of Cracow (Poland).

Year 1290: A huge silver disk was seen in Yorkshire (England). After the appearance of supposed comets, the Black Death began: « *The origin of the plague falls in China; It is said that the storm began there already in the year 1333, after a terrible fog that emitted a horrible stench and infested the air.* »

February 21, 1345: A luminous light coming from the mountains of Monserrat in Catalonia moved through the air until it stopped over the town of Manresa, whose inhabitants have continued to celebrate the "Vanguda de la mysterious Ilum" every year since then. The historian and writer William Bramley commented: " *Men faced with the terror of the Black Death were impressed by the chain of events suffered until the end of the plague, and by the accounts of the arrival of the pestilence in the fourteenth century, a case that was selected as an example of ominous events among those that must have occurred in the years preceding the epidemic outbreak of 1348, which was rather like the ten plagues of the pharaohs: disturbances in the atmosphere, storms, strange invasions of insects and celestial phenomena* .

Year 1492: Christopher Columbus claims that he and his crew observed lights in the sky, entering and leaving the sea. Almost a century later, in the famous book published in 1557, "A Chronology of Wonders and Portents" by Conrad Lycosthenes, a "supposed" description of a comet observed in the year 1479 appears on page 494: « A comet was *seen in Arabia in the shape of a pointed wooden beam.....*" The accompanying illustration, based on eyewitness descriptions, points to what clearly appears to be the front half of a rocket tucked into some clouds. The object described seemed to have many windows.

Year 1527: In the text that appears in the annals of the Inquisition, Dr. Eugenio Torralba affirms that he made trips moving through the air guided by a cloud of fire. From that year, Bernal Díaz del Castillo, chronicler of Hernán Cortés, narrates in his "True History of the Conquest of New Spain" that in 1527 the Spanish expeditionaries observed in the air, above their heads, an enormous long sword, like between the province of Pánuco and the city of Tezcuco, which did not move from heaven for more than 20 days. In his same work, Bernal Díaz del Castillo mentions: « *the Mexican Indians said that they saw a sign in the sky that was green and red and round like a cart wheel, and that next to the sign came another line and a path from where The sun rises and came to meet the red stripe.»*

Year 1528: The city of Utrecht (Holland) was under siege, « *when something cruel and strange was seen in the sky, which terrified the citizens and made the enemy believe that they would take the city. It was cross-shaped right over the city, high in the sky, yellow in color, and scary to look at,*" witnesses said.

December 13, 1547: Near Rome, at 3 in the afternoon, with good weather and clear skies, a red stick and a red cross were seen in the air for 3 hours. Also on January 3, 1551, red sticks were seen in the sky over Lisbon (Portugal). Likewise, the appearance of apparent extraterrestrials was notorious in Europe: « *In Brandenburg, Germany, some horrible men appeared in 1559, of whom some fifteen and later twenty were seen first. The first had their little heads set on the back side, and the others had hideous faces and carried long scythes with which they cut the oats, so that the cracking of the scythes was heard at a great distance; but the oats remained standing. When some people approached him, seeing them they ran away with their mowers.*» This was followed by a horrible plague throughout the region. « *During the plague of 1565 in Italy, roars of thunder were heard day and night, as in war, together with a riot and the noise as of a huge army. In Germany, in many places a noise was heard as if a hearse was passing through the street ...*"

From the year 1568 it is recorded: « *When in the Sun and the light of the Moon, a beautiful rainbow and a fiery lightning were seen above the church of Saint Stephanie, all this was followed by a violent epidemic in Austria, Swaboa. Augsberg, Wuerttemberg, Nuremberg and other places, laying waste to humans and herds.*"

October 7, 1571: A "brilliant column" appeared before the battle of Lepanto. Other superhuman beings were seen in those times: «*... in the year of Christ 1571, a very great disturbance, the greatest of all, when over Schuelesberg, there appeared so many black* *horsemen that the opinion prevailed that the Turks were making a secret invasion, but who promptly disappeared again; and at this point a terrible plague broke out in the neighborhood.»*

In the "Report on his first trip to the Strait of Magellan" by the great Spanish navigator Pedro Sarmiento de Gamboa, he refers in one of his parts to what happened on February 5, 1580. It reads like this: «... Tonight at *a At night, on the south-eastern side, fourth to the south, we saw a round thing come out, red as fire, like a dagger, which was going up through the sky or wind. On a high mountain it was prolonged, and being like a high spear on the mountain, it became like a half moon between red and white. The figures were like this (and three figures follow: one in a circle, another an ellipse, and the third a semicircle) ...»*

According to the writer Johannes Noel, he describes in his book "The Black Death, a chronicle of the plague" (1926), that *«In the year 1606 a comet was seen, after which a general plague crossed the world. In 1582 a comet brought such a violent plague over Majo, Prague, Thuringia and Holland and other places, that in Thuringia alone it devastated 37,000 people and in Holland 46,415.* »

XVII century

In that century, flying cylinders were seen over Nuremberg, likewise, an "aerial beam" as well as some igneous balloons that flew over Basel, observed by Benvenuto Cellini. In the year 1604 unidentified flying objects fly over Catalonia. The data was collected by the "Diari" of the historian Jeroni Pujades in the early morning of September 30 where the inhabitants of the bishopric of Urgell attended a low-altitude aerial combat. Later in 1621 flying objects were seen over the south of France. Then in 1640 a "flying host" was observed that flew over Braga.

May 10, 1643: A bright sword-shaped cloud was sighted heading north, it was as bright as the Moon, but the rest of the sky was very serene. It started around 11pm and disappeared around 01am, this happened in the south of England.

Year 1663: A flying ball was observed in the skies of Robozeno (Russia). The following year another event was recorded: «*Late, in the dark nights of December in the year 1664, the citizens of London sat down to look at a bright new star*», it made a "huge noise" above all: «*King Charles II and the Queen were staring at her from the window in Whitehall*." The star rose more or less in the east, not reaching a high altitude and sinking below the horizon in the southeast, between two and three in the morning. In a week or two it disappeared, and then letters arrived from Vienna reporting the sight of bright light like a comet, and " *in the air the appearance of an object like a coffin, which caused great anxiety of thought among the population*." Erfurt saw with this other terrible apparitions and some heard noises in the air like fireworks or sounds of cannons and musket shots (an ancient firearm heavier than the arquebus). " *Rumor had it that one night in the following February, hundreds of people had seen blazes of fire for a full hour, which seemed to run from Whitehall to St. James's and then back to Whitehall again, until they subsequently disappeared.*"

«*In March of that same year the brightest visible comet appeared in the sky for two hours after midnight and continued like this until dawn. With such portents came accompanied the most terrible and great plague in London.*" Other related phenomena were described in 1680: «*That between Eisenberg and Dornberg thirty funeral coffins all covered with black clothes were seen in broad daylight, between them and on a coffin a black man stood with a white cross. When all this had disappeared, there came a great heat that the people in this place could hardly bear. But when the sun went down, they perceived a sweet perfume as if they were in a rose garden. By this time they were all in the midst of a disturbance. After this the epidemic settled in Thuringia in many places.*" Further south, in Vienna: "...

And stinking fog with the culprits, as indicative of the plague, and of these, of course, several were observed last autumn."

July 9, 1686: « *At 1:30 am, a balloon of fire, with a tail, appeared apparently at 8.5° of Aquarius and remained motionless for an eighth of an hour. Its diameter was about half the Moon. It gave off so much light that, at first, one could read without a candle. Then it disappeared back into place, but very gradually. This phenomenon was also seen by others at the same time, in a city 17km away from Leipzig (Germany)."*

In 1802 the German astronomer Fritsch saw "strange objects" in the sky. Later, in 1816 a flying object was seen crossing the sky in Edinburgh (Scotland). Also in 1818 an astronomer in Ipswich (England), saw a strange object that was suspended near the Sun for 3 hours and a half. But we also found that UFO formations were seen in Emburn, northern France at that time. They moved quickly and made 90° curves. This was observed on February 12, April 27, and September 7, 1820. Later, in 1822, another astronomer saw 2 objects crossing the solar disk.

In the year 1826, in Saarbrucken, a "gray torpedo" was seen to fall to the ground, but no explosion was heard. Likewise in 1833 a bright hook-shaped object was seen suspended over Ohio (USA). That same year, in November, a "big and bright" flying object was seen over Niagara Falls. Almost three years later, a giant vehicle is seen hovering over Cherbourg (France), it was oval in shape and seemed to rotate.

Year 1845: Stationary orange objects in the sky of London, alarmed the population; an Italian astronomer observed a fleet of disks crossing the sky of Naples; A ship on the high seas observed 3 giant discs rise out of the water and remain stationary in the sky for 10 minutes. The artifacts were so huge that they were seen 1,500km away by other ships; a flying disc crossed the sky of Florence (Italy).

Year 1846: A large, bright disk was seen over Lowell, Massachusetts, which dropped a piece of "weird jelly" ashore. UFOs were also seen over London and over Inverness (Scotland). That same year one of the first signs of what could be a UFO occurred in an official North American report, some 35 years before the first known flight: "The Democracy" the old-fashioned Missouri newspaper of October 19, 1865 gives a report of an unknown object sighted under the title of "A Remarkable Strange Discovery in History". The story was reported by one James Lumley, who was a trapper. The report indicated that what Lumley divulged was true and this would break the foundations of the scientific world. Lumely claims that in mid-September of that year, he was intercepting in the mountains in a zone between 75-100 miles above the Great Falls of the Upper Missouri River. Just after sunset, Lumley saw a "bright, luminous body" in the skies. This body moved very quickly to the east. After 5 seconds, the unknown object burst into pieces. Soon he heard an explosion and a crash followed by a "rushing sound". This explosion shook the Earth. According to him, you could smell the sulfur in the air.

The relationship between flying objects, epidemics and fog is seen again in history: « *When cholera broke out aboard Her Majesty the Queen of England's ship Britannia, sailing in the Black Sea in the year 1854, several of the officers and sailors positively stated the following: Immediately before the outbreak, a curious dark mist spread over the sea and passed over the ship. Hardly had the ship emerged from the mist than the first case of the disease was reported.* A blue mist was also reported in connection with the outbreak of cholera in England in 1832 and between 1848 and 1849.

During the wars in South America, striking events were also seen. Simón Bolívar, a high-ranking Freemason according to researcher William Bramely, wrote a poem called "Delirio del Chimborazo", in which he clearly exposes a supernatural experience with non-human beings. In fact, his narration is very similar to the case of Admiral Richard E. Byrd, but in this case, he describes himself being carried through the air over mountains towards what is presumed to be the pole, where advanced beings They would reveal great knowledge.

Year 1870: A "rare object" was seen crossing the Moon's disk, which took 30 seconds. On March 22 of that same year, the sailboat La Señora del Lago observed a strange object in the sky and the crew called Captain FW Banner, who described what he saw as a circular cloud, with a semicircle divided into 4 parts. This was seen for half an hour. The following year a giant red disc was seen over Marseilles (France) for 9 minutes. Four years later, on July 6, 1874, a huge ship, about 120m tall, was seen in Oaxaca (Mexico), for 6 minutes. Likewise, in the circulation of L'Année Scientifique, the news of the sighting of a large number of black objects crossing the Moon appears published in 1874.

Year 1879: Strange objects are seen in the sky, in the middle of the Pacific Ocean, by Admiral Miguel Graú and his crew aboard the Huáscar monitor; the following year, a cigar-shaped object with a disc coming out of it was seen in France. The same year several UFOs appeared over Germany; two years later, the famous Greenwich observatory in England detected a "torpedo" flying in the sky, which was also seen in Belgium and Holland; a year later, a flying object crossed the entire Atlantic ocean, it was seen on one side and the other. It had a light coming out of the center.

Year 1885: A "round and rare" object was seen on the island of Bermuda. In November of the same year, an astronomer, among many witnesses, saw a giant object (about 5 times the size of the Moon) cross the sky of Turkey. Likewise, the astronomer José A. Bonilla published an article in the magazine L'Astronomie, in which he explained that on August 12 and 13, 1883, he watched from the Mexican observatory of Zacatecas, the passage of a total of 447 UFOs that in successive waves they crossed in front of the solar disk.

May 4, 1888: A flying disc crossed the sky over New Zealand. Three years later, on November 22, 1892, in the San Francisco Bay area, a large cigar-shaped object with small wings was seen by hundreds of people. He was traveling northeast, toward Oakland. Hours later the ship was seen by thousands of people in towns in northern California. On November 30 the object returned to San Francisco again, traveling upwind. That same year a UFO is seen carrying out aerial maneuvers over Bahía Blanca (Argentina).

Year 1893: A luminous apparatus is seen over France, and in May the English ship HMS Caroline, sailing between Shanghai and Japan, observed a flotilla of disks for 2 hours. A year later, in March, a luminous object was seen over Omaha, Nebraska. Then, on April 6, a skyship made of metal, 4 or 5m long, is seen by hundreds of people, again in Omaha. Three days later, on April 9, 1894, at Mount Carroll, 120 miles from Chicago, witnesses observed an "egg"-shaped object move toward Wausau, Wisconsin, where about 100 other people saw it. The next day, April 10, a UFO was seen for 15 minutes over Galesburg, Illinois. Later the same object was seen in Eglin, also in Illinois, and then flew over Leedora and Newton, in Iowa. After this, on April 16, a UFO with green and red lights was seen from Benton and other towns in the US. On the same day, a UFO flew just 200m above Washington DC, and a month later, on August 26, an English astronomer saw a large disk with a "tail".

Year 1895: Several sightings are recorded throughout England and Scotland. Two years later, on April 20, 1897, a cigar-shaped ship about 200 feet long crossed the sky over Sisterville, Virginia. It emitted green, red and white lights. Many people came out to watch her.

Between the years 1899 and 1905 the Wright brothers managed to put gliders in the air and thus began the creation and modification of the first airplanes. For this reason flights cannot be justified before this date. On February 24, 1904, the American ship USS Supply observed a mysterious light moving at high altitude and at high speed. In 1905 unidentified flying objects are seen in the sky of Wales, even witnesses saw them coming out of the sea. Two years later, on July 2, 1907, a dark "torpedo" remained over the city of Burlington (USA), it changed color before moving and a disc was observed coming out of the "torpedo", then both disappeared.

The Tunguska Accident

On the morning of June 30, 1908, a great ball of fire devastated the Siberian region of Tunguska, which was such an exceptional event that it sparked a controversy that still continues. The area where the object fell -or where it exploded, as some researchers maintain that the object exploded before hitting the ground-, in the Tunguska river valley, was sparsely populated by the Tungus, a nomadic people of Mongolian origin dedicated to herding animals. reindeer. Near the center of the explosion, north of Vanavara, several Tunguses were thrown into the air by the blast and their tents were blown away by a violent wind. Around them, the forest began to burn. When the astonished Tunguses cautiously inspected the site of the explosion, they found scenes of terrible devastation. In a 30km circle, trees had been struck down like wooden matches and the intense heat produced by the explosion had melted metal objects, destroyed warehouses and reduced several reindeer to ashes. Reports from the Kansk district, 600km from the point of the explosion, described events such as boatmen being thrown overboard and horses knocked over by the blast wave, while houses shook and chinaware smashed on their shelves. The

Trans-Siberian driver stopped his train fearing a derailment, noticing that the wagons and rails were vibrating.

Other effects were perceived in places very distant from the globe, but their cause remained unknown for a long time, since the news of the fireball and its explosion did not reach the ears of the general public for several years. Seismic waves similar to those of an earthquake were recorded throughout Europe, as well as various disturbances in the Earth's magnetic field. Later, the meteorologists found from their microbarograph records that the atmospheric waves produced by the detonation had circled the Earth twice. Actually, there is no report that anyone died as a result of the Tunguska explosion, but the Tungusians explained that the reindeer in that area had scabs on their skin, which modern writers, such as Baxter, have attributed to burns caused by by radiation.

A 2008 report quoted: *"Russian scientists claim to have found the remains of an alien artifact in Siberia."* (Europa Press) In this report, the information came from Moscow and said that scientists from the Tunguska Space Phenomenon Public Fund, in Siberia, announced that they had found remains of an alien artifact in the place where a meteorite is believed to have fallen in 1908, according to reported the Russian agency Interfax – that is, the Tunguska accident. The first expedition to investigate the supposed meteorite that fell in this desert region of Siberia was organized in 1927 under the direction of Professor Leonid Kulik, who at that time did not claim to have found any extraterrestrial material.

The Fund's scientists also claimed to have found a rock weighing about 40kg next to the alien remains, which they have sent for analysis. The head of this latest expedition, Yuri Lavbin, expressed his wish that the results of this investigation solve the mystery that exists around the apparent meteorite coinciding with the 100th anniversary of its fall. The Tunguska cataclysm constitutes one of the main scientific mysteries of the 20th century, since the exact nature of the body that exploded and its origin are unknown.

Other studies highlight that whatever the object that exploded did not fall directly, but descended and, before touching the ground, diverted its direction and then exploded. That could not be done by a meteorite but by a directed object. It is even believed that it was a mother ship or a nuclear vehicle since it caused a shock wave perceived hundreds of kilometers away and that devastated more than 2,000 km 2 ^{of} Siberian forest.

One year after the Tunguska accident, in 1909, immense tubular ships are seen over England, moving at great speed, as well as parked on the ground. On November 29 of that year, there was a wave of sightings over Belgium; On September 21, 1910, approximately one million people watched a monumental UFO procession over New York City. The disc-shaped objects flew over the city and paralyzed traffic and commerce. All this lasted 3 hours. Another report claims that there were many other sightings in the US mainly in Boston, Huntington, Virginia and Tennessee.

In 1912 sightings of tubular or cigar-shaped ships were repeated. On February 9, 1913, from the Toronto Astronomical Observatory, they sighted several unidentified objects orbiting the Earth. Two years later, in 1915, the famous disappearance of the English Norfolk Regiment, made up of hundreds of men during the war with Turkey, occurred. It is said that they entered a mysterious cloud that was attached to the ground, when the last man had entered the cloud, it rose and moved away at great speed against the wind. The fate of these soldiers was never heard from again.

The Miracle of the "Virgin" of Fatima

In Fátima, Portugal, there were several simultaneous events, initially from 1915 to the end of 1917, although there were others until the 1930s where one of the 3 children who witnessed the miracle continued to receive visits from an enlightened woman who came from heaven. It is said that one of the messages that were provided to the children was addressed to the world for the collapse of socialism, even Pope John Paul II himself would try to dissolve it with the help of the CIA knowing the events in Fatima, according to some. researchers. It is also affirmed that in Fátima there were some 70,000 people as witnesses in the fifth apparition, which gives this event a touch of historical relevance.

On May 13, 1917, the famous "Miracle of the Virgin of Fatima" occurred, although the main witnesses had received "divine visits" for two years. Lucía, 10 years old, and her cousins Jacinta and Francisco, nine and seven respectively, were taking care of the flock in Cova da Iría, about 2km from Fátima (Portugal). After seeing two strange flashes of lightning, the little shepherds observe " *a most beautiful lady, brighter than the Sun* " on the already famous oak tree of apparitions, which they naturally identified with the Virgin Mary. Officially, this is the first of six apparitions officially recognized by the Catholic Church; However, Lucía herself confessed that she had previously experienced various strange experiences in the company of other children.

In the middle of 1915, Lucía Abóbora, together with María Rosa Matías, Teresa Matías and María Justino, contemplated something similar to a cloud above the grove, inside which a woman without a head could be distinguished. Until the beginning of 1916 they had new encounters with another mysterious being that they associated as the so-called "Angel of Portugal". These first experiences lead us to wonder to what extent the religious convictions of the child witnesses influenced the interpretation of the phenomenon. What is more interesting, to what extent were the initial testimonies manipulated by the ecclesiastical hierarchy? The researchers located a woman who in 1915, also in Fatima, starred in numerous visions of "the Virgin." Her name was Carolina

Carreira and, unlike in the case of the three "seers", she went completely unnoticed. The result of lengthy interviews with the fourth witness from the aforementioned Portuguese city is enormously enlightening. The entity that communicated with Carolina appeared inside a frustoconical light source that gradually advanced and receded. This came from " *a cloud that moved against the wind.*"

On June 13, the supposed Virgin appeared again to the "shepherds" in the holm oak. An underground thunderclap was heard and "*a little white cloud* " appeared in the sky, to which the woman was ascending by a path of light, according to witnesses. In the third apparition, the woman revealed to the children the secrets that would give so much to talk about.

On August 13, some 20,000 people were waiting for the little ones, however, they were detained by the authorities with the intention of making them confess that it was all a hoax, which they failed to do. In the place of the apparitions, strange luminous phenomena occurred and " *a rain of white flakes of unknown substance* " fell on those present, as published in the Diario de Noticias. This substance could correspond to what is known in ufological media as "angel hair", which sometimes appears after a UFO sighting. In the fifth apparition, on September 13, about 30,000 souls contemplated " *a luminous globe revolving through the clouds.*" These phenomena made the apparitions of Fatima become the most important social event in Portugal.

On October 13, some 70,000 people, including numerous correspondents from the newspapers of the time, expected to witness the great miracle that the Virgin had promised through the "pastorinhos". The situation was very tense and if the long-awaited miracle did not take place, the children could have been lynched by the crowd. This date marked a turning point in subsequent events and led to the recognition of the veracity of the apparitions by the

Catholic Church. Thousands of witnesses coming from different points of the Portuguese geography, and even from abroad, contemplated the "Dance of the Sun" in astonishment. It seemed as if the star king began to move violently until it rushed into those present. At that time, hundreds of blackouts and conversions occurred. In addition, those gathered there received a strong heat stroke at the time that the atmosphere took on a pink color. There was not the slightest doubt, either the scorching Sun had detached itself from the sky approaching the Earth, or something that emulated it had done a great prodigy. This is how the correspondents of the Portuguese newspapers wrote it, even those of an anti-clerical ideological line.

However, if we carefully study the testimonies, we can come to the conclusion that something did come close to those present, but not precisely the sun. That day the clouds completely covered the sky, so the king sun was not visible. In addition, many of the witnesses referred to " *a silver disk* " when they wanted to describe the dancing object which, and this is an illuminating fact, did not damage the eyes when staring at it.

The secrets that were revealed by the Luminous Woman were studied by the MJ-12 (UFO research group mentioned by the military man Bill Cooper in the 90s) resulting in its veracity: it was the warning of the end of the First World War, the fall of the communist regime and the end of time due to the exploitation of the planet's resources, as well as the advent of a World War superior to the 1st and 2nd, added all this to the return of Jesus Christ himself. , on an approximate date between 2011 and 2013 – according to a detailed study by the CIA and the SIV. Let us bear in mind that neither the First nor the Second World War had yet been developed.

During the following years and parallel to the appearances of Lucía, other UFO cases were seen: In 1929, coinciding with the arrival of the Graf Zeppelin airship, 3 objects flew over the sky of Tokyo (Japan). The following year and also the following years, several fireballs are seen, over the European sky, several military pilots are witnesses of this event.

In 1934, the Roerich Expedition observed a bright disk in Mongolia. Nicholas Roerich, who looked at it through binoculars, said that it reflected sunlight, like a polished plate and had an oval shape; it was huge. It changed course to the southeast and disappeared. In 1940 and the following years, the so-called "ghost planes" made an appearance, flying all over the world, especially over Europe. It is believed that they could have been German flight prototypes to interfere in air combat.

The Battle of Los Angeles

The headline news in Los Angeles on February 25, 1942 read: " *We can hear original news from CBS radio station with Byron Palmer talking about the aerial confrontation.*" One newspaper claimed: " *Los Angeles Area Under Attack!* », Another had on the cover: « *US military attacked a UFO in 1942 over Los Angeles? – The army says: "Royal alarm"* .» A few years before the Roswell Incident, a few years before pilot Kenneth Arnold experienced the "flying saucer" milestone in the Pacific Northwest, three years before the Battle of the Bulge, two years before "D-Day," and Years before the so-called "modern UFO era" officially began, the Battle of Los Angeles occurred.

Very few have heard of the Battle of Los Angeles. Imagine a visiting ship from another world, or dimension, hovering over a panicked Los Angeles city in a long blackout, in the middle of the night, just weeks after the Pearl Harbor incident at the height of World War II fear and paranoia. World War. Imagine how this huge craft, which was assumed to be some unknown Japanese aircraft, was then attacked when it hovered over the area, stationary nearby, over Culver City and Santa Monica. Then it was attacked by dozens of US Army flak batteries, firing about 2,000 rounds of 12-pound, high-explosive shells in full view of hundreds of thousands of residents.

The sudden appearance of the huge round objects shot over all of Los Angeles and much of South Calorina within an immediate war alarm blackout with thousands of Air Raid Vigilantes running around the city in pitch black as the drama unfolded across above the skies... a drama that resulted in the death of 6 people and the rain of missile fragments on houses, streets and buildings by thousands around. Dozens of gun groups and searchlights from the 37th Brigade of the Army Coastal Artillery easily took aim at the huge ship which hung like a surreal magic lantern in the brightness. Few in the city could fall asleep after the Coastal Defense guns began firing hundreds and hundreds of shells up at the shining ship which was apparently first seen as if it seemed motionless on some sort of west side of the area of MGM studios in Culver City. The pounding of batteries and the ignition of air missiles resounded from one side of Los Angeles to the other as the gun groups easily hit their targets in what some described as "direct hits," but all to no avail as the objects they remained inert. The black skies of Los Angeles looked like they were under gunfire.

A year after the end of World War II and after the first official incidents in the Bermuda Triangle, in July 1946, another phenomenon appeared in the Scandinavian area, the "ghost rockets", which shot across the sky. Only in July, more than 500 cases of these strange objects were registered. Later more cases were reported, only in Sweden and Finland about 2000 were counted. The descriptions indicated that they were cigar-shaped, gave off flames from the rear and flew at a height between 300m and 1000m, going at great speed and also slowly, without emitting any noise, something that a conventional rocket cannot do. It should also be noted that no nation was officially testing rockets in Europe in 1946. That year there was also a wave of UFOs over Russia and Greece.

✶✶✶✶✶

THE BERMUDA TRIANGLE

The Bermuda Triangle, space also known as the Devil's Triangle, is a geographical area of 3,900,000 km ^{2} between the islands of Bermuda, Puerto Rico and Melbourne (Florida). It is located from 55° W to 85° W and 30° N to 40° N, where numerous unexplained disappearances of ships and planes have occurred. The mystery goes back further than the mid-19th century, as is believed, and since then more than 50 ships and 20 planes have disappeared in the triangle, with hundreds of people missing as well.

One of the most famous cases was the disappearance of Flight 19. This consisted of 5 US Torpedo-type bombers that left Fort Lauderdale (South Florida) on December 5, 1945, on a routine training flight and in good weather conditions. None came back. Even the seaplane that was sent looking for them disappeared. It is said that these planes appeared intact a few years ago in the middle of the Sahara desert, as well as a gigantic ship, and the US military did not take long to dismantle and remove them. Other stories from the region tell of ships being found abandoned with food still hot on the tables and planes disappearing without ever issuing a distress call. The Bermuda Triangle has always been a dangerous and mysterious area, since the disappearances of sailors, pilots and tourists have never been solved.

The elements of information around this area are intriguing: in a part of the western Atlantic Ocean, more or less triangular in shape, between Bermuda, Florida and the 40th meridian, numerous planes and ships were disappearing without leaving any trace of what that could have been theirs, mainly in the last 30 years of the mid-20th century, since in the vast majority of cases no remains or survivors have ever been found.

Messages from some planes before their disappearance did not give any indication of abnormality; in fact, at one moment everything was going normal and the next minute everything had disappeared without the slightest warning. The number of disappearances without discovery is completely impressive and the most mysterious thing is that it could not have happened because of a hurricane or cyclone because most of the disappearances occurred in good weather. According to accounts from the days of sailing, Bermuda and the area further south were indeed spared for hundreds of years by missing ships whose fate went on to fill the long list of lost ships in the ocean, disappearances usually attributed to piracy, storms or riots. In addition, a good number of such strange disappearances affected only the passengers and crew; otherwise the derelict vessels appeared to be in perfect order, with their logbooks, lifeboats, cargo, and even personal effects in place.

Most relevant verified disappearances:

· 1840: Rosalie, a German ship found without a crew.

· 1872: The ship Mary Celeste. His crew disappeared.

· 1882: British frigate Atalanta with 290 people.

· 1924: Raifuku Maru, a Japanese cargo ship that was asking for help by radio when it disappeared.

· 1945: Flight 19 and the seaplane that went in search of it.

· 1947: US Army C-45 Superfort aircraft 150km from Bermuda.

· 1948: Four-engine Tudor IV civilian with 31 passengers.

· 1948: A DC-3 disappeared with 32 passengers and all its crew.

· 1949: Another Tudor IV disappeared.

· 1950: The ship SS Sandra disappeared without a trace.

· 1952: York, British plane with 33 passengers.

- 1954: US Navy ship Constelation and its 42 crew members.
- 1956: Martin P5M seaplane, with 10 crew members on board.
- 1963: The Queen of the Sulpher ship. Without a trace.
- 1967: YC-122 military freighter.
- 1970: The Milton Latrides, did not reach its destination.
- 1972: The German ship Anita, 32 crew members and 20,000 tons.
- 1997: Disappearance of all the passengers of a German pleasure yacht.

The hypotheses are given of all kinds, from beliefs that an alien population hijacks ships and people in order to find out what we humans are like, until Atlantis is submerged in the Triangle area and, because of this, they are the "Atlanteans"." who could have a more powerful energy than the one known to us with which they "electromagnetically suck" the boats. But other theories assume that it is about the existence of certain particles that suggest the presence of antigravitational matter of a totally different nature from those known on this planet. However, none of this has been proven. Some military sources have made up the story that they are subterranean volcanic eruptions possibly opening fissures in the unexplored depths. The pressure created by the hot gases in the Earth's core would then expel remnants of densely magnetic radioactive material that would move at tremendous speed. As a consequence, an aircraft located within the magnetic field of such rays would be affected along with all its electrical instruments, including the engine ignition systems. And the fact that the disappearances occur discontinuously would confirm that they are cyclical, just like volcanic eruptions. In any case, none of this has been proven.

The hypotheses can be as absurd as they are illogical, but the truth is that the mystery of the Bermuda triangle and its companion, the Dragon Triangle, in Asia, remain unknown. Less fanciful analyzes suggest that strong currents and deep waters could explain the absence of remains, underscoring that several of the disappearances attributed to the Bermuda Triangle actually occurred 600km away, but certainly no official answer is convincing. Some believe that once deep-sea diving techniques are perfected, most of the lost ships are likely to be recovered, as civilian and military vessels pass through the region every day without mishap. At the moment the most common theory continues to be in relation to UFOs.

The mysterious Dogon tribe

The Dogons are a people located in the Republic of Mali, in West Africa. A truly amazing enigma falls upon this town, possibly one of the most extraordinary enigmas science has ever encountered. The wisdom of this people contains precise and detailed data on the solar system, which in many cases have only recently become part of the heritage of modern astronomy: they describe the Moon as "dry and barren", they know that the planet Jupiter (which they call "Dana Tolo") has four large satellites, they know about Saturn's rings, and that the planets describe elliptical orbits around the Sun. The notion that celestial bodies follow elliptical orbits around a main body that is located in one of the foci was only accepted by Western astronomy after Kepler, in the 17th century. They also describe the Milky Way as a spiral galaxy made up of millions of stars.

Apart from all this, the Dogons even refer to the nature of the Sun. They say that our Sun and the star Sirius, that star of the first magnitude, the brightest in the Southern Hemisphere, are actually two sister suns that broke off one from the other and two different star systems were formed but they have the same origin. It must be said that the star Sirius is 8.7 light years from our solar system, thus being one of the five closest stars to this solar system. However, the fundamental concepts of the Dogon myths do not refer only to the solar system. The Dogons claimed to know of the existence of a star (Sirius B) that is impossible to see with the naked eye. For them it is the most important in the firmament and revolves around Sirius A, the brightest in the sky in the constellation Canis Major. Both stars do not offer the human eye more than a single and powerful source of light in the firmament, which makes it impossible to distinguish one star from another. Thus, the circumstance existed that the Dogons knew Sirius B, being also aware that it was invisible. Their representative drawings of Sirius B's orbit around Sirius A are exactly identical to those of the modern astronomical diagram.

Your knowledge about Sirius A, B and C

They also ensure that Sirius B is a very small star; they call her "Po Tolo". They continue with the affirmation that despite being very small, it is very heavy, the heaviest that exists, made of a material that is brighter than iron, which they call "Sagala". Official astronomy knows that Sirius B is a "white dwarf", a very small and very heavy star. According to their mythology, "Po Tolo" goes around Sirius every 50 years (according to official science their calculations are currently estimated at 50,040 years), but the Dogons also say that apart from "Po Tolo", the Sirius' companion, there is another star that is 4 times larger than "Po Tolo" but nevertheless much lighter in weight and that has a more external orbit and that also lasts 50 years to go around Sirius, and the Dogon call it "Emme Ya" (for the first time, in the year 1862, the American astronomer Alvan Clark managed to see in the star Sirius, which was not just one, but two stars. With a 47cm diameter objective he was able to distinguish the one that was known from that moment as Sirius B. Later, in a much more recent era, the existence of a third star that completed the Sirius system was detected, Sirius C, the "Emme Ya" of the Dogons.

The Dogons say that "Emme Ya" is the second companion of Sirius and in turn has a small satellite that revolves around it and that they call "Nyan Tolo", the star of women. They also draw the trajectories of their orbits (it has been discovered that the trajectory that the Dogon draw is exactly the same as that discovered by astronomers). The Dogons assure that all their knowledge comes from some beings who came to Earth from "Nyan Tolo", a satellite of "Emme Ya", from the Sirius system, approximately around the year 3,000 BC, and whom they call "Nummos" – see the relationship of the name with the event in Spain of the "umo" case of several decades ago. The "Nummos" descended to Earth in an "ark" red as fire initially and turning white when it landed. Upon landing it looked as if four huge rocks collided with each other, raising a gigantic cloud of dust, the Dogon say.

It should be noted that the Russian astroarchaeologist Vladimir Rubtsov affirmed that the word with which the ancient Iranians referred to Sirius was Tistrya, a word that comes from the Sanskrit Tri-Stri, and which means three stars. That is to say, that the knowledge that Sirius is a triple star system was widely known by all the cultures of our most remote past. Not being appreciable from our planet, who disseminated such information? The Sun and Sirius rise at the same point on the horizon, which is why many temples are oriented in that direction. Since Sirius' solar rising was delayed by four days each year, both stars coincided again at the same point : 365 x 4 = 1,460 years. This led to the making of a parallel calendar, known as the Sothic calendar, which goes back to Ancient Egypt to mark events that occurred 43 centuries BC. When, then, did they make their observations of Sirius to establish their calendar? Was this knowledge received from the Dogon gods themselves and a new clue about their origin? In the tomb of Ramses III you can see a being gravitating in space around a red star: Sirius.

Electronic Geniuses

Nicola Tesla was the greatest genius in history, but there were men after him, who, as with Tesla, discovered and made incredible scientific breakthroughs that were not known by the general public. Mario Rojas Avendaro wrote his story based on statements made to him by a former disciple of Guillermo Marconi: the physicist, philologist, and humanist Narciso Genovese, a professor at an institute in Baja California. According to N. Genovese, Marconi's disciples, upon the death of their teacher in 1938, decided to continue their studies and experiments on the use of solar or "cosmic" energy, but taking all the necessary precautions so that these could not serve to war or criminal ends.

Ninety-eight scholars and technicians from different nations would have formed a society analogous to the Pugwash Committee and would have withdrawn to a deserted region of the Andes Mountains (or jungle), where they live isolated and ignored. His job was to "*tame the electrical forces of peaceful and universal space.*" The confidences that Narciso Genovese made to the press, were later reflected in a book entitled "I have traveled to Mars" (1958), controversial and controversial, due to the statements that were collected there. « *A group of people, deeply immersed in the secrets of the physical sciences, gathered in a secret place in the South American jungle, form a community of the physical sciences, dedicated solely to scientific research. Free of any commitment to governments or powers, they nevertheless have unlimited economic support that has allowed progress without obstacles with the achievement of astonishing and practical results that will be shared with Humanity little by little to the extent that this is convenient.* »

Three basic principles united this community:

1. A single religion: God, infinite and most wise architect of the Universe.

2. A single homeland: Earth.

3. A single purpose: To make our allies the inhabitants of other planets of the Solar System.

« *The teacher, the scientific guide of this Movement, Guillermo Marconi, whose investigations, the majority of which are unknown, have marked the path that we have followed up to now. Marconi, with his discoveries, united all the inhabitants of the Earth and preferred death rather than divulging amazing scientific findings that in those historical moments would have been instruments of destruction. But Marconi had close friends, partners in his work, his theories and projects; and the master's dreams are crystallizing."* Genovese avoids giving an exact location of the alleged scientific alliance and its underground facilities, although everything suggests that the extinct craters of the Venezuelan jungle are the true home of these Marconi imitators.

In another of his disturbing chapters, he alludes to his contacts with Martians and his interplanetary trips: « *Convinced that the inhabitants of other worlds are distant but separated from us, we devoted ourselves to the obsessive task of converting solar energy into a vehicle and trying to communicate with them. distant beings. Therefore, we rule out the disintegration of the atom as erroneous and dangerous, as it also seemed absurd to us to be able to leave the reach of the Earth with terrestrial forces alone [...] Since 1950 we were certain that we were being visited by devices from some other planet and deducing from our progress we arrive at the absolute certainty of them. The Earth was subjected to examination by inhabitants of another world and everything showed that their intentions were friendly, but at the same time they seemed not daring to make contact and there were serious reasons for them. So we decided to get your attention. Their ships must be very similar to us; His way of proceeding indicated it. Noticing their appearances, we initiate the release of powerful light signals and short-wave sound waves. We had no response at first, but we were certain that we had not been heard or seen, as the strange ships repeated their visits. »*

« At the end of 1955 we received certain signals of response. We arranged in our little test field all kinds of signals to invite a landing. On December 16 of the same year, at five in the afternoon, to our great joy, a formation of five aircraft made its appearance above us and almost immediately the first of the five aircraft made contact with Earth while the other four returned. to rise, staying at a short distance and at the same height [...] He extracted from a scroll of very fine gold a sheet, thirty centimeters of brilliant white metal, the thickness of our ordinary paper, the metal sheet was embossed with gold letters, an inscription headed as a shield by an engraving, also in relief, representing the Solar Planetary System r.» According to the author, the Martians have been monitoring the planet for almost 2,000 years and even had an opinion on the countries of the Earth in the 50s.

Guillermo Marconi (1875-1937) was born in Bologna, Italy. A precocious genius, at the age of 12 he impressed his physics teacher Vicente Rosa, an electricity enthusiast, who managed to interest him in magnetism and the production of electric current using hand-built batteries. At the age of 20 he managed to make the first wireless transmission, inspired by the work of the German physicist Heinrich Rudolfh Hertz. His invention garnered little interest in his native country and he decided to move to England where he founded the Wireless Telegraph and Signal Company, Ltd. On December 12, 1901 «the *letter S of the Morse Telegraphy Code was able to traverse the ether across the Atlantic Ocean. Thanks to his discovery, he was awarded the Nobel Prize in Physics (1909).»* The inventor would die a victim of angina, a death that seemed mysterious to many of his compatriots. Little is known about his later years. Apparently the Italian wise man, free of economic worries, dedicated himself in the 30s to clandestine experiments, helped by the physicist Landini.

A yacht he owned, the "Electra", was converted into a laboratory ship. "*It is said that at that time he would have managed to send wave beams from Genoa to Australia, where the light bulbs went on for no apparent reason to the uninitiated.*" He also became interested in the problem of extraterrestrial civilizations, "*as well as that he claimed to have picked up signals, if not messages, from a people in space.*" The most outrageous rumor credits him with the invention of the death ray, which is believed to have been presented in a demonstration to the Duce, Benito Mussolini. However, that merit had already been given to him before Tesla.

5.

HITLER AND THE THULE COMPANY

"Since the Earth in its primitive state is not suitable for our expansion, man must chain himself to satisfy human destiny."
Jean Vorst (Curator of the French Museum of Natural History)

THE ARYAN RACE AND secret German technology

Occasionally, for racist reasons, some theorists claim that the Aryans were the founders of the ancient Mesopotamian civilizations and thus the world's first civilized people, but Aryan merely means "Martian." Aryan dominance theory was promoted during the brutal Nazi regime to support its idea of "Aryan superiority". The Nazis always held that the Aryans were originally created by supermen as gods from a different world. A similar belief was expressed earlier in history, when the Spanish conquistador Francisco Pizarro invaded South America in 1532, the natives referred to the Spanish invaders as "Viracochas", which means "the white masters". Native American legends in South America tell of a dominant race of huge white men who had descended from the skies centuries before. According to the legends, those "masters" had reigned over the South American cities before disappearing again with the promise of returning. The native South Americans thought the Spanish were returning Viracochas, and initially allowed the Spanish to appropriate American treasures and gold without resistance. Let us keep in mind in any case that the indigenous people were a minority. What I mean by this? That 6 million people disappeared from America before the conquerors arrived, and everything indicates that they were taken from this planet.

Actually, when talking about Aryans, Nazi philosophy should not be confused with Indo-European, since the original Aryans were, according to other myths, descendants of the Atlantean continent. From them a group of Atlantean survivors established in the Ural mountains would have emerged, creating various branches and genetic crosses that would result in racial groups such as the Celts, Basques, Nordics, Siberians and Aryans. Thus, the fame that was given to the Germans was more an intention of the Allies to discredit and sink German power from any area or terrain that they could use – in addition to the actions of the Nazis that gave them their fame. For example, while the Germans developed a military and social totalitarianism, and mistreated Jews, blacks, and people of other ethnic groups, the Americans and Russians had been using concentration and extermination camps for years. In fact, many images of deaths presented as part of the Nazi holocaust were actually crimes carried out by the US military itself in order to further blacken the Third Reich's infamous reputation and eliminate large numbers of Japanese who had migrated to the US. In this way, the world should see only the Germans as the common and diabolical enemy, not realizing with this the atrocities that the US, the Soviet Union and the Republic of China were doing. Simply put, some believe that wars happen between good guys and bad guys, but they really happen between bad guys and bad guys, because the good guys don't seek war.

The Third Reich was for Germany a time of progress in all fields: Germany had the fastest cars, the fastest planes with the longest flight range, the first television (during the 1936 Olympic Games), the best entertainment movies, the most pioneering pharmaceutical industry, etc. Soon the first jet aircraft (Me-262) and the first long-range missiles (V2) flew. All this is known. Much less well known is another technology that, for obvious reasons, the Germans in the Reich kept secret and about which the Allies, once they got word of it, kept the most absolute silence. Based on the occult philosophy of the Third Reich (Thule and Vril societies), Hitlerite scientists would have achieved accredited advances (especially aeronautics and astronautics) of an unimaginable magnitude. The knowledge of mysterious German circular aircraft powered by anti-gravity engines with the code names of "Vril" and "Haunebu", which were supposedly developed not based on conventional technique, but on a new technique stemming from NS occult philosophy, has always been denied by the Allied forces. Many may think that it is impossible for the Germans to develop such a fabulous technique in such a short space of time, but they forget that they were not based on classical scientific principles, but on the occult philosophy of Germanic societies such as Thule and Vril.

Thus, for example, the German scientist Viktor Schauberger was a convinced advocate of "implosion instead of explosion." He rejected the internal combustion engine, since it is based on destruction (explosion), but divine Creation is always constructive. Therefore, a technique based on destruction is contrary to the laws of God and could be termed as a satanic technique. Instead, he proposed implosion engines. This is just one example of the philosophy of these scientists. Thanks to the way of thinking of the Third Reich, the Germans advanced in technique in a few years what the Allies would not advance in decades.

Hitler's UFOs

In 1919 the Thule Society was founded in Germany, its founder was Haushoffer. Many German bosses met there. This individual is responsible for choosing the swastika – a classic symbol or emblem in the Indus Valley – placed behind a shining sword as the ultimate symbol of Nazism. The name Thule was chosen in memory of the legendary, and for them existing, kingdom of Thule, which is another name for the legendary Atlantis. They thought that an advanced civilization had once existed in the Gobi desert, destroyed by a great catastrophe. Its inhabitants had had to emigrate to northern Europe and others to the Caucasus. These inhabitants, according to their theories, would be the original race of humanity, that is, the first pure Aryans. His ideal was to return to the origins and make the corresponding conquests to reborn this civilization, the initial Aryan trunk. Their beliefs led them to have knowledge and contact with Hindu colonies and Tibetan circles that had a vision very close to their principles, and even with races that are not from this planet.

Hitler's plan was to found a thousand-year-old empire and was inspired by members of the Thule society and by the renowned satanist Aleister Crowley. The political ambitions of the society generated the formation of small independent groups, one of which was the society "Sisters of Light", internally called "Die Vril Chefin". Hitler's scientists for many years worked on the design of strange flying objects. According to recently uncovered secret reports, the Third Reich possessed technology so highly advanced that it allowed it to build flying saucers of terrestrial origin. In 1919 von Sebotendorf, Klaus Haushofer and Dietrich Ekar founded the "Thule Society ", an amalgamation of secret societies with branches throughout Germany. Its headquarters were in Munich and many members of this society rose up in clear opposition against the brief Socialist Republic of Bavaria – let's remember that Adam Weishaupt had founded the Illuminati society there more than

150 years ago. They founded a political party and in 1921 they appointed Adolf Hitler, a young man known for his fondness for the occult, as political spokesperson. Hitler's project of founding a thousand-year-old empire was inspired by the doctrine of the Thule Society.

The political ambitions of the Thule Society spawned the formation of small independent groups, one of which was named the "Vril Society." At the end of 1919, a select group of members of the Thule and Vril societies met in a mansion in Berteschgarden. On that occasion, the meeting was chaired by Dr. Schumann, his specialty is what we would call today "Alternative Energies". However, the medium María Ostich and a young woman named Sieggrund, who also acted as a medium at times, were also present at the meeting. Maria read some texts that she had received from such spirits in the Sumerian language, and another encrypted in the secret code of the Templar Order, both texts were translated. Those who studied these topics wondered: were they messages from the gods or signs of an extraterrestrial civilization? Or were they plans to develop a technology capable of reaching the stars? The truth is that from then on, the members of the Vril Society dedicated themselves to the realization of what would be one of the most unusual ideas that the human mind has conceived: propulsion by levitation.

The sinking of the Titanic

Although the Germans were the most powerful country in the world at that time, some sources even point to them as the culprits of the sinking of the most famous ocean liner in history, the Titanic. According to some researchers, the Germans had discovered some kind of technological marvel in the Atlantic Sea, precisely where the Bermuda Triangle is located, part of the area that millennia ago would have covered Atlantis. There the Germans would have discovered a device capable of teleporting or pulverizing anything, according to some theorists. I cannot confirm this assertion, only to say that the rumors were such that they assumed that the English secret service was afraid that the Germans would decipher the information they wanted to send to the Americans about what the Germans had discovered and therefore preferred to send it on the Titanic.

Although, other information, much more reliable and, in this case documented, came to reveal that the Germans sank the ship with the help of a German U-967 series submarine, not because they had secrets about Atlantis, but to remove the treasures of the billionaires who were on the boat. This submarine would have fired at the ship and sunk the Titanic, as has come to be known, where it was already known that they were waiting for them at depth to plunder the wealth stored on the ship (for this reason, when they came to look for the Titanic in the middle of from the 1990s, nothing of value was found). Logic tells us: who knows a ship that has been sunk by an iceberg before? I mean, statistically speaking, since when does ice break steel? How is it that there are ships that go to the Arctic and Antarctic and as they go they break the ice sheets in their path without making a single dent? It's obvious. Why, when the location of the Titanic was officially discovered, were no jewels found? Wasn't it a cruise ship full of millionaires? Who could have looted the ship if the best underwater research projects were being developed so far? At such a depth, what company could descend to steal the treasures left there by the most prominent millionaires of the 1910s? All this makes us think, especially if we analyze the shape of the hole made in the fuselage of the ship's bow, the speed at which the adjacent compartments filled with water, the size of the crater, the fact that witnesses claimed to have heard a sound of Very strong explosion, not to mention the fact that the bridge officers did not perceive such an "iceberg" is ridiculous. This has all the earmarks of what is usually called a "conspiracy theory".

By itself, many researchers did not accept the official thesis that it was an iceberg that submerged the huge ship, for the simple reason that ice cannot break steel, otherwise ice picks could not exist! And let's not forget that when the famous Titanic treasure was brought to light, the safe only had some papers... The fact is that some theorists believe that the most terrible thing is that perhaps that area was one of the escape routes for escaped Nazi hierarchs, as famous as Marshal Hidjoff Putten, although others believe they hid at the South Pole, in the New Swabia region. A much stronger theory.

Secret societies and secret rites

After the National Socialist Party came to power, the occult societies went underground. The Tule Society – a variant of the name of the mythical Tholan, an extraterrestrial civilization that is believed to have lived on Earth in the prehistoric era, and which is often confused with the missing Atlantis – created within the SS a secret organization called "Schwarzesolenoid" (Black Sun), alluding to the central sun of the intraterrestrial world. The Vril Society continued with its scientific investigations, until in the middle of 1934 it created its first circular-shaped experimental ship, propelled by anti-gravity energy. Those responsible for its construction were Doctor Schumann and an engineer from Wochum, probably Andreas Epp, according to some experts on the subject. Starting in 1929, the young Gertie Woch directed the Vril Society, taking charge of attracting risk-loving private investors. By the end of 1934 the Vril Society had built a new aircraft, the RFZ-II, equipped with an improved "Vril propulsion" and for the first time with a magnetic drive steering system. It measured just over 5m in diameter, and also had some of the distinctive characteristics of the famous unidentified flying objects: optical disappearance of the contour and color variation depending on the power level: orange, yellow, green, white, blue or violet.

Despite their technical sophistication, the circular airships hardly caught the attention of the political leaders of the time, yet, encouraged by Victor Schaurberger and Vril's recent achievements, the SS research department begins to build their own craft. circular. Based on Captain Hans Koler's "Tachometer Converter" and adopting some Vril components, they developed their own "Tule engine". At the end of 1938 they had built a small circular ship, propelled by propellers, the RFZ-IV, to study the flight behavior of those prototypes. In 1939, the SS had already built the RFZ-V, the first large spacecraft, 25m in diameter and renamed with a mysterious name: Haunebu-I. The first flight of the Haunebu-I took place amid tight security in August 1939. There are documents that show that in 1941 the British had information about this top-secret SS project. Compared to the simple Vril prototype, the Haunebu, it was highly complex, on the other hand, the shape of the engine allowed it to have more usable space.

With the outbreak of World War II, competition in the arms market intensified and alternative forms of energy appeared that tried to emulate traditional systems. A compromise formula was adopted regarding experimental flying saucers such as the RFZ-VII. While other UFOs crossed the sky, some German vehicles were already seen flying, such as the small Vril RFZ-II, which had begun to serve as a reconnaissance ship in the late 1940s, or the RFZ-VI and Haunebu-II. In June 1942, the "Fliegengyroskop" (Flying Gyroscope) began to be talked about insistently, "Schrieber-Habermold", known as the "Flying Top", was a jet-propelled vertical ascension circular aircraft. At the end of July, the first practical tests began until April 12, 1945, when Richard Niet told Hitler: « *Today under my direction and in the presence of three Luftwaffe officers, the V-7 has been tested over the*

Baltic Sea. The features and characteristics of this ship were superior to its predecessors: the V-7 was a supersonic helicopter equipped with 12 BMW auxiliary engines, which in its first test flight reached an altitude of 23,800m and which in its second elevation reached 24,200m, in addition, in principle, the device could also be raised by non-conventional energy sources.

During the winter of 1942, a new circular ship crossed the skies of the Vril test range, the Vril-I, 11m in diameter and with a single crew member, it had the typical dimensions of a fighter-bomber, that was its purpose, its armament: two MK-108 300 caliber cannons and two MG-17 machine guns. At the time that the Vril-I was being developed, attempts were being made to re-establish "supernatural" contacts and plans already existed to build a larger ship, the Vril-VII. At the end of 1942, the SS research department began work on an improved version of the Haunebu, the Haunebu-II, 31m in diameter and 11m high. The Haunebu-II, had to reach a speed of 6,000 km/h within the Earth's atmosphere and was believed to be capable of traveling through outer space. Some versions of the Haunebu-II clearly showed its military vocation, such as the anti-radiation protector. But the SS had an even more daring project, they had designed a giant Haunebu 120m in diameter and according to certain reports there was already a 71m Haunebu-III, built shortly before the end of World War II.

The SS research department had even planned the construction of a gigantic space station that bore a strong resemblance to ancient airships and was named the "Andromeda Maschine" (Andromeda Machine). Its 100 tons of weight did not seem to constitute any difficulty to place the device in orbit. On January 3 and 4, 1944, Hitler and Himmler supposedly met with the Vril Society to address the "Vril Project," which involved launching a gigantic spaceship through the dimensional channel, an unexplored space at speed of light, towards the ends of the

Universe. No wonder Adolf Hitler went so far as to say: " *This war will not be won by anyone.*"

foo fighters

The allies called them Foo-fighters and their German creators "Kugelblitze" ("lightning-balls") or "Feuerbälle" ("balls of fire"). Beginning in 1944, Allied pilots flying over Germany to bomb it began reporting reports of strange, almost transparent glowing balls hovering alongside them and accompanying them for miles. According to these reports, they could not shoot them down, even if they were shot, and any maneuver to mislead them was useless. Much has been speculated about the function of this anti-aircraft weapon, but apparently it interfered with the electrical systems and radars of the allied bombers. Sometimes their presence was so annoying or disruptive to the pilots that a planned bombing raid had to be called off and the bomber squadron returned to base.

On December 13, 1944, the South Wales Argus published a startling article stating: « *The Germans have manufactured a secret weapon to coincide with the Christmas season. The new device, which appears to be an air defense weapon, resembles the crystal balls that adorn Christmas trees. They have been seen suspended in the air over German territory, sometimes alone, and sometimes in a group; They are silver in color and seem transparent.*» Shortly after, on January 2, 1945, it was the New York Herald Tribune that expressed itself in the following terms: « *It seems that the Nazis have projected something new into the night sky of Germany. It is about the mysterious and strange balloons foo-fighters that run on the wings of the Beaufighters that secretly fly over Germany. For more than a month the pilots, on their night flights, have come across these fantastic weapons that, apparently, nobody knows about. The fire balloons appear suddenly, accompany the planes for kilometers and, according to official reports, appear to be radio controlled from the ground.*»

The "foo" are identified with a secret anti-radar weapon: « *In the autumn of 1944, in Oberammenrgau, in Alpine Bavaria, an experimental center sponsored by the Luftwaffe, in OBF, will have completed a series of investigations related to electrical devices capable of to interfere with the operation of the motors, up to a maximum distance of 30m, through the production of intense electromagnetic fields. Defecting the ignition circuit of an airplane engine would inevitably have caused the aircraft to crash. In order to make the invention practically effective, the German technicians intended, however, to triple the radius of action of the weapon at least, but when the conflict ended, experiments in this regard had barely been outlined. Meanwhile, as an underproduct of these investigations for immediate use in warfare, another center, run jointly by the Sperr Ministry and the SS Technical General Staff, had adapted the idea of "proximity radio nuisance" to interference on the much closer delicate and vulnerable electronics from American night fighters. Thus was born an original flying machine, round and armored, more or less similar to the shell of a large turtle. It would move with a special reaction engine, also flattened and circular, which recalled the famous Heronian aeolipile as a physical principle and generated a vast halo of very luminous flames. That is why it had been called "Feuerball". He had no weapons or pilots. Remotely controlled in the act of taking off, it then automatically followed the enemy aircraft, attracted by their exhaust flames and approaching them without colliding, which was enough to put their radar aircraft in critical condition.* »

The Führer's spaceships

• RFZ-1: Prototype reconnaissance flying disc, propelled by antigravity energy.

• RFZ-2: Improved version of the original model, propelled by an SSM-L levitating motor.

• RFZ-3: Operational version of RFZ-2. Also powered by the SSM-L.

- RFZ-4: Version of the RFZ-4 with a conventional piston-driven propeller engine faired in the fuselage in a horizontal position. Basically a saucer shaped helicopter.
- RFZ-5: 26m in diameter and two SSM-L engines, heavy transport version of the "production" model RFZ-3.
- HAUNEBU I (H-1): First flying disk for space flight, powered by three antigravity generators.
- HAUNEBU II (H-2): Version designed for ground attack and high-altitude interception. Technical characteristics similar to those of the H-1.
- HAUNEBU III (H-3): With a diameter of 20m and four generators. Specifically designed to reach destinations outside Earth orbit: The Moon or Mars.

High Jump: Hunt for Hitler

In 1947, the so-called Operation High Jump took place, which was officially the polar expedition of Vice Admiral Richard Evelyn Byrd of the US Navy, sponsored by the Rockefeller Foundation. However, this was also the name given to an apparent military test at the South Pole carried out by the US and the USSR, since they were, to the public, in a strong and heated political division. It is possible that the name of High Jump as a polar expedition then became a cover to hide the real battle that took place in those days: the War of the Penguins, as it was ironically defined by the media.

Between the end of 1946 and the beginning of 1947, the largest expeditionary military force that the US has sent to Antarctica to date begins to deploy from US bases in the Ross Sea (south of New Zealand) to the continent, divided into three converging groups, initiating a far-reaching invasion. Task Force 68, the invasion force, was made up of 13 ships (including icebreakers, destroyers, cargo ships and supply tankers), 2 hydrofoil launchers, a communications ship, a submarine (Sennet) and an aircraft carrier (Phillipine Sea); the embarked troops totaled 4,200.

The operation was led by Admiral Richard Byrd. Officially, Operation High Jump were simple maneuvers that were intended to " *test military equipment and troops in Antarctic conditions* ."

The expedition was planned and equipped for a duration of 6 to 8 months. The military said: " *The mission is essentially military, the participation of foreign observers has been ruled out and it has had the assistance of a limited number of specialized scientists, which highlights its primarily military nature.* " It all had to do with the German plans carried out before the start of World War II. In 1938 and 1939, the German Society for Polar Research supported explorations led by Captain Alfred Ritscher, who was sailing on the ship Schwabenland. The expedition arrived in the region known as Queen Maud Land and aerially photographed more than 600,000 km ^{2} . The circumstances experienced under the NS regime would lead one to assume that beyond their civil and scientific nature, strategic and military considerations had a decisive influence. During the war, squadrons of German submarines had been tirelessly and frantically flying back and forth from Antarctica. The Germans were building huge underground complexes in the Antarctic lands, sparing no resources or scientists. It is claimed that this is where almost all the NS leaders who "disappeared" fled, starting with Adolf Hitler, who left several of his "doubles" and scenes in Berlin to make believe that he had committed suicide. That would be the final destination of many Nazis after passing through South America —although quite a few stayed there.

From South America, reports were collected saying that German ships and submarines arrived in various groups on a few occasions in places such as Brazil or Argentina. According to the Portuguese researcher J. Garrido, a week before the German surrender in 1945, the commander of the German submarine fleet, Admiral Doenitz, stated that he would never surrender to the Allies. For this reason, Richard Byrd was sent to participate in

Operation High Jump as the officer in charge of it, while the command of Task Force 68 falls to active Admiral Richard H. Cruzen to win a war that had not ended. During this operation, Byrd had flown, at least once, over the entire territory of Neuschwabenland, from the southwest direction to the Ritscher Highlands (Ritscher Hochland) and the areas east of the South Pole. Without knowing why, Byrd returned to the United States in February 1947 and declared in an interview with a reporter that it was "*necessary for the United States to take defensive actions against enemy combat aircraft coming from the polar regions*" and that in the event of a new war "*the United States would be attacked by planes that can fly from one pole to the other with incredible speed.*"

Other strange statements made in the United States by Byrd and other soldiers at press conferences spoke of sightings and encounters with high-capacity aircraft not comparable to the most advanced jet aircraft of the time. Admiral Byrd had to face a secret and meticulous interrogation by the American authorities. After that, the United States withdrew from Antarctica for almost a decade. But even after Operation High Jump ended, strange things continued to happen: James Forestal, Secretary of Defense during the operation, was admitted to a hospital in 1948, where under strange circumstances he fell from the tenth floor, when days before he had been strongly interested in declaring the information about the UFO phenomenon. It was officially a suicide. Years later, military officer Milton William Cooper affirmed that Forestal had been assassinated by CIA agents. Immediately after this operation, on February 19, 1947, Byrd himself once again flew over the North Pole, by order of his country, reaching "*new unknown lands.*" His cryptic and unique testimony about this new mission, which is reproduced in fragments by the press, is initially ignored, although it will continue to feed a kind of legend about enigmas existing in polar latitudes, which added to the relative inaccessibility of them by non-military or scientific sources, will make them endure. It should be borne in mind that a book was written about a Byrd diary that was promptly withdrawn from the market by the US secret service. What did they fear would be revealed?

It is very strange the fact that in Operation High Jump Soviet forces participated, for example, some ships. Soviets and Americans collaborating together at the beginning of the Cold War? Did the new enemies reconcile for a short period to finish off the common enemy, the German Reich? The main group, magnetic and photographic aerial reconnaissance, operates from a continental runway built to launch DC3 type aircraft adapted for long-range aerial photographic survey flights. 70,000 aerial photographs were taken in two weeks, demonstrating the extensive air resources employed in the operation. What were the Americans looking for?

Were atomic bombs taken on this expedition, as some sources indicate? Some authors suggest that atomic bombs were detonated in Neuschwabenland. These atomic explosions would be the cause of the current hole in the ozone layer in Antarctica. Either way, the German bases at the South Pole would not be on the surface, but would be underground. Did the Germans in the Reich count on the possibility of an atomic attack? Definitely. Let us bear in mind that the Americans had no qualms about dropping two atomic bombs against the Japanese civilian centers of Hiroshima and Nagasaki, in which hundreds of thousands of innocent people were charred to death and many others left with serious consequences for life. Could they then have prejudices when it comes to launching atomic bombs against a continent only inhabited by Nazis and penguins? For this reason the operation was nicknamed "The War of the Penguins."

According to certain sources, it was certain that at least in 1956 or 1958 - around the actual date of Adolf Hitler's death -, the year in which a new American "expedition" to Antarctica took place, nuclear weapons were brought and three times: August 27 and 30 and September 9. None of the three atomic missiles exploded on the Antarctic soil, but, without explanation, they exploded in mid-flight over the sea as they headed for their target. Although Operation High Jump was estimated to last 6 to 8 months, the invading forces had to withdraw after 6 weeks, after numerous undetermined losses in materiel and men. Other sources indicated that the withdrawal began after 3 weeks, after decisive fighting between attackers and defenders of Neuschwabenland.

It is not officially known what the actual casualties of the invaders were, but it is known, for example, that the Sennet submarine, officially due to the Antarctic ice, suffered serious dents in its hull, having to be withdrawn during the operation to a port in New Zealand to be repaired. It is also known that several combat planes and high-tech aerial equipment were lost and that there were human losses, specifically deaths of US Marines. All this in a training operation? In the United States it was very difficult to justify to public opinion the casualties that occurred in Antarctica, but the case was officially closed. The military dubbed this operation "the war of the penguins" after the federal government repeatedly declared to the suspicious American public that only penguins lived in Antarctica and that the casualties of military personnel were due to unfortunate people. accidents. Also officially, the expedition was a "great success" because it *made it possible to discover many new aspects of the use of military equipment under extreme conditions."* So why did Byrd return to the United States in February 1947, months ahead of schedule?

So what happened to Richard E. Byrd? The expedition to which he was sent after the War of the Penguins, was the one that collects his diary. In this he claims to have been received by blond, light-eyed human beings who live beyond the polar regions, those kingdoms below the surface of the Earth, in which they have lived for millennia. On January 8, 1956, several researchers from a Chilean scientific expedition in Antarctica observed, for several hours, UFOs in the form of "cigar" and disc evolving in the sky of the Weddell Sea area. In that same year of 1956, a new military operation was attempted by the Americans, Operation Deepfreeze, and the results were worse than those of the previous one. Then, on August 27 and September 9 of that same year, the South African government declared that it had detected two high-energy electromagnetic emissions, comparable to nuclear explosions, in the Antarctic area near its coasts, which corresponds to the Neuschwabenland area, a manifestation of an underground character and another on the surface. Other known sightings of UFOs in Antarctica were declared in the following years, especially those of 1964 and 1969, by personnel from both Argentine and Chilean military bases.

Whenever the Americans have attempted to invade Neuschwabenland, mysterious forces have repelled them. Everything indicates that the Germans of the Reich already have a wide network of bases, spread throughout the world and certain non-human forces that helped them develop a technology that was not of this world, as described by the information revealed by the services. Russian secrets - even English and American - and contact groups, where it is ensured that specifically the Germans were helped by extraterrestrial beings. It is emphasized that these forces came from Orion (Source: ERKS. At the address: http://www.unglaublichkeiten.com/unglaublichkeiten/htmlphp/basenx.html. You can find a map with the main more or less known bases).

The relationship between Byrd and the UFO issue is also remarkable. In his famous diary, he wrote that after High Jump he made a polar reconnaissance flight where his plane was remote-controlled by intraterrestrial entities that kindly welcomed him and stressed the importance of warning his government about the use of nuclear weapons and the damage to the biosphere.

Germany and Orion

Sources claim that the Nazis, through their sectarian ties, were receiving help from Orion entities. As I have already mentioned, the German military elite and many politicians, during World War 1 and 2, were involved in the Vril and Thule secret societies. The Germans were famous for their ties to the occult, both among royalty and the power elite. We see that Germany was a hotbed of occult groups and fertile ground for the birth of secret societies, such as the Illuminati, or religious debacles.

But the close link between hermetic groups and the Orion Constellation is very old. Orion plays a very important role in our history and in the history of our galaxy. In fact, already in antiquity the representation of Orion was very important: in the Hellenic culture, Orion was an avid hunter who, trying to rape the goddess Athena, was punished; for the Egyptians it must have been very relevant since the three main pyramids are aligned to Orion; even in the Bible it is highlighted that the Pleiades and Orion were the work of Iehovah (Job 9:9, 38:31 and Amos 5:8).

Contact groups generally agree that the Orionites are human beings like us, with fair skin, light eyes, and blond hair. At least that's its generic description. The Orionites would have been the emblematic example of the galaxy from which life was brought to our planet. It is said that in Orion there were legendary and arduous battles, very similar to George Lucas's novels in the Star Wars saga, where several rebellions originated. Furthermore, many UFO researchers and contact groups say that the Biblical Lucifer Rebellion was in fact an uprising in Orion that later brought serious consequences to our world.

It is argued in the same way that the Orionites would have had a strong influence on the Sirians (Sirian civilizations) and would have consolidated a "real" alliance creating a new lineage, called "Nibiru". Some theories assume that these are the ancestors of "those who came down from heaven" or Anunnaki. Not all the hypotheses are plausible or related to each other, but what links them is the fact that they agree that the Orionites have had a strong negative influence on our world, mostly under the Third Reich. However, this issue was not only permeated in the Old World, since in pre-Columbian America the representations of Orion are very frequent, so they seem to have also had an important implication on this continent.

A remarkable similarity is the indisputable symbol of the pyramid, which in many cases is projected with an eye at the top. The pyramid represents the Celestial Organization Chart, that is, the political, monarchical and military hierarchy of the kingdom of heaven, that is, of outer space or universe. Likewise, the eye represents the one who "sees everything", or in Greek "Thea" or "Theos", which also means "god", and goes into Latin as "deus", and then into Spanish: "God". For that reason, the main Illuminati and Freemason symbol is a pyramid with the eye at the top, but whose top is separated or cut, which means that the main objective of the Masons is to "remove God" or "prevent the top of the pyramid reigns", or in other words, that Jesus Christ take his place as King. For this reason Jesus could have said of himself: « ... *Have you never read in the Scriptures: The stone that the builders rejected has become the head of the corner. The Lord has done this, and is it a wonderful thing in our eyes?* » (Matthew 21:42) Builder, or its similarity "mason", is said in English "mason". However, due to the intricacies of this topic, we have left the details for the book "Recognizing the Time of the End".

South America and Orion

A huge stone world map was found in 1984 in Ecuador while extracting gold from underground tunnels. This stone was discovered along with 350 other artifacts that do not fit any existing or known pre-Columbian culture. On this map there is a natural line of quartz that has an eye drawn at the height of what would be the Sinai desert, something very significant in the divine symbolism palpated in the Hebrew scriptures: « *The chariots of the gods are tens of thousands of thousands; the Lord comes to Sinai in the sacred [vehicle].*» (Psalms 68:17. Hebrew version). Likewise, in said stone there is expressed a continent in the Pacific (Lemuria), that is, this world map must be more than 10,000 or 12,000 years old, since Mu (Lemuria) and Poseidonis (Atlantis) disappeared in the Last Ice Age, approximately. On the other side of the map you can also see the Atlantean continent. This similarly shows a circle in the Bay of Guayaquil, in Bolivia (the place where the artifacts were found).

In the same place they found the famous "Pyramid of the Eye" mentioned by Klaus Dona, which if placed under bright light or "black light", the eye glows strongly. Let us remember that a large jade cup with twelve smaller jade cups next to it was also discovered in that place, and in the large cup you can see a perfect inlay of the Orion constellation, and other stars. Another pyramid-shaped stone was also found with the eye at the top of the pyramid, and at the bottom of the stone you can see the stellar constellation Orion, highlighting the three main stars of Orion's belt. All this is very similar to the positions of the three Egyptian pyramids, which are oriented to Orion, Sirius, and Tuban (Alpha type star, of the Constellation of the Dragon).

The geniuses of martial arts

The Sumerians, Atlanteans, Mayans, Egyptians, Hebrews, Germans, Russians, and North Americans were not the only ones to receive continued advice, influence, or control from extraterrestrial entities, as were the Orientals. Among other curiosities of our history, let us remember that Japan was founded around 660 BC by Emperor Jinmu but was strongly influenced by Buddhism and the Chinese empire. Still, the Japanese have their own ways of looking at life and their own religions such as Buddhism, Shinto, Confucianism, and Taoism. Its ancestral culture of martial arts has its origin in beings from space and this is how close to Kyoto is, as the tourist guides announce, the abode of gods and demons, Mount Kurama, from where they say superheroes have emerged.

Mount Kurama is a wild area with dense and shady forests where, according to mythology, it was at the top where the destination was chosen for the Tengu to descend from the stars. But who are the Tengu? Some sources believe that the Tengu are descendants of Susano Wo no Mikoto, the storm god brother of Amaterasu, the Sun Goddess. Founders of schools of saber and Jujutsu claim the divine origin of their Ryu martial techniques, as already stated. became clear in the case of the Tenshin Shoden Katori Shinto Ryu school. But according to different accounts, the Tengu were also the provocative element to capture these techniques. These beings are classified in the pantheon of minor divinities, but they are still quite respected and feared.

We have the O Tengu and Karasu Tengu as supernatural creatures, clad in feathers and cloaks, and whose human appearance differs in their red skin, white hair, and prominent nose. The Tengu should not be confused with the Shura, which according to ancient culture are reincarnations of warriors killed in combat, spirits introduced into Japanese mythological legends by Buddhism. It is said that the Shura live in heaven, where they meet to fight each other, divided into antagonistic groups. They have the appearance of warriors, under a spectral appearance. They utter screams like thunder and are responsible for darkening the sun and moon. They symbolize the spirit of hatred and revenge. The Tengu are in charge of divine messages and legends tell that their demonic appearance can only be observed by evil people. The Tengu are the best intermediaries between the immortal gods and people. In relation to the Bushi, there is a reference that each warrior had a Tengu assigned, with the role of being his secret advisor, offering intuition more than reasoning. The Tengu symbolizes an inner illumination, something powerfully associated with the ideas of archetypal beings of which Plato and Socrates philosophized.

As we can see, Asian culture is rich in stories of all kinds, whether from Tibet, Vietnam, Cambodia, China, Korea, India or any other place in Indonesia and Oceania, but everything always focuses on the appearance of gods from the stars. In some anecdotes we have the testimony of some who say that Asians are a genetic cross between the "homo" race and aliens, which would explain their morphology: straight hair, slanted eyes and medium height. This "genetic" intervention that the gods would have made is seen in many other parts of the world where, for "x" or "y" reasons, the gods crossed man with their own race. This is how a scientific theory prevails among a certain group of scientists who believes that the Chinese and other peoples of the area are descendants of a mixture between extraterrestrials that in one way or another interbred with other humanoids that already lived on Earth. It is necessary to know that the Chinese themselves believe that they were created by divine beings from the stars.

return of the gremlins

Not all have been pleasant visits, in many cases the relationships with non-human beings have been bad or simply disconcerting. In 1979 a Peruvian soldier was attacked by a "thing" that carried him and carried him several meters, finally dropping him, bruised and bleeding, onto some nettle bushes that ended up damaging him. The battered man swore by all the saints that he had encountered the "devil" himself. On another previous occasion, in 1954 the Republic of Venezuela suffered a wave of appearances of extremely aggressive hairy "things" despite their short size. On November 28 of that year, one of the most significant meetings of this type took place on the outskirts of the city of Caracas, when Gustavo González was driving a truck through the outskirts of the city, then he and his companion saw a strange object circular, metallic in appearance, perched on the ground. Gustavo González stopped the vehicle and both men got out. Very close to the object was a "being" with an apelike appearance, then Gustavo González's assistant; José Ponce ran towards the supposed "anthropoid" and taking it by the waist lifted it up - the "being" weighed just over 16kg. He tried to take it with him, but the strange hairy humanoid knocked Ponce off his feet and immediately attacked him with long claws that he hadn't noticed before. José Ponce defended himself with his knife, but this was useless as the strange "being" seemed to be made of metal. At that moment Gustavo González intervened and the matter ended with two injured truckers arriving at the nearest police station to complain about the attack by the strange "being" who was apparently a master in the art of self defense. This would be yet another urban tale, if it weren't for the fact that the skeleton of a very small humanoid with a highly disproportionate head was found in Venezuela not many years ago.

the alien indians

In addition to the fact that even today aliens may continue to live under the Earth or in Nepal -like the dropa-, or even have their blood run in our veins, there are other little-known cultures that may not be indigenous to this world or may have been some result of a genetic machination by foreign beings.

There is a remote tribe in Ecuador, the Waorani, who, far from the size of their ancestors, have a normal size. A tribe with 6 fingers and toes, a tribe with 2 rows of teeth, a bloodthirsty and ferocious tribe. The Waorani were discovered in 1940 by an expeditionary group searching for oil, who were assassinated as soon as they made contact. 12 Shell employees died at the hands of this ferocious tribe. It took a decade to be able to establish contact with them again. The next contact also ended in a massacre at the hands of the bloody Waorani. After many deaths, it was possible to establish a peaceful contact and some chilling data was discovered. The Waorani maintain the highest homicide rate in the history of humanity, above 50%. They kill their elders when they can't stand them anymore or kill any unwanted newborn or have malformations, even burying them alive. On the other hand, this bloodthirsty tribe has superior genetics, being the healthiest human beings in the world. « *Medically the Waorani have become an enigma, there are no traces of cancer, heart disease, increased blood pressure, allergies, or any of the diseases known to date. They also have hands and feet with 6 fingers and 2 rows of teeth. Descendants of a race of giants that in ancient times mixed with the natives, also bequeathing them unparalleled ferocity and violence.*»

6.

CRASHED SHIPS AND MODERN VISIONS

"Walker there is no path, the path is made by walking."
Antonio Machado (Spanish poet. 1875-1939)

THE ROSWELL ACCIDENT

On June 24, 1947, the flight captain, Kenneth Arnold, was flying in his small airplane over the Rocky Mountains in the state of Washington (USA), when he saw nine giant boomerangs flying in formation between distant peaks and some 1,900 km/ h (almost twice the speed of sound). From that moment on, one of the most fabulous sociological phenomena of all time was born: Ufology.

A few weeks later, an aircraft crashed in Roswell, New Mexico, and the United States Air Force immediately classified the event as TOP-SECRET. It was officially the first X-Files in history, although unofficially we have seen that there had already been many more, even in that same decade. Friday, July 4, 1947, was a day that had passed through the water. At the end of that festive day in the United States, a terrible electrical storm shook Lincoln County, New Mexico. There, most farmers were on alert for the possibility that the storm, which never broke out, would reach their cattle. One of them, the foreman of the Foster ranch, William

MacBrazel, was destined, without knowing it, to be the man who starred in one of the most spectacular discoveries in the history of Ufology. In the midst of that impressive storm, MazBrazel heard something out of the ordinary: a very violent metallic thunder that led him to think that a plane had crashed somewhere on his land. With the first rays of the sun, MacBrazel, accompanied by a neighbor, searched the surroundings of the ranch. A short distance away, they discovered a wide expanse of land completely covered with thin metal plates and some kind of small beams. The covered area was 1km long by about 100m wide.

On Sunday, July 6, the rancher headed in his van to Roswell, the most important city near the ranch, and asked the sheriff to send someone to remove those remains that made it difficult for his sheep to pass through. George Wilcox, sheriff of Roswell at the time, in his office examined in astonishment one of the pieces of metal that MacBrazel brought him. It was a very thin silver plate, but extraordinarily resistant, and a kind of beam-like rulers and covered by pink hieroglyphics, engraved on one side. The sheriff decided to alert Major Jesse A. Marcel of the Air Intelligence Service at the nearby Roswell military base to take up the case. The military's response was not long in coming. Minutes after the Sheriff's call, Major Marcel appeared in his office and, after chatting with the rancher, launched an expedition to recover those remains. Late in the afternoon, an official Army truck, a cargo-carrying jeep, and MacBrazel's old van set off for the Foster Ranch. Your goal: pick up the scattered debris and determine what kind of artifact might have fallen there. Servicemen from the Roswell base first examined the MarcBrazel field on Monday, July 7.

Just seeing the remains, Major Jesse Marcel determined that those sheets did not correspond to anything that hit the ground or exploded on it. And he added: *"It was something that exploded in the air, traveling at high speed."* In any case, according to the military, the main body of the ship was missing. After collecting the material and meticulously combing the land, the older Marcel had enough time to stop at his home and show the remains of the object to his son Jesse and his wife. Jesse Jr., who is today a leading doctor in Montana, as well as a helicopter pilot, remembers that on that occasion he was very surprised not to see electronic devices such as resistors, connectors, cables or tubes among the remains. There was nothing to guess what kind of device this belonged to.

Increasingly interested, the Roswell military went to great lengths to track down the location where the main object had impacted. One of the intelligence officers from the Roswell base visited Dr. Lincoln La Paz, a prestigious expert in meteorite research and professor at the University of New Mexico in Albuquerque. The military provided the doctor with all available data on the case, apparently including details of the wreckage collected by Major Marcel, in the hope that he would determine other collision points for the object and determine its approximate path. Even today the results of his search are officially unknown. Despite their attempts to control the situation, the military could not keep the case secret. A Roswell firefighter, part of a team notified by the military to help search a desert area near the city, came across the remains of what appeared to be a discoidal ship, embedded against the side of a ravine. Also a team of archaeologists led by a professor from Texas Tech University and two young hikers camped in the place were able to see the fragments of that plane without wings. But there was more than iron there, there were the bodies of several of its crew: some strange beings with a weak complexion, a large bald head and black eyes without pupils. (Source: Javiera Sierra of Secret Files)

Several witnesses in the Roswell case confessed, years after being forced by the military to silence the facts, that one of the

UFO crew members arrived at the base alive. What Roswell firefighter Dan Dywer saw on the morning of July 7, 1947 is not something that can be easily forgotten. Among the twisted irons of that strangely designed aircraft, were the bodies of three unusual beings. Two of them lay inert; the other was clearly alive. He was a small being, about the height of a ten-year-old child, he would explain to his relatives when he returned home, after being evicted by the military when they arrived at the scene of the events. But Dywer could see that the humanoid was loaded into a military van, which transported it to the Roswell base. There, according to another witness, the strange creature entered the hospital under its own power.

Minutes after that scene took place, Glenn Dennis, an employee of Ballard Funeral Homes of Roswell, arrived at the Roswell Military Hospital. Dennis was also an ambulance driver, he had taken a wounded military man to the hospital. He was very surprised by the frenetic activity that took place that day in the corridors of the base and, in the midst of the confusion, he went deeper into its rooms until he met a sick friend of his, who urged him to get away from that sector of the hospital, as an elite medical team was secretly working *"over the bruised bodies of three non-human beings."* What Dennis found out from his conversation with that nurse has confirmed details provided by other witnesses: The beings had four long, fragile fingers on each hand, had a larger cranial capacity than humans, had eyes set deep in their faces, and lacked protuberances on their heads. the places where nose and ears should be. The most disconcerting thing for Dennis was that one of those three subjects was alive, and that the military had not commented on that finding.

This account by Dennis is one of the most complex of the Roswell plot. Even today, he himself remembers that hours before going to the base to take the wounded soldier, he received a call at the offices of his funeral home. A voice identifying himself as a Roswell base officer inquired about the smaller coffin models he had, interested in ordering several airtight pieces with some urgency. What caught Dennis' attention the most was that the base ordered children's coffins... when no children lived in the military installations! In 1988, the unknown American researcher Jerome Clark -editor of the prestigious International UFO Reporter magazine- echoed some rumors circulating in military intelligence circles, which claimed that the Roswell survivor was given the code name of EBE, which means, according to Clark, Extraterrestrial Biological Entity. Number 1 is believed to have lived well into the year 1952.

In January 1990, the NBC television network replaced one of the episodes of the series, "Unsolved Mysteries", dedicated to reconstructing the Roswell incident. Watching it, to the memory of 48-year-old Gerald Anderson, brought up a forgotten memory of a summer morning in 1947, while vacationing in Albuquerque, New Mexico. That morning, as he later told the investigators, he was traveling by car with other soldiers on a country road, near a place called the Llanos de San Agustín. Halfway, they stopped by a stream. «*We were about 50m or 100m from where it happened. Suddenly, we saw a silver, circular object lying on the ground at an angle to the ground. There were also the members of his crew on the ground, under the object. One of them was standing up and the others were lying on the ground, not moving at all.*» The crew members wore very tight metallic overalls, had a large head with no hair, huge dark eyes, and very thin 4-fingered hands. Finally, an army convoy drove them out and cordoned off that area. Anderson's testimony is one of the most revealing clues added to the "Roswell File" in recent years. Years later, military footage of the autopsy of these non-human bodies leaked and was seen around the world, although speculation continues about its authenticity. The only military alternative to avoid ridicule was to bribe, pressure and resort to other "methods" to pass off the tape as a fraud, although it is believed today that what was projected was a recreation as faithful as possible of an original tape that by its age and poor state of conservation deteriorated.

On the same day of the famous accident, two other ships crashed in the area, one in Magdalena - New Mexico, where they found 4 dead EBEs; and the other was in San Agustin, also in New Mexico, where 4 dead EBEs were also apparently found. Some theories say that they were space travelers who, upon reaching our time, suffered an "entry" accident. Another theory says that they were ETs that had a misentry or failure to enter the atmosphere, while others suggest that positive ETs and negative ETs are waging a millennia-old war, and they would have been struck down in that contest.

On August 1, 1947, a United States Air Force B-25 crashed while flying from a base in Tacoma, Washington, to another in Novato, California. In the accident, Captain William Davidson and Lieutenant Frank Brown, two military intelligence officers who had investigated the Maury Island case near Tacoma, an alleged UFO crash, died. Some newspapers reported in the days that followed that the plane was carrying fragments of an alien spacecraft in its hold and that it had been shot down by saboteurs.

That same year of 1947, specifically in October, a ship crashed in Paradise Valley (Ariz) in the US, and 2 dead EBEs were found; also in this year another ship crashed in Great Falls (Montana) and found 3 dead EBEs. The following year, in 1948 another ship crashed in Globe (Arizona), and in Aztec (New Mexico) there were two falls of VEDs, one on February 13 with 12 bodies found and another on March 25 with 17 deaths. This was undoubtedly the most terrible and surprising of all, since a large number of human remains were found inside the ship. Panic and consequent demoralization gripped scientists, so documents initially classified as "secret" immediately became "strictly and highly confidential." " *An even thicker veil of silence was thrown over them than that of the MANHATTAN project,"* said military man Bill Cooper. « *The alarm went off in the government and a general panic was created among the leaders of the USA before a threat of extraterrestrial invasion where we were inferior in technology.*»

At this point, the time travel theories were ridiculous, for what government would send their pilots one crash after another to their certain death, and the re-entry accident theory would say that they are fools not knowing entering a planet or that strangely our atmosphere has some problem for its vehicles, however, this is debatable. So the "space war" theory is much more convincing, as they could be being shot down by opposing factions. And it must be noted that between January 1947 and December 1952, no less than 16 spacecraft crashed or had to make an emergency landing. Then 65 dead aliens were found and one survivor who was immediately hidden. Another spacecraft exploded, of which practically nothing was left. Among them, one on January 30, 1949, also in Roswell (N. Mexico) with an EBE that was found alive, and another on December 6, 1950 in Indio Guerrero (Texas). A question that does not stop rumbling why do they always fall in the US? Perhaps they fell in other places but the means to study them or control the airspace like in the USA did not exist in other countries.

The alien that survived on that occasion was found far from the wreckage of the Roswell crash. He was named EBE. This name was proposed by Dr. Vannevar Bush and was an acronym for "Extraterrestrial Biological Entity" (Extraterrestrial Biological Entity). «*EBE showed a propensity for lying, and if asked about something he did not want to answer, he would simply remain silent. However, during his second year in captivity, he began to collaborate and the information he provided was surprising. The compilation of his revelations forms the basis of what was later called the "Yellow Book." Bill English and myself, during our activity in the GRUDJE 13 group, have been able to see photographs of EBE, as other people did later too.»* (Bill Cooper)

In late 1951, EBE fell ill. The medical staff was unable to determine the cause of his illness. There was no experience on which to draw. EBE's bodily functions were based on chlorophyll and it transformed food into energy in a similar way to plants. The depositions were also similar to those of plants. Consequently, it was decided to call a botanist, Dr. Guillermo Mendoza, a specialist in botany, who was in charge of looking after his health. Dr. Mendoza made an effort to save EBE's life, although he died in the middle of 1952. In this way, Dr. Mendoza became a specialist in the biology of extraterrestrials.

more important cases

Simultaneously, while the unsuccessful attempt to save EBE's life was being carried out, and in order to take advantage of this situation to curry favor with a race so superior to ours, the United States began in early 1952 to send the cosmos calls for help. Calls were not answered, although the project was maintained as a sign of goodwill. In this year of 1952, among other accidents, one in May in Spilzbergen (Norway) with 2 dead EBEs; another in Germany (North Sea); another on August 14, 1952 in Ely (Nevada) with about 16 deaths, and another on September 10 in Alburquerque (N. Mexico), resulting in 3 dead EBEs. In this case, the data is not concise if it was in 1952 or in 1950.

UFO sightings were so numerous that the means available to seriously examine and evaluate them proved insufficient. For example, in Baurú, in the Brazilian state of São Paulo, on July 23, 1947, less than a month after Kenneth Arnold's aerial encounter near Mount Rainer, a surveyor named José Higgins and several of his companions saw a large disk metallic that approached and landed on the ground. While the others fled in terror, Higgins remained motionless, suddenly finding himself in front of three beings over 2m tall wearing transparent overalls and carrying metal boxes on their backs. One of the creatures pointed a tube at him and moved towards him as if to grab him, but Higgins was able to dodge it and saw that it was reluctant to follow him as far as the sun was shining.

All three beings had bulky bald heads, large round eyes, no eyebrows, and long legs. They jumped and leaped, picking up large stones and hurling them far away. They also made holes in the ground, perhaps trying to indicate something like the positions of the planets around the Sun, and marking in a special way the seventh from the center: did they refer to Uranus? Or according to the Sumerian order, would they point to Mars? Then the creatures reentered the ship, which took off with a whoosh. Higgins' account appeared in two Brazilian newspapers.

Three weeks later, and very far away, there was another extraordinary observation. On August 14, 1947, Professor Johannis was walking on the mountain near Villa Santina, Carni, in the Italian province of Friuli, when he suddenly saw a red metal saucer in a rocky cleft. The professor came out from among the trees to get a better look at him, and then he noticed that two beings that looked like dwarfs were following him walking slowly, with their hands fully glued to their sides and their heads motionless. As the strange creatures approached Johannis, his strength failed him; he seemed paralyzed. The little beings, less than a meter tall, wore transparent blue jumpsuits, with a red belt and collar. The witness, who did not see any hair on the heads of the creatures, described the skin color of their faces as earthy green. He also made out straight noses, slash-like mouths that opened and closed like those of fish, and large, round, bulging eyes. Johannis stated that, on a sudden impulse, he yelled at them, waving his mountaineering pick. Then one of the dwarves reached for his belt, from the center of which it blew out like a puff of smoke, and the pick flew from Johannis's hand, and he fell backward. Then one of the beings picked up the beak and went with his companion towards the saucer, which immediately took off and, after hovering for a moment above the terrified professor, suddenly seemed to shrink and vanished.

The case of Thomas A. Mantell

In 1948, the strange death of the war veteran, Captain Thomas A. Mantell, occurred when he absurdly died while chasing an Unidentified Flying Object of gigantic proportions on the afternoon of January 7, when many people observed a huge round object and very bright over Madisonville, Kentucky. Several F51 Mustangs tried to chase the object without success, so they gave up the chase, but Mantell continued to climb, when he communicated: "...ca *n't reach it, I'll have to give up the chase soon...* " It is believed that this was the last thing the pilot was able to say to the control tower, although others say that he managed to shoot the object but not without first notifying the base. That same day, around sunset, the lifeless body of the veteran pilot appeared near the wreckage of his wrecked Mustang F51 fighter, some 145km from the airfield. Witnesses said the plane suddenly seemed to explode in midair. The ATIC, was the one that only offered explanations, although somewhat confusing and of course nobody believed, because they sounded false: «... *Captain Thomas A. Mantell, died while chasing the planet Venus...*»

Some objective analysts affirm that Captain Thomas A. Mantell actually saw what he described, possibly his device entered the magnetic field of the colossal alien spacecraft, by getting too close to it. Others say that Mantell warned the base that he would fire at the object and when he did, and the object when attacked, fired a metal beam at Mantell's P-51 Mustang, knocking it down on the spot, which would be documented based on eyewitnesses.

incidents of the 50s

After these incidents, in August 1949 a 3km platform flew over Cinnati-Ohio (USA), for several days. The following year, on May 11, 1950, a UFO passed over Mc Minnville, Oregon (USA). That year, several circular unidentified flying objects were also recorded overflying Montana (USA). On August 19, in California's Death Valley, two mineral prospectors observed what appeared to be a saucer crash landing. As they approached, they saw two small beings coming out of the device and they ran after them until they were lost among the dunes. When the men returned to the landing site, the saucer was gone.

On March 18, 1950, Argentine rancher Wilfredo Arévalo saw an aluminum saucer land on the ground, while another hovered a short distance away. The object that landed was surrounded by a blue-green vapor, and in its center was a transparent cabin in which Arévalo made out four tall, well-built men, dressed in clothes that seemed to be made of cellophane. When the crew realized they were being watched, they focused a beam of light on the estanciero, and then the saucer turned a brighter blue, flames sprang from its base, and it rose from the ground. The two objects quickly disappeared in the direction of the border with Chile. Although these reports promised to be interesting material for future research, they did not seem to indicate a serious threat of alien invasion. Perhaps the resistance of the official media to take them into consideration was simply due to fear of ridicule. To name these beings, the researchers adopted the word humanoids.

Similarly, in 1950, astronomer Seymons Hess saw UFOs in May of that year. Also in the north of the African continent there were countless witnesses of many sightings. The following year, two cigar ships were seen in the Bay of Inchó and when they left the sea they raised a column of water about 30m high. During several nights in August and September 1951, waves of UFOs were seen and photographed over the sky over Texas (USA). From the summer of 1951 to the summer of 1952 there was a spate of sightings in the California desert area. On August 25, 1951, a group of five professors and one post-graduate saw a formation of brilliant lights flying rapidly across the sky. The teachers estimated his speed at about 2,900km at an altitude of about 1,500m. Skeptics claimed that the lights were nothing more than reflections from the bellies of a flock of ducks; The curious thing is that they flew at more than 2 times the speed of sound and that some teachers, given their profession, did not realize this obviousness.

Year 1952: On May 7, a UFO is photographed near Rio de Janeiro (Brazil); that year a UFO is also seen over the uranium mines of the Belgian Congo. At dawn from July 19 to 20, the so-called "Invasion of Washington" takes place, several UFOs are detected by radar, photographed and seen by several people, flying over the American sky and blatantly hovering over the White House and the Capitol. In the same way, UFOs in formation intercept an American fighter plane. The story of July 19 and 20 repeated itself on the 26th of the same month, when formations of several UFOs were detected by radar, as well as commercial pilots observing the flying discs, where military planes chased the UFOs to no avail and where thousands of witnesses from the ground were observers of the event. In the year 1952, thousands of cases of UFO sightings were reported around the world, such as a surprising case in South Korea.

On July 29 of that year, an unidentified flying object flew over New Jersey (USA). On October 17, in the town of Oloron-Ste-Marie, French Basque Country, a cylindrical device was seen, camouflaged in a kind of "cloud", it was accompanied by about 30 smaller objects that looked like balloons; In the US alone, more than 3,000 cases of sightings were classified that year. The most interesting thing happened at the end of 1952, when a 1 km long cigar-shaped mother ship landed in the sky over Krasnovodsk on the shores of the Caspian Sea, in southern Russia. At the same time, in the last days of December 1952, many sightings occurred over Marysville (USA). It should be noted that astronomer H. Percy Wilkins also observed several of the UFOs of that year.

Year 1954: On January 9, several unidentified objects fly over Sweden. There is also a wave of sightings in Europe, in general, especially over France, Italy and Germany. Consecutively there are several cases of UFOs over Brazil, where they flew over cars along the desolate highways, approached several planes and interfered with the transmission of electric power. The following year, on May 4, 1955, the French Forcalquier astronomical observatory photographed unidentified flying objects that were at high altitudes; UFOs are also sighted in formation flying over Budapest.

In May 1956, radar units from the Hungarian Air Defense Command base captured unknown flying objects, which again flew over Budapest in formation; on December 8, unidentified aerial phenomena occur that coincided with the launch of the Viking I of the Vanguard program. A year later, a UFO wave was recorded over New Jersey (USA). On January 16, 1958, a spectacular photograph of a UFO was taken over Trinidad Island. That year there is also a UFO wave over Japan.

The George Adamski case

But in 1953 something happened that shocked the most rigorous researchers. During that year a certain George Adamski made his appearance in the world of UFOs with a book co-authored by Desmond Leslie: "Flying Saucers have Landed". In this controversial work, Adamski claimed that he had spoken to a human being from Venus, that he came in a flying saucer, and that he had taken photos of the spacecraft. The book, which quickly became a best-seller, was of great use to researchers although they never admitted it, as it got thousands of casual readers interested in ufology. George Adamski (1891-1965) was an amateur astronomer who operated his Newtonian reflecting telescopes from his home in Palomar Gardens, California. He was obsessively interested in reports of flying saucers, and claimed to have seen and photographed them telescopically on several occasions, such as on March 5, 1951, when he managed to film a gigantic cigar-shaped object surrounded by scout ships, and on May 1, 1951. from 1952, when he took a photo of another gigantic cigar-shaped mother ship. Later, on November 20, 1952, Adamski headed with a small group of friends to a location near Parker Highway, Arizona, to search for and photograph UFOs. After setting up a portable telescope with a 15cm diameter objective in a convenient location, Adamski settled down to await events, while his companions withdrew to observe from a distance. It didn't take long for him to be rewarded with the sight of an object landing among the hills in front of him; he photographed it from afar.

Then a person appeared and approached him. The stranger, who must have been around 1.70m tall, wore clothing resembling a skier's and had shoulder-length blond hair. Adamski claimed that they were able to communicate telepathically about various things, and that the visitor had indicated to him that she came from Venus. Then a scout boat arrived, and the stranger, refusing Adamski's request to be allowed to accompany him, left taking one of his rolls of film with him. On December 13, the Venusian returned to Earth bringing it back, and that was when Adamski was able to take close-up photos of the spacecraft. In his second book, "Inside the Space Ships," Adamski claimed that he had finally taken a trip around the Moon and that a companion pointed out the rivers and lakes on the far side.

Years later, in March 1960, a series of sightings of unidentified flying objects over Finland followed. On September 26, a formation of discoid-shaped objects is seen over Italy. Subsequently, on October 6, 1961, a large and luminous object flew over Lake Maracaibo in Venezuela, at a low altitude, causing panic among the lake's fishermen, many of whom jumped into the water. One of them drowned.

In 1962, many UFOs were seen over Japan, the US, Spain, Italy and Argentina. In February 1964, at the Badalona observatory in Barcelona (Spain), he photographed an unidentified flying object that was flying over the Sahara desert. The following year there were many sightings in Chile. Likewise, an image was taken by Deputy Sheriff Strauch, during a hunting expedition in Gibbon (Minnesota, USA), on October 21, 1965, and illustrates the difficulty of taking correct color photos of UFOs in bad conditions. light conditions. The strange color of the sky suggests that the original object was probably red, another feature that links it to other UFO sightings. UFOs were also observed in Antarctica that year, specifically in the summer of 1965. These were observations reported by the Argentine Navy and corroborated by personnel from the English and Chilean bases on Deception Island. In general, that year there was a strong wave of unidentified objects in Central America.

The New York Blackout

At 5:00 p.m., on November 9, 1965, apparently a protection relay for a 230,000 volt line from Ontario (Canada) tripped, thereby starting one of the most terrifying electrical accidents ever known in the world. Western world. Immediately the means of transport that use electrical energy were totally paralyzed. Communication systems, the press, radio, and television were submerged in the most absolute silence, which caused even more alarm and confusion. A gigantic city plunged into darkness (New

York) and millions of people trapped in the most unlikely situations, elevators, subways, public establishments, that was gigantic chaos. Police stations were inundated with calls for help and people requesting information. In total, 8 states of the Union and 2 of Canada were gradually affected. An area of about 187,000 km^2, which was home to more than 30 million people, was affected by darkness for about 14 hours.

The situation reached extremes of great tension. Many citizens thought that the American nation was the object of aggression by the Soviet Union. The Fort Bliss, Giggs and Holloman air bases were also affected by the lack of electricity, triggering a maximum security alert. A pilot from Syracuse, Mr. Weldon Ross, reported by radio that when attempting to land at the Hancock airport in that town, he suddenly saw an enormous luminous sphere of about 30m in diameter, suspended over the high-voltage power lines, which came from the Niagara Falls. He was able to accurately calculate that this luminous phenomenon was located at the point where the two 345,000 volt power lines intersect near the Cay station. Roberto C. Walsh, delegate of the Directorate of the Federal Aviation Agency, claimed to have seen that same mass of light a few kilometers south of the aforementioned airport. All this coincided with the first moments of the gigantic blackout. Life magazine photographer Arthur Rickerby obtained an impressive graphic document from New York City at the start of the breakdown. To the west, a silver object with strange characteristics appears. It was published by Time magazine on November 19, 1965, and although some believe that it was the planet Venus, the author is totally against such criteria.

When the years passed and military informers began to release information, despite the persecutions and assassinations by the CIA, it was learned that the reason for said blackout had been the capture of an alien by the US government. According to the sources, the US was ordered to return the alien to an area of Canada, where, according to some investigators, it had been the site of a previous UFO crash where the little guy would have been recovered. Apparently the US had refused, so the blackout was only a small test of the capabilities of these aliens. The report concludes that the US government was forced to return it to an area of Canada, and in fact this would not have been the only similar incident that would have occurred with "blackmail" and kidnapping of aliens by the US armed forces.

On October 10 of the same year, in the north of France, in Pournoy-la-Chétive (in the Moselle area), at around 6:30 p.m., three children who were skating saw a shiny machine land. A kind of very short man appeared dressed in a black dress, similar to a priest's cassock. His face was very hairy and he had large eyes. He was carrying a flashlight that dazzled the boys and was saying words that they did not understand. Frightened, they sped away, and when they looked back they saw the machine rising rapidly. The next day, three men were driving through Tapignac, near Royan, on the Atlantic coast of France, when they saw a red glow in the fields and in the sky; It was more or less 7:30 p.m. They stopped, got out of the car and saw a disc-shaped object with a reddish dome about 250m away, floating about 10m above the ground. After a few seconds it moved away through the trees, but its light was still visible. The men grabbed a lantern and headed toward the light; From the object that had landed some 400m away, four 1m-tall beings came out and went to work under the ship. Seeing them, the little creatures disappeared into the disc which, after quickly changing color, took off at full speed.

Encounters in the Third Phase

The diversity and variety of humanoid behavior is evident from even these few examples – since the story of UFOs in our world is clearly longer. Tall, gangly, jumping beings, who wore transparent suits; armless dwarfs in diving suits and big helmets; rectangular creatures like sugar cubes that carry a concealed weapon; hirsute, bug-eyed monsters in black robes. Certainly in many cases it seems more as if some aliens saw it more prudent to send "guinea pigs" or laboratory beings to carry out study or analysis functions. There were also reports of beings giving friendly taps on the shoulder, or passing by; beings who threw rocks or played hide-and-seek, or simply fixed the breakdowns of their ships. Some pointed lights or beams at human witnesses; some experienced temporary paralysis. All this is very different from the style and demeanor of the gentle, long-haired Venusian who was said to have had a polite telepathic discussion with George Adamski, and obviously totally different from the parameters that the cinema teaches about aliens: invaders or cannibals, spiral marrow eaters.

When talking about cases of personal encounters with extraterrestrials, we refer to the expression coined by Dr. J. Alien Hynek in his book The UFO Experience, and which is already widely used spectacularly by filmmakers: Encounters in the Third Phase. The list of these cases includes supervisors, mineral prospectors, a rural owner, businessmen, children, a farmer, a laborer, and a teacher. And if you add to the list the doctors, police officers, soldiers, housewives, scientists, laborers and aviators who have had similar experiences and with whom you reach a very representative sample of the public, they begin to appear. uniquely coherent patterns of behavior.

In the early hours of October 12, 1963, Eugenio Douglas, a truck driver, was dazzled by a bright light that appeared in front of him on the highway near Córdoba, Argentina. The truck went into the ditch and Douglas got out, then seeing a large metal object in the road. Three beings that looked like robots, whose height he estimated to be about 4m, left through a door. They wore helmets and skin-tight suits. Douglas fired multiple shots at them and then fled. The UFO buzzed and he felt a sting from lightning as he ran.

Another terrifying encounter took place in Belo Horizonte, Brazil. At 7:30 p.m. on August 28, 1963, three children were in the garden of their house, playing next to a well. They saw a spherical object floating in the air, about 5m above the garden. It was transparent and lit from within, so that they could see its four occupants, seated on stools. One appeared to be manipulating an instrument panel and all wore clothing similar to that of divers. One of them emerged from the bottom of the ship and descended, motionless and upright, between two beams of yellowish light. Walking purposefully and swinging its arms, the being came toward them. He looked at the children with his one eye, made some gestures with his hands, made strange noises, and then sat down on the well rim. One of the children fought against the paralysis he felt in the presence of the creature and managed to pick up a brick. Instantly, the being emitted a ray of light, coming out of its central part, towards him and the brick fell from his hand. After gesturing more, the creature moved away and floated up the shaft of light to the ship; at that moment there was a great flash and the sphere rose through the dark sky. Suddenly released from their strange paralysis, the children ran toward the house, shouting for their mother.

In October of that year, 1963, a woman who lived in Washington DC, saw three occupants in a cylindrical UFO. One came out through the wall of the nave and closed in on her. He was wearing gray overalls, with some sort of slit for the eyes, though the eyes were not visible. Later, the being returned to the ship in the same strange way. A month later, on November 16, 1963, two boys from Kent, England, were walking with their girlfriends, when they saw a bright star come down, float, and move through the trees just over 70m from where they were. The golden oval UFO stopped instantly, a human-sized figure emerged and shuffled toward them. When they saw that it was totally black, had no head, and had bat wings, the four of them panicked and ran away.

In many of these cases, both the UFOs and their occupants use light beams or rays, or some kind of invisible force. In addition, the instantaneous appearances and disappearances, the passing through walls and the floating rays seem to indicate that, in many cases, the witnesses saw images projected by intelligences located inside the ships. There is evidence, according to some, to suggest that UFO occupants choose clairvoyants and hypnotizable subjects as contacts.

In a brilliant series of articles that appeared in the Flying Saucer Review, titled: A Long, Cold Look at Extraterrestrial Intelligences, the author, C. Maxwell Cade, a radiologist, suggested that UFO occupants could read witness fears: «*My God! A flying saucer! Will there be a furry monster inside?* » That emanation, amplified, could be retransmitted to the mind of the witness and... a hairy monster appears! Maxwell Cade points out that there are many ways to cause hallucinations, from a simple overdose of alcohol, hypnosis, suggestion, and drugs (such as LSD) to irradiation of the brain with high-frequency waves; all of them are more or less dangerous for the subject. If such techniques are within our reach, who can imagine methods of influencing the mind that could be used by higher intelligences?

Contact persons feel uneasy, shocked, or frightened and feel an obsessive obligation to discuss the incident with friends or an imperative to report it to the authorities, although they often wish they had kept it to themselves afterwards. Very few of the thousands of witnesses seek publicity, give lectures, or write books about their encounters. However, the very nature of the contacts with the humanoids: their rarity, the disturbing quality of many of the reports, the many questionable or futile activities of the creatures argue that the accounts may be correct.

The flow of reports about humanoids is not abating. At about 3 pm on February 5, 1971, two forestry workers in Kinnula, Finland, saw a UFO land on long legs in the clearing where they were. A creature less than 1m tall, dressed in a green jumpsuit and a lensed helmet, emerged from an opening and headed towards them. His hands seemed round and no fingers were visible. One of the workers came forward with his power saw running; the being withdrew and floated towards the ship, in which other entities were now visible. The worker caught the creature's foot and burned his hand. The alien entered the ship which took off immediately.

A year earlier, on January 7, 1970, two Finns who were resting during an alpine ski race in a clearing in a forest, saw a domed disk appear, surrounded by mist with a ray of light that was directed directly at the ground. When the lightning struck the snow, sparks flew, and suddenly a small being appeared in the beam of light. The creature had spindly arms and legs, a hooked nose, green overalls and boots, a shiny conical helmet, and was less than four feet tall. He pointed a box in the direction of one of the skiers, Aarne Heinonen, and then both the beam and the being vanished in the direction of the saucer that suddenly disappeared. Heinonen was ill for several months after the incident.

The fantastic year of 1966

On the night of January 19, 1966, numerous witnesses observed 2 bright objects over the city of Acarigua (Venezuela). One of them came from the North, the other from the South. When they crossed paths, the city suffered a brief but total power outage. On March 23, dozens of people in Joppa, Illinois (USA), saw an elongated object with several lights, with a much brighter one in the center, moving slowly and silently over the city. On March 24, a formation of lights is seen maneuvering in a strange way in the sky, near New Orleans (USA). That same day, an object with bright red and white lights crossed a highway near Holland, Michigan (USA). On the same day, an orange-colored object, tinted blue around the edges, flies over the city of Valparaiso (Chile), circling its trajectory at an altitude of about 2,000m. Also that day, a circular object that gave off an orange glow and a bluish glow in its lower part, was seen by numerous people crossing the sky in Girardot (Colombia), at 9:40 p.m.

Is it likely that in this case it is the same object seen in Chile on the same day? Also in March, near Haiderabad, India, two army officers reported that while on patrol, they were forced off the road by a brightly illuminated circular object emitting a loud buzzing noise that stung several times towards the vehicle. On April 3, an oblong object equipped with several pairs of lights was seen near the international airport in Los Angeles (USA). On April 21 in Mexico, an American Airlines pilot contacted the airport to report that a bright object had followed his plane for several minutes. The control tower's radar did not detect the object. Two months later, in May, in Natal, South Africa, a blue-green discoidal object chased a commercial airliner. On June 6, in the town of Grafton (Australia), a UFO made an appearance for 2 hours, drawing the attention of numerous people who notified the police of what was happening. Two agents go out in a patrol car to chase the UFO, which through the binoculars looked like a large ring of light that changed from white to red. The object ended up moving away at breakneck speed.

Already in the middle of the year, on July 16, thousands of Romans saw a series of unidentified lights in the sky, south of the city. Days later, on July 27, UFOs are seen in 5 cities in North Carolina (USA). The official explanation was that what was seen was nothing more than gases expelled by military reactors. Later, on July 31, a group of patrolmen from Prince Georges County and the state of Maryland, stood along the highway in the vicinity of Beltville and saw 6 glowing objects moving in the direction of Baltimore. That same night many people saw fantastic objects in the skies of Columbia and other nearby areas in the state of Maryland. The Federal Aviation Agency detected several of these objects on its radars. At 5 a.m. on October 3, several people in Gulfport, Mississippi saw a blimp-like UFO with rows of lights pass by, heading toward New Orleans. Minutes later he is seen near Gentilly, suspended in the sky for several minutes. At the international airport and at the Lakefront airport they assured that there were no airships in the area. Several sightings of unidentified flying objects were also recorded in the central region of Africa. Also that year a photograph was taken during the Gemini XII space mission, on November 12. Analysis has shown that the UFO in the upper right corner is a distant object, but NASA claims that it is actually debris that had been ejected from the Gemini capsule itself.

strange cases

On the early morning of January 13, 1967, dozens of police officers and civilians from the states of Kansas and Missouri (USA) saw a strange flying object pass by at a very low altitude (300m), moving slowly without making noise and radiating an intense white light. I cross those regions in 2 hours, between 4 and 6 in the morning. According to the authorities, at such hours there was no experimental balloon in that part of the country. In that January of 1967 several luminous objects were seen at night in the area of Cape Girardeau, Sikeston and Cairo. On the night of the 19th of the same month, 2 policemen witness the dematerialization of a UFO before their eyes. They described it as having red and white lights, turning green every 5 minutes. That year, on March 16, several UFOs fly over a missile station in Montana (USA). Also that year Russian astronomers appreciate UFOs in formation.

If these detailed and different reports narrate cases of projections, how do they do them? In an article published in the Flying Saucer Review in 1980, JG Adams considered some features of other reports on humanoids in which they were only partially visible, and to which can be added the case of Oscar Iriart, in Argentina, who was intrigued to see that the beings he found in 1968 had only transparent legs. Mr. Adams makes a list of beings that have been seen standing in the air, others gliding on the ground, those that appeared surrounded by a halo, and those that vanished or disappeared abruptly. All these phenomena, he says, are typical features of holograms. Technically, we have the possibility of projecting into open space an object that is visually solid using a beam of light, especially a laser beam, and a transparent sheet that contains the image and does not have to be as large as the resulting image of the image. projection.... Anomalies such as partial images can occur when the beam is obscured. Are the humanoids so frequently observed produced by a variant of holography that has the possibility of penetrating the human mind? It would not be strange, since the late 90s NASA has been developing space holographic montage programs.

On September 4, 1971, in an airplane, it was possible to film a discoidal object of about 200m, at the precise moment in which it emerged from the Cote lagoon (Costa Rica), at a speed of 3,000km/h. Two years later, in 1973, UFOs are observed over Mount Musine (Italy). Then 26 cases of UFO sightings were reported in Spain, only those registered, between September 1973 and June 1974. On February 28, 1974, a UFO described 3 very wide irregular circles, which covered the entire north of Portugal, the Spanish territory and part of the Atlantic Ocean.

At around 8:40 p.m. on January 7, 1974, a Belgian businessman was driving his car near Warneton, on the French border, when suddenly the headlights went out, the engine stopped and the radio went mute. He put the handbrake on and saw in a field, some 150m away, an object similar to the helmet of an English soldier standing on three legs. Then, feeling a growing fear, he realized that two strange figures were approaching him. The smallest, who looked very much like the little man in the Michelin ad, wore a round helmet, had eyes like marbles, and a gash for a mouth. The taller one wore some kind of uniform, a belt with bullets and a cube helmet. Their faces looked identical. The taller being opened its mouth and the alarmed businessman felt a shock at the back of his neck and heard a modulating sound. At that moment, another car appeared in the distance. The two beings turned in unison and headed stiffly but agilely, making identical movements and undisturbed by the thick mud, toward their ship where they met a third, similar creature. They all entered the object; the legs of the machine disappeared, it rose and vanished, just at the moment when the other car arrived at the place.

Within the broad electromagnetic phenomenology that UFOs seem to cause, their influence or relationship on sudden blackouts throughout the world is of the first order. Without any convincing explanation, population centers and even extensive regions have been deprived of electrical power when in the vicinity it has been possible to detect the presence of these incomprehensible failures at the time a UFO appeared in their vicinity. Neither electrical surges nor other conventional answers can replace the technical enigma.

At 11 p.m. on July 13, 1975, two towns in the province of Huelva, Bollullos del Condado and Almonte (Spain), suffered a sudden blackout that lasted 45 minutes. A farmer, Diego Sánchez Matamoros, and a graphic arts worker, Diego Salas Campo, were at the Bollullos cinema at that time. When the power failure occurred, the session was suspended, so they decided to return home in their car. At the exit of the town and descending a hill, they saw a yellowish light that produced intermittent flashes, but they did not stop. Coming out of a curve, the two witnesses saw at a distance of 50m and to the right of the road an unidentified object 5m in diameter and ovoid in shape, which was located on one of the poles of the electricity line that supplies the zone. It gave off blinding bursts of yellow light that changed to white. They traveled 100m from where the object was located, stopped the car and backed up to the height of the electricity pole. That artifact seemed to be made of metal and was located about 30m high.

The driver Francisco Esquivel got out of the vehicle, approaching the farm where the UFO had been located. At that moment, everyone saw that sparks began to appear from the power lines. The object was still motionless emitting flashes. After a quarter of an hour, the driver returned to the vehicle and started continuing his journey to the nearby town of Bollullos, seeing how the UFO rose slowly and the car's engine began to fail. That strange phenomenon followed them at a certain height, until they reached the town. Subsequently, technicians from the Sevillana Electricity Company discovered that the power line was cut exactly in the place where the UFO had been located. However, the supply to the towns in the area was perfectly normal. This fact lacks an explanation and is possibly related to the disconcerting effects produced by the Unidentified, mostly in nuclear plants.

Subsequently, splendid photographs of a UFO are obtained over Río Negro (Argentina), on January 3, 1975. In March, the flight of strange objects was reported in the sky of Algiers, and a cigar-shaped UFO flew over Korsor (Denmark) in February. On July 26 a flying disc is seen in the skies over Switzerland, it was a case in which three witnesses observed an object near Saas Fee. Those present assured that it seemed metallic, and it was difficult to distinguish it because of the fog that covered the mountain; it hummed softly. It was photographed and the image has been rigorously analyzed by the UFO specialist organization Ground Saucer Watch. The following year, on January 2, 1976, a UFO is photographed while slowly flying over the sky of Butterworth/ Penang (Malaysia), and in August several UFOs fly over the sky of Tunisia. Then, on September 10, the pilot of flight BEA831 from Moscow to London witnesses the sighting of an unidentified light, when asking the Soviet authorities about the source of that light, he was told not to ask questions; nine days later, on the afternoon of September 19, unidentified objects are seen north of Tehran (Iran).

In 1977, in Dyfed County and also near St. Bridesbukten in Wales, there were several UFO-related events. Later in April 1978, three mysterious fireballs fell on Canadian territory, devastating buildings, knocking out power, tripping light switches and leaving 3 mysterious burn holes in the ground. Later, on August 8, a very bright UFO flies over Johannesburg (South Africa), and on December 20, the Wellington (New Zealand) air traffic controller, captures through the radar the presence of several UFOs, which had appeared surprisingly. to a total of 6 aircraft. That was the start of a UFO wave in New Zealand.

Other Encounters in the Third Phase

Physical or mental abduction by UFO crew members is now called the Encounter in the Fourth Phase (E-4), although it is not part of Dr. JA Hynek's original classification of encounters. The connection between E-3 (or contact reports) and E-4 claims can be clearly seen in the following cases:

At 11:30 p.m. on March 17, 1978, mechanic Ken Edwards, who was returning home from a union meeting in Manchester, England, took a motorway exit. This exit is flanked, has embankments on both sides and runs past an atomic power plant surrounded by a 3m high security wall, which is built on top of the embankments. The high beams allowed Ken to see a 2m tall figure coming down an embankment. She was leaning forward as she walked, keeping her arms in the same direction, so that it seemed impossible that she could keep her balance. Also, the arms seemed to come out of his chest, not his shoulders. The being wore a silver jumpsuit and a helmet that only allowed Ken to make out two round eyes. Ken pulled his van to the shoulder and watched in alarm as the figure stopped in the middle of the road and, from about 15 feet away, looked up at him. Two shafts of light, narrow as pencils, shot from the figure's eyes and struck him. After a while, the figure moved on to the left side of the road, up the embankment, through the security wall, and disappeared. Ken later stated that he felt a kind of paralysis while the rays were focused on him. When interviewed by the UFO Investigator Network (UFOIN), Ken added that the entire encounter lasted between 4 and 5 minutes, and it took him an additional 5 minutes to get to his house. However, his wife was pretty sure he got home at 12:30 and not 11:40 as expected. There is an unexplained time lapse. In this case no UFO is mentioned, but it would not be strange if there had been one around.

In 1979 a UFO is seen over the skies of the island of Tenerife (Spain), even coming out of the sea, and there are many people as witnesses. On the night of November 11 of that year, a UFO causes a commercial plane from the TAE company to land at the Manises airport, also in Spain.

In March 1983 there is a wave of triangular UFOs in the Hudson Valley. Years later, on November 8, 1989, one day before the fall of the Berlin Wall in Germany, a UFO is seen for 1 hour and 40 minutes making an appearance, something very common in transcendental events. Months later, on April 1, 1990, a triangular UFO is seen over Verviers (Belgium). This is part of a strong UFO wave that year across Europe.

On May 29, 1991, a UFO makes its appearance in Curitiba (Brazil), it is seen by several people. On July 11, during the solar eclipse in Mexico, a huge wave of UFOs was seen, witnessed by hundreds of people. These were photographed and filmed. On March 31 , 1993, a triangular UFO is seen over Great Britain . On May 31, a UFO is filmed flying over Mexico City. On January 28, 1994, about 70 km southeast of Paris, the crew of a passenger plane witnessed the passage of a discoidal object, whose diameter was estimated to be about 100 m. The radar detected the object and estimated its speed at about 200km/h.

On August 27, 1995, a strange elongated object is seen in Colorado (USA). In January 1996, a UFO was photographed "floating" at low altitude in the skies of Denver, Colorado (USA). A formation of UFOs is appreciated over Phoenix, in Arizona (USA), on March 13, 1997: In October, unidentified flying objects make an appearance in the skies of Moscow (Russia). On June 16, 1998, a UFO flies over Sao Paulo (Brazil). On January 8, 1999, the London night sky was the scene of the appearance of hundreds of strange lights, which were seen by many witnesses. Many other sightings occurred between January and February 1999 in the Buenos Aires Triangle (Argentina). Later, on May 23, a UFO is seen for 1 hour and a half perched in the air over Santiago de Chile. Also that year, there was a wave of UFOs in Peru: sightings were recorded in the cities of Lima, Tumbes, Cuzco, Chiclayo, Huanuco, Pucallpa, etc. In the same way, there is a wave of UFO sightings over Turkey in August, coinciding with the solar eclipse and the earthquake that occurred in those days. Would there be a relationship? It would not be strange, in fact, it would not be new.

Close Encounters in the Fourth Phase have spawned countless science fiction movies and books. The protagonists of these encounters, where the victim is uploaded to a spaceship in which traumatic experiments are carried out, are usually carried out mostly by little men with big heads, bald heads, big eyes, and short stature. However, the notion of said "martians" was not popular until the 50s, and the reason for this will be explained later. I will now cite a few modern examples of the phenomenon:

On July 10, 1965, farmer Maurice Masse was walking through a vineyard adjoining one of his lavender fields in Valensole, Basses Alpes, France, when he saw an object in the field that was shaped like a rugby ball and the size of a rugby ball. of a Dauphine car. Nearby were two small beings (described as the size and build of an eight- year-old child) who were picking lavender flowers. Masse made for them without hesitating, but was seen by one of the creatures who pointed a staff at him; He stood still, paralyzed. When the creatures returned to their ship, they did so by rising like bubbles in a beam of light. The immobilized farmer saw them through the transparent walls of his machine. There was a thud, the ship's legs turned, the object floated away, and ended up vanishing 20m away. It seems significant that the facial features of the Valensole creatures were similar to those of the beings that participated in a classic E-4: the kidnapping of Betty and Barney Hill in New Hampshire in 1961, for a medical examination and of those they abducted. to António Villas Boas in Minas Gerais, Brazil, in 1957, to examine him and carry out sexual experiments.

As more reports become available, fascinating resemblances and patterns of humanoid behavior have begun to emerge from them, even in cases where witnesses were unaware of the stories of other contacts in other parts of the world. In the early hours of May 31, 1974, a young couple, Peter and Frances, were driving from Salisbury (in what was then Rhodesia) to Durban, South Africa, over the Beit Bridge. His car, a Peugeot 404, was escorted by a shiny object from near Umvuma to the vicinity of Fort Victoria. All the lights went out, except for a strange glow on the outside of the car that was apparently not controlled by its driver; it was very cold; the radio continued to broadcast a Lourenco Marques program long after its normal range had been exceeded. At Fort Victoria, when they stopped for gas, the UFO rose up and temporarily disappeared. They resumed the march at 5:30 am. Now they were escorted by two UFOs: one was directly above them. The familiar dry terrain suddenly changed into tropical vegetation and swamps; the path became straighter. Peter was in a state close to a coma; a force outside of him controlled the car. Frances fell asleep at 6:15 am. He woke up around 7:00 a.m., when they were a little over a kilometer from the Beit Bridge. Again, the UFOs rose high, as if obeying a signal.

Border officials laughed when they saw the couple wrapped in blankets on a wonderfully warm morning. When they crossed the bridge and went to get gas in South Africa, they discovered to their astonishment that the tank was still full. The car had consumed practically nothing on a 280km trip! That was all Peter and Frances remembered of their strange trip. But six months later, still uneasy about their bizarre experience, they contacted the Durban Natal Mercury after reading an article dealing sympathetically with UFO witnesses. Investigator Carlvan Vlierden was called in who, assuming they had lost track of time, arranged for a doctor to question Peter under hypnosis. The result was a much more detailed account of the extraordinary encounter. According to him, when they left Fort Victoria behind, the UFO overhead sent beams of light onto the car; using the and using the radio they managed to control it. They placed screens around them and projected onto them scenes of tropical vegetation. The car was teleported over the road. Peter sensed what was about to happen and mentally fought off the invasion. He added that he and Frances were programmed into the car and that his wife fell asleep because of their voices speaking over the car radio. It seems that Frances is not a subject capable of falling into a deep trance but Peter is, and he also has psychic abilities. Under hypnosis, he stated that they had figured it out in just seven seconds. A being came down the shaft of light and sat down beside the sleeping Frances; he could take any shape he wanted. Peter said that they then showed him the inside of the UFO, through the beam that attached it to the car. He was also told a lot of information about extraterrestrials. A large number of whom you were told live among us, on Earth. They never intervene directly in our affairs, but they are the planners, the influencers, the persuaders.

Waking up to the 21st century

On the night of January 4 to 5, 2000, a triangular object with intense lights around it was seen in several towns in the state of Illinois in the US and also in January, a UFO was photographed in the mountains of Las Vegas. On July 22, during a period of more than 30 minutes, a large UFO was sighted in the northeast of Caracas and with enormous luminosity that made it necessary to use dark glasses to observe it. Despite the fact that it was hidden behind a cloud, its metallic structure and a kind of fin at the bottom were noticeable. In September of that year, an unidentified object made an appearance over the spectators of a professional American football game in Arizona (USA), being filmed by television cameras that broadcast the match, incredibly the news was not disseminated by no media. On October 5, 2000, a metallic and luminous sphere, which reflected the light of the Sun, was seen over Resistencia, in the Argentine province of Chaco, later another flying sphere would appear making smooth movements. On October 13, light formations were seen in the skies over Kansas, Nebraska, and Witchita in the United States. Days later, on October 19, an elongated object of dark gray color and an approximate length of 1 and a half km, flew over at a low altitude (approx. 45m), the town of Elk City, Oklahoma (USA).

On January 27, 2001, a UFO is seen in the vicinity of the airport in Siberia (Russia), the device vanished after an hour and a half of remaining "floating", interrupting the activities of the airport. On February 11, 2001, the crews of two commercial airplanes (Lan Chile and Avant Airlines) observed the presence of a gigantic silver UFO suspended at an altitude of 18,000m in the vicinity of Antofagasta (Chile). The object was registered on the radar screens of the capital Santiago, and in Calama. On March 28, 2001, in Mexicali (Mexico) a formation of unidentified flying objects demonstrated precisely at the transit point of commercial airplanes. On July 3, dozens of witnesses saw a huge silver object in the shape of a cigar or cigar, which crossed the sky at low altitude, coming dangerously close to several buildings in Liverpool (England). On August 11, a formation of UFOs is seen in the sky of Naucalpan (Mexico). Also a month later, on September 11, 2001, during the attacks on the Twin Towers, a huge silver disc-shaped object with two powerful lights was filmed next to one of the buildings that is receiving the impact of an airplane. The news didn't get much attention given the fact that the WTC attack was more important. Days later and as the impact on the news subsided, there was talk of the sighting, making it clear that it was a UFO, since at that time there were no other objects flying in the sky in the area, much less of such a magnitude.

On December 1, 2002, a bright UFO was seen over Caracas (Venezuela), from which 5 smaller objects were seen leaving. Later, in January 2003, several sightings took place in Necochea (Argentina). Eight unidentified flying objects manifest themselves on the night of July 4, 2003 over Marseilles (France). On December 28, unknown objects appear on the Popocatépetl volcano, moving against the wind for several minutes.

Months later, a group of UFOs fly over Mexico City, on January 31, 2004, the objects were in formation representing a figure similar to a "cane". On February 10, a luminous red object is seen in Kansas (USA), which remained motionless below the clouds and then quickly disappeared. After 5 days, on February 15, a UFO of about 100m in diameter was sighted in the Cachipampa area, 120km south of Salta (Argentina). On March 4, 2004, a UFO is casually photographed by David Michell in Oregon (USA). On March 6, a disc-shaped flying object flies over a rural area in Alabama (USA), emitting a strange buzz, it ended up moving away at high speed. Five days later, on March 11, 2004, a very bright silver-grey rounded object is seen in San Pedro (Argentina). On March 14, two strange objects fly high over the south of Mexico City.

UFO crashes

The most important UFO accidents that we have been able to document, with their corresponding crew members, are:

1897 (April 17) Aurora (Texas, USA) 1 dead.

1908 (June 30) Tunguska (Russia)

1935-41 - Germany (North Sea)

1939-46 - Spilzbergen (Norway)

1941 - Goszevo and Dubroski (Belarus) Russia.

1947 (July 2/4) Roswell (New Mexico, USA) 6 dead and/or 4 badly wounded.

1947 (July 2/4) Magdalena (New Mexico, USA) 4 dead.

1947 (July 2/4) San Agustin (New Mexico, USA:) 4 dead, although one is believed to have survived.

1947 (October) Paradise Valley (Ariz, USA) 2 dead.

1947 - Great Falls (Montana, USA) 3 dead.

1948 - Globe (Arizona, USA)

1948 (March 25) and/or (February 13) Aztec (New Mexico, USA) between 12 and 14 dead.

1948 (July 7) Nuevo León (Mexico) 1 dead.

1949 (January 30) Roswell (New Mexico, USA) 1 live.

1950 (December 6) Indian Warrior (Texas, USA)

1952 (May) Spilzbergen (Norway) 2 dead.

1952 (August 14) Ely (Nevada, USA) between 12 and 16 dead.

1950-52 (September 10) Albuquerque (New Mexico, USA) 3 dead.

1953 (April 18) Southwestern Arizona (USA) 4 dead.

1953 (May 20) Kingman (Arizona, USA) 1 dead.

1953 (June 19) Laredo (Texas, USA) 4 dead.

1953 (July 10) Johannesburg (South Africa) 5 dead.

1953 (October 13) Dutton (Montana, USA) 4 dead.

1954 (April 12) New Mexico (USA) 4 dead.

1955 (May 5) Brighton (England) 4 dead.

1955 - Kazakhstan (Russia) A ship was recovered in perfect condition.

1955 (end of the year) Cerro Macón Salta (Argentina)

1957 (August 21) Los Corrales Entre Ríos (Argentina)

1957 (July 18) Carlesbad (New Mexico, USA) 4 dead.

1957 - Semipalatinsk, Kazakhstan (Russia)

1958 (April 1) Zone of Neuquén Neuquén (Argentina)

1958 - Kazakhstan (Russia)

1961 Timmensdorfer (Germany) 12 dead.

1962 (April 18) Las Vegas (USA) The ship was recovered in perfect condition.

1962 (April 28) Korb Lake, Leningrad (Russia)

1962 (June 12) Holloman (New Mexico, USA) 2 dead.

1962 - Semipalatinsk, Kazakhstan (Russia)

1962 - Northern Russia.

1964 (November 10) Fort Riley (Kansas, USA) 9 dead.

1964 (November 24) Tío Pujio, Córdoba (Argentina)

1965 (January) Villa María, Córdoba (Argentina)

1965 (January 13) Lavalle, Mendoza (Argentina)

1965 (December 9) Kecksburg (Pennsylvania, USA) 4 alive.

1966 (June 17) Elista, Caucasus (Russia)

1966 (October 27) Northeast Arizona (USA) 1 dead (UFO managed to take off)

1966-1968 - 5 UFOs crashed in the states of Indiana, Kentucky and Ohio. (USA) 3 dead and a ship recovered in perfect condition.

1968 (November 29) Urals, Sverdlousk.

1972 (July 18/28) Sahara (Morocco) 3 dead.

1973 (July 10) Arizona (USA) 5 dead.

1976 (May 12) Australian desert - 4 dead.

1976-1977 Puebla (Mexico)

1977 (June 22) Arizona (USA) between 5 and 11 deaths.

1977 (April 5) Ohio (USA) 11 dead.

1977 (August 17) Tobasco Region (New Mexico, USA) 2 deaths.

1978 (January 18) McGuire (New Jersey, USA) 1 dead.

1978 (May) Bolivia – ship without occupants.

[...]Nepal (?)

[...] Spain - 1 dead.

1978 - Kazakhstan (Russia)

1978-88 (November) Afghanistan - 7 dead.

1979 - Ural Region, near Rinburg (Russia)

1983 (May 5) Ordzhonikidze, Caucasus (Russia)

1983 - Kazakhstan (Russia)

1984 (June 20) Baku, Azerbaijan (Russia)

1984 - Taymyrian (Russia)

1987 (August) Vyborg, Leningrad (Russia)

1988 (November 22) Al'myakovo, Tomsk (Russia)

1989 (May) South Africa - 2 alive.

1989 (June) South Africa – 1 or 2 ships recovered in perfect condition.

1989 (July) Siberia, (Russia) 9 alive.

1989 (September 16) Belaya Pashnya (Russia)

1989 – Dushanbe, Tajikistan (Russia)

1989 - Omsk (Russia)

1990 (September 26) Kyzlkumy, Uzbekistan (Russia)

1990 (September 2) Megas Platanos (Greece)

1990 - Vladivostok (Russia)

1991 (November) Ezibastuz, Pavlodar (Kazakhstan) (Russia)

1992 (March 29) East of Santiago del Estero (Argentina)

1992 (June 25) Moldova, Ukraine (Russia)

1992 (November) Long Island, NY (New York, USA)

1994 (June) kyiv (Russia)

1995 (September 15) Lesotho (South Africa) 3 wounded who possibly died in military facilities.

1996 (January 20) Varginha, Brazil - 2 alive.

UFO RELIGIONS

The UFO issue has not only been locked up in what is called "paranormal", but it has also been soaked in religious movements. Some like The Church of Jesus Christ of Latter Day Saints (Mormons) and currently Catholicism have considered that human beings do exist outside the Earth. The Catholic Church has presented them as: "*The Aliens are Our Brothers*." The Vatican's chief astronomer said officially and publicly that " *there is no conflict between the Christian faith and the possibility that intelligent life exists on other planets, and that perhaps they could be more evolved than humans*." The scientific adviser to Pope Benedict XVI said that " *the possibility that life may have developed elsewhere cannot be excluded*," and likewise reiterated in an interview that, "*given the number of existing galaxies, it is impossible not to think that the life is a reality on other planets*." When asked if he was referring to beings like us or more evolved, he assured that " *in such a large universe this hypothesis cannot be excluded*." John Paul II's scientific adviser, Monsignor Corrado Balducci, also a prominent exorcist and demonologist, said: "*I do not exclude any religion that has contrasts with UFOs*," and added: " *I hope I too can become a promoter [of this issue], so that the problem of ufology is always better known.*"

But other ideological strands have gone further than this. The Church of Scientology and the Raelian Movement consider that the supreme deity is represented in extraterrestrial gods or "Elohim". The founder of the controversial Church of Scientology, L. Ron Hubbard, notable member of the OTO (Ordo Templi Orientis) and partner of the satanist Aleister Crowley, assured that the maximum deity is the Extraterrestrial Spirits called: "Theta". Its main leader is Heber C. Jentzsch as President and has maintained the status of the congregation as it is known today: a UFO religion. The sacred text of this organization is Dianetics. Scientology is a system of beliefs and teachings, originally proposed as a secular philosophy in 1952 by occultist L. Ron Hubbard, and later reoriented since 1953 as an *"applied religious philosophy."* About this religious denomination so famous for incorporating film artists and musicians, its founder said: « *I would like to start a religion. There is the money!* » (L. Ron Hubbard).

Another group is the revolutionary Raelian Movement, whose founder is known as Rael, who has been denounced for the violation of several constitutional laws of the United States. In fact, his wife and other people have received sentences for violation of other laws. That is to say, this religion is not exempt from continuous controversy, especially due to its lack of certain moral principles. According to Rael, the maximum deity are the extraterrestrials called: Elohim. This is also designated as the UFO Religion, and its sacred text is called: "*The aliens took me to their planet and to others.*" The Raelian Movement is a religious organization that promotes the belief that highly scientifically advanced extraterrestrial beings, known as the Elohim (one of the words used in the Torah for God), created life on Earth through genetic engineering. This notion is by no means new, but according to Raelian doctrine, a combination of human cloning and "mind transfer" could ultimately provide humans with the gift of immortality, and would have been part of what It happened with the Adamic parents, according to its founder. It is obvious that the Raelian Movement is considered as a new religion by its supporters and as a sect by its detractors.

The French Claude Vorilhon (born in 1946), better known as Rael, was in his day a sports journalist who came to have his own magazine on the motor world, "Auto Pop", with great success. Vorilhon claims to have had contact with an Elohim on December 13, 1973 in a volcano crater near Clermont-Ferrand in central France. Following instructions supposedly given to him by the alien, Vorilhon founded the Raelian Movement, which boasts 55,000 members in 84 different countries. Membership is particularly high in France, Japan, Canada (particularly Quebec) and the US (particularly Florida). The Movement spreads its messages through Rael's books, his speeches and his website.

According to Vorilhon, in December 1973, some beings that came in a UFO, coming from a 25,000-year-old civilization, had several encounters with him and gave him a message about human origin. This message says that after the formation of the Earth, some beings from another planet (the Elohim, which for the Raelians means "those who came from heaven") created humans and the rest of the living beings on Earth through manipulation. of DNA and genetic engineering, as also argued in Mesopotamian writings. The message dictated to Rael during his encounter with the Elohim affirms that they sent all the prophets who established the origin of the main religions (Abraham, Buddha, Jesus, Muhammad, etc.). The Raelians believe that the Elohim will return to Earth when there are a sufficient number of people living in peace and interested in them. According to the Raelians, this had already been announced in all religious texts. Rael assumes that the Elohim wish to hold this meeting at an embassy to be built for them, and they will share their scientific knowledge with us, their creation. One of his main goals is to inform as many people as possible about his alien race.

The symbol initially chosen by Rael for his movement was truly controversial: a Star of David with a swastika inside. According to Raelian statutes, the swastika " *represents the infinity of time, and its origin comes from Sanskrit and Buddhist symbols, through the Chinese character that identified temples, to ancient catacombs, synagogues and mosques.* " In 1991, the symbol was changed to remove the swastika, which is not respected by Jews. The original symbol is still used in some parts of Asia. Another possible reason for removing the swastika was to help in negotiations with Israel to build the "Raelian Embassy" or "Third Temple of Israel" there, to greet the imminent arrival of the Elohim, although Israel flatly rejected this request. The official reason for the change was that the Elohim requested it so. It is clear that the relationship between the realinos and the followers of the New Age places them as victims of the same swindling gods, who in Sumer were known as Anunnaki, opposed for thousands of years to the Hebrew deity called Jehovah and clear deceivers of the world, of many different ways, especially through religions, sects and secret societies.

The Raelians seem to have an interest not only in immortality, but also in reincarnation, the same vision of many other religious groups that have been seduced by this unprovable idea. Another of his goals would be to bring famous individuals like Jesus or Hitler to the present – understanding that they believe that Jesus is dead – either to receive divine inspiration, or to apply retroactive punishments. They don't really believe in reincarnation as described in mystical writings, since they don't believe in the existence of an ethereal entity free of physical ties (what is understood as "soul" in monotheism). In their books, the Raelians explain that the soul is a primitive state of human DNA. They consider that human cloning is the only way to achieve eternal life. Ultimately, DNA should be enough to bring someone missing back to the present. However, reincarnation would require a "recording" of the individual's mind, for use in "mind transfer" into a fully grown cloned adult, who has not been exposed to any "sensory activity". But the Realians must carry out their cloning research in secret or outside of North American territory and other countries, given the law against human cloning.

Raelians promote a new form of government they call geniocracy, or "rule of the jinn." To aspire to occupy a government position, it would be required to have a potential intelligence (they do not refer to the IQ) of at least 50% of the average, and to be able to vote it would be necessary to have 10% of the average. Rael, in his book, Geniocracy, maintains that nations function as a human body, in which each individual is a "cell", thus each one having a main task, arguing «all cells are important, but the cells of *the foot fulfill the function to walk and those of the brain, to think.*» He also maintains that with the geniocracy, manual work will no longer be necessary, since in a short term, it would be replaced by robots until a self-sustaining life system was created.

Remembering that Mormons believe that God is an immortal human who lives on a distant planet and from there came Jesus, Satan -who they say were brothers and sons of God- and the angels -the younger brothers-, we understand that the roots of all these absurd ideas come from the same dark mind: the Anunnaki (called Nephilim in the Bible). If we look at the New Age thought system, they also talk about energies, dimensional beings, and extraterrestrials, in the manner of defenders of the galaxy, but they communicate by possession (a person who acts as a "medium" and allows a "channeling" through your body). Although some information is true, but in its context, and the vast majority of references, are pretty, embellished, distracting, dissuasive verbiage and out of the real context of what the documented information supports. Moreover, the same situations are repeated among the world power elite in their occult and satanist practices.

7.

GALACTIC DIPOMATIC RELATIONS

"When humans are not doing their job, they, as well as the Earth where they live, are also in a state of deficiency. Healing fails to occur, because it is much easier to harm another than to heal yourself."
Vernon Howard.

DIPLOMATIC RELATIONS *with aliens*

According to what the military of several countries and secret service informers affirm, several governments have had contacts and agreements with extraterrestrial races throughout history; but the US has had crucial diplomatic relations with a particular race since the 1950s. This race was identified as coming from a planet in the red star system in the Orion Constellation that we know as Betelgeuse. They claimed that their planet was going extinct and that they could not live there much longer. According to M. William Cooper, these humanoids have a flag that is called "the Trilateral", and are known as "Rigelians". Contact groups affirm that these individuals belong to the Dragon confederation as well as the beings they define as Insectoids, Cybernoids, Syntosoids, Androids, Civor, Reptiloids, Draconians, Purpurados, Ezezanis and others, who appear throughout the folklore of ufology. It is said that these individuals have the physical characteristics of an animal, being bipedal and with high technological development, each race having its specific negative functions on Earth. This was one of the main conclusions drawn by the military and researchers after decades of study on extraterrestrial races for purely negative purposes.

When speaking of the so-called "Dragon Confederation" or "Brotherhood of the Serpent", the references are lost in time. According to contact groups, some extraterrestrials claim that the political-military division created in the cosmos arose some 4.3 billion years ago. According to them, all these strange races were "created" at that time with the sole purpose of serving as armies for the Satanic Empire or Empire of the Dragon. This mix of ufology, occultism, religion, science fiction, demonology, angelology, and New Age are the highlight of many groups that have started to investigate models of conspiracy theories, the so-called pseudoscience, and alternative history. The problem when it comes to discrediting these arguments is finding such a significant number of badge people talking about the subject, but that in all cases there is still no coherent and healthy common thread.

According to the American soldier Milton William Cooper, who worked for many years in Naval Intelligence, a first contact with EBEs was formalized in 1953, and from then on mutual agreements were initiated between them. The agreement was based on the fact that the US would allow them to kidnap people for medical purposes, because according to the Rigelians, they are on the verge of extinction and desperately seek help from glands and living cells. According to MW Cooper, around 17,000 of them live in Nevada in the area known as "Dulce", in which there are underground citadels where many EBEs live in complete comfort. There are tunnels in these cities or facilities, which even reach places like Puerto Rico, Argentina and other places in South America, and these complexes are also designed for the future survival of "certain" families of the human race, after the 3rd World War that Bilderberg have planned.

In 1953, diplomatic relations began between the US and the extraterrestrial race of the grays or also called "Trilateral", from which the name for the government committee, TC (Trilateral Commission), was adopted. In the first year of US President Dwight Eisenhower's term, at least ten other flying discs crashed and were hidden, resulting in 26 deaths and 4 survivors. Four of these ten incidents occurred in Arizona, two in Texas, one in New Mexico, one in Louisiana, one in Montana and one in South Africa. There were also hundreds of UFO sightings. Eisenhower knew he had to get down to the alien problem and solve it. He also knew that he could not, while he was at it, update Congress. The accident data during his term in this year 1953 were mainly: one on April 18 in southwestern Arizona with 4 dead EBEs; another on May 20 in Kingman (Arizona) with 1 EBE dead; another on June 19 in Laredo (Texas) finding 4 dead; another on July 10 in Johannesburg in South Africa, finding 5 dead EBEs; and another on October 13 in Dutton (Montana) resulting in 4 dead EBEs. In 1953, likewise, astronomers discovered objects in space that were approaching Earth. At first it was believed that they were asteroids. Other observations proved that it was spaceships.

Project Sigma picked up radio emissions from approaching aliens. When the flying objects reached Earth, they placed themselves in orbit on the Equator Line: « *It was a number of huge ships, whose intentions were unknown.* » Radio contacts were made, thanks to the use of a binary computer language, which allowed the Sigma project, as well as another new project called Plato, to organize a landing that allowed direct contact with these beings from another planet. The Plato project was entrusted with establishing diplomatic relations with aliens from space.

In the same period, another race of human aliens had also contacted the United States government. The latter warned them against the extraterrestrial race that surrounded Ecuador with their ships and proposed to help us in our spiritual development. These are what humanity has long called "angels" and who made contact with the government through Richard E. Byrd, George Adamski and others (Adamski, despite being publicly mocked, received the honors of a decorated military man at the be buried, after his death, in Arlington Cemetery). As a preliminary condition, these human aliens – also called "blondes" or "Nordics" – asked the Americans to dismantle and destroy their nuclear weapons. They refused a technology exchange arguing our lack of spiritual maturity and our inability to handle the technologies we already had. They said that we would only use new technologies to destroy each other. They explained that we were on the path of self-destruction, that we should stop killing each other, polluting the Earth and depleting its natural resources; and likewise that we should learn to live in harmony. However, these conditions were regarded with extreme suspicion, particularly the main demand for nuclear disarmament. It was estimated that accepting these conditions would make us totally vulnerable to a possible extraterrestrial threat. *"There was no reference to a similar situation in the history of humanity that could have helped us in this circumstance,"* Cooper added in a letter with 536 copies that he sent to each member of the US Senate and House of Representatives. UU. on April 26, 1989, as an indictment essay against those who manage all this conspiracy and its secrecy.

In that letter he went on to state that nuclear disarmament was ultimately deemed contrary to the interests of the United States and the offer was rejected. So, during 1954, the grey-colored, fat-nosed race of extraterrestrials, those who had encircled the Earth, landed at Holloman Naval Air Base where a compromise principle was established. Then-President Dwight Eisenhower met with those aliens and, like something out of a Hollywood movie, a formal agreement was signed between the alien nation and the United States of America. The first Rigelian diplomat was then received. It came with the title of "Most Excellent Lord Plenipotentiary Krll". You can see many movies that directly or indirectly allude to all these events, such as Transformers and Independence Day, which claim that the secret US government has captured alien spacecraft and other technology and He has even replicated it. Also in Monsters vs. Aliens, Close Encounters in the Third Phase, The Day the Earth Still Stood (Ultimatum to Earth), agreements, diplomatic relations or what an official and public face-to-face encounter with space entities would be like.

Terms of agreement

« *These two mentioned landings and encounters were filmed, and the films still exist today. The signed agreement provided that aliens would not interfere in our affairs and that we would do the same with them. We should keep his presence on Earth a secret. They would make the US beneficiaries of their technology and help them in their scientific development. In addition, they could not reach any agreement with another terrestrial nation; they were authorized to abduct men in a specified number and at limited intervals, for the purposes of medical research and study of our development, on the condition that the people were not harmed and that they were returned to the same place of their abduction. The kidnapped persons should not keep any memory of what happened. The aliens were also required to regularly provide MJ-12 with a list of their human contacts and any abductions they carried out. It was agreed that each nation would host an ambassador from the other, and this, for as long as the agreement remained in force. The alien nation and the United States were to exchange 16 people permanently, in order to learn to know each other.*" Bill Cooper.

The Vatican, informed of the facts

The Vatican collaborated closely with the United States Government to keep all extraterrestrial information Top Secret, hiding the truth from all countries of the International Community. The Vatican Secret Office for Extraterrestrial Affairs cooperated in the manipulation of information to the media, being co-responsible for spreading lies to the population of the United States and the entire world. Necessary accomplices in the pact of silence before the crimes committed by the secret government agencies towards UFO witnesses and people who possessed confidential or privileged information. People were being killed, and the Vatican leadership was silent as if it knew nothing. Cardinal James Francis Mc Intyre, Bishop of Los Angeles from 1948 to 1978, attended the secret meeting on April 16, 1954, which took place in California, at Muroc Airfield, the same location that would later become the Air Force Base. Edwards Air Force. The meeting was attended by the then President of the United States, Dwight Eisenhower, and a series of people related to the Secret Agenda of the Majestic-12 group and collaborating figures in government secrets. Among them, and in addition to Bishop McIntyre as secret representative of the Vatican, as well as government officials of the highest level, were also special assistants such as Gerald Light, President of the Association for Paranormal Studies, the journalist Franklin Allen, and the economist Edwin Nourse, all of them in the service of the Government.

The secret meeting coincides with a mysterious disappearance of the President, leaving the White House for several days, which worried officials. It was officially reported that the President had gone to the dentist in Palm Springs. The site, by the way, was near the Muroc Base. The military had closed and shielded the Muroc Base for 3 days. In this secret military base, a first meeting between an extraterrestrial delegation and President Eisenhower took place. The meeting was filmed by the military with three

16mm cameras, placed at various points, loaded with color film. In total, 20 minutes were filmed, in 7 rolls of 30 meters in length each, which are in a safe place. Two days later, Pope Pius XII received Bishop Mc Intyre. The Pope then decided to create a Secret Department of information, with a structure similar to the departments of military intelligence, called SIV (Vatican Intelligence Service). In confirmation of all this, upon McIntyre's return to the United States, he together with Archbishop Edward Mooney of Detroit, at the request and direct order of the Pope, were the first coordinators of the SIV, for the entire information exchange operation. extraterrestrial secret between the Vatican and the US government.

Few people know that precisely on that event, the secret meeting between the extraterrestrial delegation and President Eisenhower's delegation at the Muroc Base in 1954, is based on the film directed by Steven Spielberg, entitled: "Encounters in the Third Phase". Many data come from the story narrated by the personal secretary of Pope John XXIII where the religious leader claimed to have had an encounter in the gardens of the summer residence with an extraterrestrial being that descended from a ship, to later talk with the Pope for a few minutes, the Vatican has always been involved with stories of extraterrestrials as evidenced by this recently published article in which serious acts of complicity between the church and the US government are denounced.

Now, with all these advances in knowledge about extra-planetary life and contact with their civilizations, progress was made in the development of special access facilities. Underground bases were built, and the exchange of technology would take place in those common bases. The bases reserved for aliens were built under the Indian reservations that were located in a square located between the states of Utah, Colorado, New Mexico and Arizona. Another base was built in Nevada, in the region called S4, about 7 miles south of the western border of District 51, called Dreamland (commonly known as Area 51). All the land used by the aliens, as well as the personnel assigned there, are still controlled exclusively by the Ministry of the Navy. *"Although work began immediately, construction did not really get off the ground until 1957, when the funds allocated to the project increased significantly."* Cooper continued to state in his document.

Secret Projects

Many projects were created since 1947 and were "covered up" and distorted to dissuade the media and the curious:

(MJ-12) Majestic 12. Those who control power.

(CIA) Central Intelligence Agency. Those who handled the information and were in charge of the first years of information security, mostly on the extraterrestrial theme.

(NSA) National Security Agency. Who control almost all the information.

Project Sign. The first project to study the extraterrestrial theme.

Grudje project. Created to deter the media and change the information of the sources.

Project Blue Book. Created to Grudje framework to get more information.

Blue Teams. Groups destined to hide the recovered flying devices.

Pounce Project. Next project for media misinformation and information gathering.

Alpha Teams. Later name of the Blue Teams under the Pounce Project.

NSC4, NSC4A, NSC10, NSC10/1, 2 & 5. Reports created in Congress to allow the CIA and NSA more and more power and scope inside and outside the US.

Already a year before the agreements began, on November 4, 1952, the then president of the nation, Harry S. Truman, created by secret presidential decree the super-secret National Security Agency (NSA). Its real function was the decoding of the aliens' communications and the study of their language, in order to be able to contact them. This task, one of the most urgent, showed the extent to which progress had been made and was carried out through the project with the callsign "Sigma". In addition, the NSA had to monitor, throughout the world, all communications and emissions of terrestrial or extraterrestrial messages, in order to obtain information for the information services, and on the other hand, to hide the existence of extraterrestrials. The Sigma project had the expected success. The NSA also maintained contact with " Moon Base" and other secret space projects. Through this presidential decree, the NSA remained above all laws. The NSA, even today, is in charge of a large number of functions, and is actually the most important service of the information services. It currently receives 75% of the budgets assigned to information services. " *The position of CIA director, today, is just a smoke screen to deceive the public since the real job of the NSA is, even today, extraterrestrial communication, in addition to other very specific operations.* "

Bilderberg, the masters of the world

Since the Roswell event, President Harry S. Truman had informed not only his allies but also the Soviet Union. And this in case it happened that the aliens became a threat to humanity, plans were designed for the defense of the Earth in a supposed invasion, despite the fact that there were no precedents for something like that. The maintenance of secrecy on an international scale therefore encountered great difficulties. It was recognized that it was necessary to create at an international level an extraordinary group to monitor and coordinate efforts to maintain secrecy and to protect the government from the indiscretions of the press. Resulting in the creation of a secret society called the Bilderberg Club (named after the place of its foundation, the Bilderberg Hotel, Knokke). The headquarters of this secret society is located in Geneva (Switzerland). Little by little, the Bilderbergs became a secret world government, which even today directs and controls everything. The members of the Bilderberg Group meet at least once a year, in different places each time: In 1988, it was in Telfz, near Innsbruck, Austria, a meeting in which the Chancellor of the German Republic Kohl participated; In 1989, the meeting took place in Colorado, USA, with the participation of Count Lambsdorff. *"The United Nations was a sham at that time, just like it is today."*

The problem with the grays

In a poll by the firm Roper broadcast in the US, it was reported that 70% of the American population believes that the government is not telling the public everything they know about UFOs and ETs. Likewise, recent media published a survey in which more than 130 million people in the US affirmed that there is some form of extraterrestrial life. 45% believe that the Earth has been visited by extraterrestrial beings. Well-known American journalists continue to turn a deaf ear to the public's demands for a true political investigation. Accepting, instead, the denial of the numerous government agencies about the facts, while refusing to interview the legions of researchers, who have carried out serious scientific investigations on UFOs and extraterrestrial contact. Despite the pressure, the government prefers not to say anything officially.

But let's travel 56 years in the past, to 1955, when it became clear that the gray aliens were cheating on Dwight Eisenhower and breaking their agreement. Dead bodies of people and mutilated animals were discovered in many places in the United States. It began to be suspected that the aliens did not provide MJ-12 with the complete list of their contacts and abductions of people and it was feared that all the abducted people had not been returned. They were also suspected of collaborating with the Soviet Union, and this suspicion was confirmed. It was admitted that aliens used and abducted large numbers of humans for the purpose of testing them with the help of secret societies and through extraordinary powers, magic, occultism and religion. « *There were aerial battles between the planes of the US Air Force and alien spacecraft, confirming the overwhelming inferiority of our weapons compared to those of the visitors* ».

In November 1955, NSC Decree 5412/2 created a committee, supposedly for the study of all the factors tending to establish and execute a master plan for foreign policy in the age of nuclear power. Once again, it was just a vulgar pretext that had to hide the real purpose of the study, that is, the question of the grays. Since simultaneously, President Eisenhower had formed in 1945 and by decree NSC 5411, a study group that had to examine all the facts, evidence and lies of the extraterrestrials and discover the truth about them. «*NSC5412/2 was created only as a cover in the event that the press began to look for the reasons why such important men met so frequently. The first meetings took place as early as 1954 and were called "the Quantico meetings", from the name of the meeting place, the Quantico Naval Air Base. The study group was made up of 35 people who knew the secret and members of the CFR (Council on Foreign Relations), known as the Jason Society group or Jason Scholars.*»

Hungarian Jewish refugee and nuclear scientist Edward Teller was invited to attend the rallies. Dr. Zbigniew Brezinski chaired these meetings for the first year and a half, followed by Henry Kissinger, a German-born American politician to a Jewish family, for the second term beginning in November 1955. Nelson

Rockefeller was a regular visitor to all sessions. In a second phase of the investigations, the meetings took place at Quantico, and the group was soon named Quantico 2. Nelson built, for MJ-12 and the study committee, a secret meetinghouse in Maryland that only could be reached. access by plane. Therefore, the meetings could be carried out without fear of the curiosity of others. This secret meeting place received the name "Country Club" (Field Club). It offered complete facilities, including a respite and meeting center. At the end of 1956, the study group was apparently dissolved and Henry Kissinger published the supposedly official results in 1957 under the title "Nuclear Weapons and Foreign Policy" published by the CFR in Harper & Brothers (New York). Although Henry Kissinger really wrote more than 80% of said manuscript during his studies at Harvard.

The study group continued its work in secret. «*One can get an idea of the importance that Henry Kissinger attached to this study group by listening to the statements made by his wife and his friends: many of them admired the fact that he left home very early and returned at night, without talking to anyone and without answering any questions. He seemed to live in a world in which there was no room for anyone else. These statements are very significant.*" The results of the study on the presence and actions of extraterrestrials must have impressed him deeply. « *Henry Kissinger was not the same during the time these meetings lasted. And he never again knew events as serious as at that time. He often worked very late, after a hard day's work. These circumstances were what finally led to the divorce.*» One of the most outstanding conclusions of this study on extraterrestrials, according to the Milton W. Cooper document, was that nothing could be said to the general public, since their knowledge would probably have led to the collapse of the economy, of religious structures and a national panic that would lead to total anarchy. In this way the conspiracy of silence continued. Therefore, since nothing could be made public, Congress evidently should not have known of this.

Money

Funding for projects and research had therefore to be obtained from non-governmental sources. As an intermediate solution, money was obtained from the military budget and from the secret funds available from the CIA. Another important conclusion was that the gray aliens used humans as animals to obtain glandular and hormonal secretions from the blood, as well as for horrifying genetic experiments. The aliens declared that their way of acting was necessary for their survival. They explained that their genetic structure was so deteriorated that they could not reproduce. They declared that if they couldn't improve their genetic makeup, their race would die out. « *The MJ-12 regarded his excuses with much suspicion. However, since our weapons were useless against theirs, MJ-12 decided to maintain friendly relations with them until they had developed technology advanced enough to allow us to defeat them militarily.* "

The Soviet Union and other powers were offered their collaboration for the survival of mankind. Meanwhile, the construction of two weapons systems involving conventional and nuclear technology was considered, which would apparently allow the US to match the grays militarily. The results of these reflections were the Joshua and Excalibur projects.

Joshua was a weapon requisitioned from the Germans and was capable, already at that time, of piercing the 10cm-thick armor of a tank at a distance of almost 2,000m using low-frequency wave beams. This weapon was thought to be effective against alien spacecraft and their beam weapons.

Excalibur was a rocket-propelled weapon that flew below 10,000m and hit its target with a 50m margin of error. This one was capable of drilling into the ground to a depth of 1,000m, it was to carry a one-megaton nuclear warhead and it was intended to destroy the aliens in their bunkers. « *The Joshua project was finished, although, as far as I know, it was never used. As for the Excalibur project, it remained unfinished for a long time, I don't know if it was finished successfully.* » We have to remember that in 2005 the US showed that it had a rapid-range weapon against flying objects which was exposed as a defense weapon in the event of an attack by intercontinental missiles. Could it be this same weapon that was being tested? The truth is that in a NASA film you can see an object passing thousands of kilometers above Earth in infrared, and suddenly a plasma laser fired from Earth forces it to withdraw. Who shot him? It may be that it was again that weapon that was already used, or was tested, in the 90s.

contact groups

According to ufologists, the Riguelians are known in our world as "the grays" -typical of abduction cases-, 1m tall and a "negative mental power". It is also stated that they subdue man with their technology and that they require blood to live, with which they feed through the skin. True or false? What matters is that a truth is being hidden from the world about inhabitants of other worlds who have been here. Well, in the case it is also said that they are bipedal, with large slanted black eyes, like a fly, and that they have hands and feet made up of four fingers each. It is said that they are totally hostile, destructive and dangerous, with an animal genetic structure, they kidnap women to fertilize their eggs with their genetic information, they implant microchips to control people's attitudes and will, they maintain men, women and animals. in their ships and bases, as constant sources of food given the continuous reproduction of blood (their food). This bad reputation is accompanied by the statement that their race is in the process of extinction and they see humanity as an alternative to propagate their existence and their species.

The extraterrestrial contact groups assure that the total number of positive and negative races in this galaxy is 76, with 136 different types of ships, ranging from 30cm to 10km in diameter, classified as Observation Ships, Manned Ships, Mother Ships and Colonies, which move between solar systems and planets, being able to live in space, under the Earth, in the air and under water. The contact groups also say that there is currently a total confrontation against all the dark negative extraterrestrial forces that inhabit and arrive on Earth, by the positive forces or biblically called "angels". We fight against all its estates, ideologies, empires, leaders and against all the forms of manipulation and subjugation that they impose on the human beings of this globe, given our unconsciousness, ignorance and numbness in which we find ourselves.

The messages of mediums in the contact groups maintain that man will free himself from his slavery and subjugation knowing his true enemies and discovering what really happens on Earth, a truth that not only the dark extraterrestrial rulers but also the countries, organizations and men who have made pacts with them, selling humanity for "30 pieces of silver." They say that despite there being thousands of grays on Earth there is an opposition to them in those other extraterrestrials that are mentioned in the Bible, and currently more than 7 million of these extraterrestrials live on our planet, acting in all strata. to intervene in humanity and help it in its spiritual advancement.

Interview to EBE-2

The interview reported below was reported by Robert Collins on his website (www.ufoconspiracy.com) While the details are not exactly accurate, the order of magnitude of the numbers provided do match (day length and year length). Rick Doty revealed the information from when he was involved with EBE-2 and shared it: "*On March 5, 1983, I was at Los Alamos National Laboratories conducting negotiations on a counterintelligence project. During my visit, a source I'll call 'LANL-1', asked me to sit in on a very special interview. Not knowing what he was talking about, I asked. However, he couldn't tell me exactly what the project entailed or who he was interviewing with."*

From this interview we can extract the following: « *I accompanied LANL-1 to an underground facility to the west of the Los Alamos complex. The area was called, site 30. Access to this facility was made by entering Area 49. Access to the underground facility was through building number 49-2091. An elevator took us down about 60 feet - calculation only. Once we arrived, access was through a large opening in the vault outside the elevator. We walked down a hall to another vault door. We entered and turned right. We walked about 200 feet turned left and entered the vault door into a large room. This site contained two tables, several chairs, and the recording equipment. I sat near the door.* »

« *About 10 minutes later, 3 people I didn't know entered the room. One, an air force colonel, asked me to sign a security document, which further distanced me, separation TS/SCI/Group-MJ-B-3. Which I had never heard of, but I signed. The colonel told me that I should listen and not make any sound during the interview. I asked the colonel with whom I would be interviewed and he told me that it was a guest from another planet. The colonel withdrew. The other 2 people set up a table with a microphone and recording equipment, including a camera. About 5 minutes later, a 4 foot 9 inch creature that didn't look human walks in. He was dressed in a tight cream uniform. It had no hair and was identified to me as EBE-2."*

«*EBE-2 sat in a chair across the table from 2 civilians and the AF colonel. I didn't know the identity of the 3. LANL-1 entered the room and sat next to me. I listened as the three of them asked EBE-2 a series of questions concerning their home planet. The first question had to do with temperature, climate and weather. EBE-2 replied in perfect English but it sounded like a voice produced by a machine.*

Very difficult to explain, it was just something coming from a device that EBE-2 had in front of him or something on his body. EBE-2 explained what the weather was like on their planet, which had a dry temperature, varying between 65-90°. There were 35 hours of constant sun and 3 hours of darkness. Rainfall occurred only during one of its months each year. The day lasted 38 of our hours. They did not have months but had years consisting of approx. 600 of our days. They were using a society cycle that I understood to be similar to our months. During this cycle of society, each EBE worked for a certain time and ran their businesses. There was also a rest cycle consisting of a regulated period of sleep. I have no memory of the exact number of hours or sleep time. EBE-2 discussed time patterns and how they were formed. I don't remember the exact words. However, EBE-2 seemed very intelligent and fully explained each weather pattern in exact detail. He used terrestrial equivalences for meteorology terms."

« The interesting part of this interview was that I did not hear any of the questions that the 3 humans who sit next to EBE-2 were asking. Either the questions were already given to EBE-2 or the 3 humans "thought the questions" and EBE-2 would respond in English. [Clarification requested by Rick Doty: this was observed on a TV monitor and Doty was not actually in the same room as EBE-2.] [Addition by Robert Collins: EBE-2 indicated that its planet was named "Sieu" - but he said it in Eben, not English. He never mentioned the "Serpo" as such. He said that according to the days of Earth, his days on his planet were approx. 37-40 hours; he liked the cool Earth climate around LANL (Los Alamos National Laboratories) and northern New Mexico; and that [was possible because] he was a scientist and provided assistance to Earth scientists in the area of space travel. EBE-1 (initially just known as EBE) was the sole survivor of the Roswell crash, and lived until 1952. EBE-2 arrived in 1964 and stayed until 1984, and EBE-3 (with two

attendants, one of whom was female) He arrived in 1978 and stayed until 1994.]»

Staff Document MJ-12

The following 12 points are part of the original 1954 US government manual, which contained recovery from a crashed UFO. It is known as "SOM1-01 Special Operations Manual". The document was classified two levels above Top Secret. July 30, 1999 - Facts regarding the exobiological life that will be transported through the "public acclimatization program" :

1) Intelligent life exists on other planets and throughout the Universe.

2) Art not of human design or manufacture is at work on and around the Earth, sea and air of planet Earth.

3) Intelligent beings other than Homo Sapiens Sapiens are conducting various missions on this planet. These beings have been coming here for tens of thousands of years.

4) Alien beings can have human-like bodies or non-human bodies (such as hybrids, insectoids, or reptilians). Intelligent beings can be physical, non-physical, or inter-dimensional in nature.

5) The variety of life in the universe is diverse, just as life on our own planet is diverse.

6) Some alien beings have the ability through advanced technology or other means to move back and forth through time and space at will.

7) The spiritual evolution of an alien life form can be ahead of, equal to, or behind its level of technological development.

8) The social orientation, motives and agendas of these beings are very diverse. Some alien intelligences are friendlier to humans than others.

9) In many cases, the "abduction phenomenon" is a real event. This activity is complex, coordinated, and purposeful. It often occurs through many generations of a family.

10) Interbreeding of humans with more than one alien species has occurred. Hybrid children and hybrid adults exist. They have characteristics of the human and alien races.

11) Although most alien contacts and sightings occurred in our modern day, Earth has been shrouded in secrecy and mystery, the veil is slowly being lifted by the activities of civilians and specially assigned government personnel. Public Acclimatization to the reality of alien life is proceeding in a manner designed not to shock or disrupt society any more than necessary.

12) A great deal of "UFO" and alien information is now in the public domain. Countless books, videos, and Internet websites are devoted to these topics. Thousands of pages of US government documents on encounters and unusual views have been made available.

Inside a crashed ship

This classified two-page document was sent on December 24 by a researcher, and appears to be a transcript of a report or conference prepared on March 24, 1995. It tells of the experiences of a number of military personnel entering a crashed ship (Kingman, Arizona, 1953). The reported symptoms correspond very closely to those reported in the Team Commander's Log in its eleventh issue.

For added consistency, in 1995, Bill Uhouse, an S-4 initiate at Area 51, who worked with a living alien (J-Rod) trying to bridge the gap between ET technology and our own in a ship delivered by the ETs to S-4, he told a researcher who provided the document on a ship recovered in 1953 from the town of Kingman, Arizona. Uhouse reported the following, as summarized by the investigator: *"The ship continued to make a noise that the engineers could not stop. Someone suggested that they bring the alien occupants of Los Alamos back, where they had been taken to a prepared habitat, and make them stop the noise. This was done, and when the aliens indicated that they would have to enter the ship to stop the noise, they were allowed. It is believed that they made contact with other of their ships while inside. Then they went back to the gate again and were loaded into the van and driven back to Los Alamos."*

Entebe operation, a cover?

One story, difficult to verify, says that Israeli researchers discovered an alien spacecraft 15m deep in the Egyptian pyramid of Snofru. According to what they say, the Israeli Ministry of Defense was notified and one of the most impressive military operations in history was carried out. This information is mixed with the "Entebe Operation" developed to rescue some Israeli hostages in Uganda on July 3, 1976. At that time the African country was under the mandate of Amin Dada. The issue is that they were the same planes, the same soldiers and almost the same distance that it is claimed had to do with the story that has spread about the UFO. In the well-known operation only an elderly woman and an Israeli soldier named Jonathan Netanyahu died. The parallels are amazing what will be the right? What is being said is that Israel sent 5 Hercules planes and a contingent armed with the latest technology and equipment to take the ship out and take it to Tel-Aviv. The Egyptian army and special commandos intercepted the convoy and made the operation The Israeli army would have managed to cross the Nile thanks to the boats that were waiting for them and reached the border. True or not, rumors say that some Israeli scientists say that thanks to the recovery of this ship they have achieved great technological advances and amazing discoveries regarding cell regeneration.

8.

AREA 51

"A cosmically healthy man living quietly in society is worth more than millions who shout for reforms."
Vernon Howard.

SPACE PORT AND GENETIC laboratories

The truth about the underground bases is not spread to the media, rather it is said that they are simply military bases. The truth is entangled and the informers are persecuted, threatened and even killed. «*Phil Klass was a CIA agent, and this was confirmed by the reports that I myself have seen between 1970 and 1973. I knew that Phil Klass had among his duties as an aviation expert, the refutation of all information regarding UFOs. All military leaders have been ordered to find out about him on how to proceed in the event of reports of contacts with extraterrestrials, as well as how to deny the press and the public any information related to them.* " (Milton William Cooper)

According to MW Cooper, certain men such as William Moore, Jamie Shandera, and Stanton Friedman were, knowingly or not, secret government paymen. « *I think rather that they did not know anything, even if it can be proven that William Moore used an ID card of the military secret services and that he had admitted, in a conversation with Lee Graham, to be a government agent; I still have doubts about that. Lee Graham called me and at my request confirmed what Moore had said. Stanton Friedmann has told me, as well as many others, that he had worked on the construction of a nuclear reactor, used to power airplanes, which was as thick as a basketball, which was clean, which did not leave any residue. except hydrogen, a true 'dream. They were his own words.* » Strangely today Stanton Friedman maintains that many UFOs are of extraterrestrial origin, although others are not. Could the experiences and the accumulation of evidence have made him change his mind?

The only possible fuel for a machine to only eliminate hydrogen is water. And it is precisely this that powers an alien spacecraft: atomic power and water, and only aliens could at that time know of such technology. At least the groups that were interrelated with the secret government of the United States. Milton W. Cooper knew that all the organisms and organizations of some relevance that deal with the investigation on UFOs are objects of manipulation in their midst by the secret government, in the same way that NICAP has been infiltrated by manipulators and is in fact run by them. « *I believe that all his attempts at manipulation have been successful. It is more than likely that all public institutions that deal with UFOs are manipulated in the same way.*"

diversionary operation

During 1957 work continued on the "Yellow Book". A new project was carried out, the "Redlight" project, and preparations were made for test flights with alien spacecraft. A top-secret facility was built at Groom Lake, Nevada, in the compound there reserved for weapons tests. This place was named Dreamland and its custody was entrusted to the Ministry of the Navy. The personnel were subjected to a "Q" security examination and a presidential authorization - to say that the President of the United States was never authorized to access the place. This extraterrestrial base, in which the technology transfers took place, is located in region 4 and was named, to confuse the curious, " The Hidden Face of the Moon", (from whose name so many misunderstandings have arisen in the press in recent years) The army was entrusted with the constitution of a super-secret organization for the protection of extraterrestrial projects. This organization, called the National Reconnaissance Organization (NRO), is located in Fort Carson, Colorado.

Special teams called Delta Teams, were created for the protection of secret projects. A second project, called "Snowbird" (Snow Bird), followed immediately, whose function was to give an official explanation to the accidental observations of luminous and red-colored flying devices, passing them through air tests of the Air Force. For this purpose, Snowbird flying devices were manufactured with conventional technology which made demonstration flights for the press. The Snowbird project was also used to discredit the true and irrefutable observations of extraterrestrial spacecraft, in order to dampen public curiosity. The Snowbird project fulfilled its mission perfectly: UFO reports decreased significantly during the following years.

The White House Military Office had organized a secret fund of US $1,000,000 which it managed directly. This fund was used for the construction of more than 75 underground facilities. To the questions of the presidents, they were answered that they were refuges for them in case of war. In reality, few of these underground facilities were built for presidents. Millions of dollars passed through this Office to go to the MJ-12 and from there, to the contracted companies. With these funds, secret alien bases, other military bases, and facilities planned for Alternative 2, which we will discuss later, were paid for. President Lyndon B. Johnson used money from this fund to build a movie theater and redevelop the road leading to his ranch (He had no idea of the ins and outs of the matter). These secret White House funds for underground construction had been created in 1957 by President Eisenhower. The budgets came from Congress, used under the guise of *"construction and maintenance of secret facilities for the use of the President in time of war"* or *"relief shelters for Presidents."*

« The location of the places and everything related to these facilities was and is a top secret. The Military Office still has these funds today, which are routed to their destination through a compartmentalized and complicated network, so that even the most experienced spies or accounting experts cannot follow their trail.» (MW Cooper) The facilities in the Nevada desert are America's most guarded and important secret facilities. Area 51 has the best technology ever thought of and is 50 years ahead of conventional and commercial technology; Dulce is an alien base that has gotten out of the control of the American government itself. Among these bases are distributed the functions of alien cryogenics, development of extraterrestrial technologies, study of mental power, manipulation of human and animal genetics, among many other secret operations.

Project Sign

In the United States, the Air Force created, starting in 1947, a commission of inquiry or investigative agency that depended on the ATIC (Air Technical Intelligence Center), which was installed at the Wright-Patterson air base, Daytona (Ohio). The mission of this body consisted of obtaining information on foreign planes and remote-controlled devices, in reality it was the Intelligence service of the Air Forces. It was at that time (1947) that the US Secretary of Defense, James Forestal, commissioned the ATIC to carry out an investigation into these strange phenomena, so on December 30, 1947, the Secretary of Forestry signed the order instituting the creation of a commission of inquiry that should function within the ATIC. This commission received the name of Project Sign. It had an ephemeral existence and in general the public was unaware that the real cause of its disappearance was that the personnel that made up this project, both officials and specialized technicians from North American Aviation, had the unfortunate idea of affirming after arduous and meticulous studies that UFOs exist and that they are machines controlled by intelligent beings and of extraterrestrial origin.

Such a conclusion put the Pentagon's senior military commanders on notice, who reacted in a typically military manner to what they considered a potential threat to national security, that is, according to the report, United States airspace was constantly violated by unknown machines with scary qualities: they accelerated abruptly from zero to several thousand kilometers per hour in a few seconds, suddenly stopped as if nothing and completely changed course without flinching, they could remain immobile in space for indefinite periods of time and then with a sudden take-off disappear from sight, etc. It was therefore quite understandable that the authorities took a stance that urged the utmost caution. It was necessary to impose the most rigid censorship on that information and at the same time "calm down" public opinion, until more information was available about the true origin, characteristics and intentions of these fabulous devices. Thus, through AFR 200-2 (Air Force Regulation 200-2), any Aviation officer who revealed "classified" reports on UFOs. This is how they began to silence those who knew too much, or who could instill in the common people making reckless statements. Some time later, the CIA added a new clause to this scheme requiring the Aviation to "explain" all observations in any way, and to "discredit" important witnesses as visionaries.

About the month of July 1948, the owners of Project Sign thought it convenient to submit a very complete and "definitive" report to the Pentagon. This report, presented as a document of many typed pages and bound in black covers on which the text TOP SECRET was read, concluded that UFOs were "controlled extraterrestrial vehicles, which from the large amount of data collected *during management, about a large number of them had not had any normal explanation.*» This top secret report was eliminated from the official archives by means of incineration, only a few copies of it survived, one of which had come into the hands of Captain Edward Ruppelt, when he began directing the "Project Blue Book" (Project Blue Book).

Project Grudge

The previous program was succeeded by Project Grudge, which meant the beginning of a dark stage in the investigation of the UFO phenomenon, an official era of totally skeptical attitudes, primarily based on the fact that UFOs could not exist. It also officially meant a change in personnel and the departure of Project Sign technicians, who had a broad and positive position on the subject, and who supported the idea of the real existence of UFOs as guided extraterrestrial spacecraft that circled our planet. This negative program for the investigation of the UFO phenomenon was officially dissolved on December 27, 1949, leaving behind a voluminous report of more than 550 pages, on the investigations carried out during the time of his administration. This comprehensive report was given the official title of "Unidentified Flying Objects - Grudge Project. Technical Report No. 102-AC-49/15-100". Its format was typically military, that is, made up of a main text that had a brief discussion of the problem, and accompanied by various Annexes with conclusions and propositions, which served as support for the main text. These Annexes detailed the analysis of the different investigations that the group had carried out on the recorded sightings, the percentage probability of their existence, etc. With the support of the psychological section of the Air Medicine Laboratory, they explained: "*There are enough psychological reasons to satisfactorily explain observations that do not have a positive explanation.*" This report added that some people see "spots or flies" dancing before their eyes, due to solid particles floating in the aqueous humor of the eye and casting shadows on the retina. Other funny observations said that they were due purely and simply to imaginative subjects, other percentages were attributed to weather balloons, or they gave an astronomical explanation, for example celestial bodies or meteors, or they were simply designated as frauds, very imprecise observations or could be attributed to aircraft sightings.

Commenting on these resolutions, Captain Ruppelt said: «...*apparently all UFO observers were myopic and/or outright imbeciles ...*» In the last Annex the members of Project Grudge declared: «... *23% remain of observations that we cannot explain, but for which, nevertheless, an explanation must be found, because we do not believe in flying saucers (sic)...* » As a final premise, before disappearing, Project Grudge ruled: "... *The United States Air Force announces that after two years of research, they can affirm that flying saucers do not exist ...*" While the ATIC continued to receive data and reports of all kinds that he automatically kept in drawers or possibly some of them ended up in the paper basket, where surely many of them were thrown away without even being read. Precisely during the month of January 1951, Captain Edward J. Ruppelt was called back to active service, being assigned to the ATIC as an information officer. A short time later, he was commissioned to carry out a meticulous study on the situation to date on the issue of UFOs, a mission that he fulfilled to the letter and with detailed reports that he delivered to the Pentagon for further analysis.

Project Blue Book

That was the way things were when the ATIC received the order to create a special agency to deal with UFOs. This agency, built on the ashes of the Signo and Grudge projects, received the name of Project Blue Book, and its direction was entrusted to Captain Edward J. Ruppelt, who was already considered a specialist in the matter. Said project in the course of its existence traveled thousands of kilometers in the way of its surveys with the different observers, verified hundreds of reports and analyzed several thousand sightings. At the beginning of 1953, Ruppelt organized an assembly of wise men, to whom he explained for two days what the ATIC, under his direction, had done to date. From 1947 to the end of 1952, 4,400 reports were received. In February 1962, the United States Air Force officially declared that: «... *after fifteen years of investigations into reports relating to flying saucers, it has been shown that none of the 7,000 UFOs that have been investigated, they were a spaceship from other planets...*» The investigations of the Blue Book project, which began in 1947, led us to believe that there was no evidence of extraterrestrial vehicles under intelligent control, nor of technological advances beyond the reach of modern science, nor of a threat to national security. Most of the reports on UFOs, according to the Blue Book project, referred to planes, satellites, astronomical phenomena, balloons, birds, lights, jokes, etc. However, despite these skeptical conclusions reached by the ATIC, the UFOs did not stop their activity, waiting for these "programs" to rule on their existence or not. On the contrary, they continued to demonstrate, so as not to let popular interest cool.

the aurora ship

Cooper wrote: "*Since our exchanges with aliens, we possess technology beyond our wildest dreams. A spaceship called "Aurora" is in Area 51, with which space travel is carried out on a regular basis. It is a first-order space device, called TAV (Trans Atmospheric Vehicle). It can take off on a 12km runway and climb into a very distant orbit, then return to earth. We currently have an atomic-powered alien-like flying device located in the S4 (Nevada) region.*" Cooper was assassinated in 2001, so he didn't have full knowledge of the number of sugar mills the US owns today. « *Our pilots have made interplanetary trips with this device, during which they have visited the Moon, Mars and other planets. We have been lied to about the true nature of the Moon and the planets Mars and Venus, as well as the advancement of technology available to us today.*"

Conflicts with certain aliens

«*In 1969, a confrontation between scientists and aliens took place in the underground laboratory called "Dulce". The latter took many of our scientists hostage. Delta Teams were called in for his release. But their weapons were inferior to those of the aliens. In the course of this operation, 66 of our people perished. For at least two years, all joint projects were suspended. Finally, an agreement was reached, and the collaboration continued, which continues today.*" Would this have anything to do with the arrival of the Apollo project on the Moon?

«*In our common history, aliens have manipulated the human race through secret societies, religion, magic, the occult and other powers. The CFR and TC completely dominate the technology of the aliens and also dominate the economy of the country. Eisenhower has been the last president who has been able to have access to everything related to extraterrestrials. The presidents that followed him have only been able to know what the MJ-12 and the secret organizations have wanted to communicate to them, and very often they told them lies. MJ-12 has exposed to every president the history of alien culture as that of a lost culture seeking a new homeland on this planet and showering us with gifts in the form of technological innovations. And in other cases, nothing has been said to the president. The presidents took history for granted and meanwhile, innocent people continued to suffer at the hands of scientists, aliens or humans, who carried out horrible experiments, even more so than those practiced by the Nazis. And if all this were not enough, other people continue to fall victim to the insatiable greed of aliens for biological enzymes, glandular and*

hormonal secretions in the blood. A large number of human beings are kidnapped, to then suffer psychological or physical consequences throughout their lives. The documents that I could see belonged to 40 people who had been implanted with instruments whose function I do not know. The government believes that the aliens intend to form an army of mutated beings that, at their command, will be activated and directed against us. Furthermore, we should not forget that up to now we have not been able to manufacture an effective weapon to deal with them. Is all this worth the technology we have received from them? »
(Milton William Cooper)

France releases its UFO reports

On February 2, 2007, the French Space Agency delivered thousands of reports and documents of Third Type Contacts and UFO interception. The French Space Agency has announced that all these 3rd type contact files are the reports dating back to 1870 when a tall being came down from a round ship and the townspeople went with machetes and torches to kill him thinking it was a devil. The crew member moved away from the ship and it exploded, killing everyone around. In principle, some 20,000 reports have already been deposited on the web and they announced that everything will be filtered to the Internet and given to the journalistic media with total freedom and without any type of censorship.

In early February 2007 while in the US with my study group, one of them told me that his mother had met an ex-FBI agent at a party a couple of weeks ago, and she told him He recounted the things his son was studying and those he now understood based on the reality of the Bible, heaven and angels. The agent was surprised and asked: *"Where do you get that information from? since what you say is true."* She told him that she was studying it with us and had understood that the heaven of which it is known is the mere universe and the angels are what science calls: "aliens". The agent told him that he was aware of many of these facts, and that also, as the Bible mentions about "The Mark of the Beast", President George W. Bush was interested in carrying out a monetary system through a chip financial inserted in the right hand to be put as world control in a few years.

In highly protected sectors, and inaccessible to the common officials of Area 51, the aliens practice dark genetic experiments protected by very powerful sectors of the US government itself in exchange for weapons technology, and they are already implanted with control chips. In fact, the gray aliens themselves have also been shown to be controlled to some degree by a chip in their heads, as if other entities, even superior to them, manipulated them.

Area 51 and Dulce

For many years a veil of theories and superstitions have been created about the North American military base "Sector 51" or "DreamLand" in Groom Lake, Nevada, popularly known as Area 51. This military base was officially non-existent until 1973 when the then president of the USA John F. Kennedy forced them to take him to that site and gave orders that it should appear on the official maps and records of US military locations.

The construction of DreamLand is part of a large number of "facilities" (underground bases) that the US Department of the Navy has under all the territory belonging to the Indian reservation. Today it can be seen from Google Earth and is known as a base for military flight tests. The truth is that access is still restricted and the upper levels are a cover to hide what is in the underlying levels. Evidently John F. Kennedy did not come to know much about these lower levels, nor about the other facilities, such as those that interconnected with the base itself, such as Dulce, which today is totally out of US control. The things that were known about this other "Facility" were from a soldier who worked inside and took out many of the documents that revealed to the media the ins and outs of the black and clandestine operations carried out by the US armed forces in said laboratories. These texts are popularly known as the "Sweet Papers".

thomas c.

When talking about the "Dulce Papers" reference is made to a series of documents, black and white photos -about 30- and a video, which would have been stolen by a high security officer from the Dulce underground base, one one of the largest and most important sites that the United States has ceded to aliens on Earth, but no, we are not talking about science fiction or a movie script. This is one of many cover-ups that the US government has carried out, and that they were already weaving since before World War II. This officer who produced the "Sweet Papers" claims to have worked in this place until 1979, when he decided to retire due to the nature of the events that occurred inside the base, which escaped all ethics and humanity, and which causes an emotional breakdown by not being able to face or assimilate the events that were occurring.

As a member of the installation's security system, and with access to many of the locations on the base, Thomas had the opportunity to personally witness many of the operations that were carried out, both scientific and technological experiments, as well as genetic and thought experiments on animals. and humans. Already determined to defect, and with the conviction of telling the world what was happening in that place, he took on the task of gathering important documents and evidence that could support the story he was about to tell. Equipped with a small camera, he took about 30 photos of the complex at its different levels, collected high-security documents, and took a video of the control center that showed various views from the security cameras of the corridors, laboratories, the aliens, and US government personnel working in conjunction with the ETs.

Turning off the alarms and security systems in one of the nearly 100 exits to the surface, he left the facilities with all the documents and evidence and those that he hid in an unknown place after making five copies. When he was preparing to flee with his family, upon arriving at his home he found that at the door of his house there was a van with federal agents waiting for him. He had been betrayed by K. Lomas, another worker friend, and as a consequence his wife and son had been kidnapped. The agents wanted to take back what Thomas had taken from the facility in exchange for returning his wife and child to him. Aware that he might not see them anymore, and that they would probably be used in biological experiments, he decided not to give in to their requests.

Thomas worked for seven years in high security photography for the Air Force, beginning in 1971 in Santa Monica, California. In 1977 he was transferred to the Dulce facilities. The Base is provided with a kind of underground tube transportation system. This tube system would be connected to an underground base under Area 51, in Nevada, to facilities in Colorado Springs, Carlsbad (New Mexico), and so on until completing a vast network of underground connections under the United States, which would extend over a global system of tubes and sub-cities. Thomas says that there were about 18,000 "Greys" at the Dulce facility, and that he also saw reptilian humanoids. In Dulce's multi-level facilities, the level of security increases as you go down to deeper levels.

Thomas had ULTRA-7 clearance, and therefore knew of 7 sublevels, but there could be more. Security at Dulce's complex is extremely high: every time an individual enters a high-security zone beyond the second level, they are weighed naked and then given a uniform. The data of the person's weight is stored in their electronic identification card every day, any significant change will require a physical examination and X-rays. These types of weights are found at the entrance of all sensitive areas. The individual must place the electronic ID card in a slot in the door, then a numeric code is entered into a keypad, and both the code and the weight must match, or the door will not open. Any discrepancy will immediately make the appearance of security personnel.

No one is authorized to carry anything in sensitive areas. Any supplies are placed on a conveyor belt, and X-rayed. The same method is used when leaving sensitive areas. The elevators are magnetically controlled, the magnetic system is in the walls of the elevator tube, there are no normal electrical controls or elevator cables. Everything is controlled by advanced magnetism, including the lighting: there are no regular lamps and the tunnels are illuminated by pentoxide-phosphor units with emission bands wider than normal. Some deep tunnels use a form of phosphoric-pentoxide to temporarily illuminate areas. Aliens hang around those areas for unknown reasons.

Level 1 contains the garage for vehicle maintenance. Level 2 contains the garage for the trains, underground transporters, tunnel digging machines, and disk maintenance. At level 4, unconventional studies are carried out, such as research on the human aura, telepathy, hypnosis, and dreams.

Thomas argues that they knew how to separate the physical body from the "soul" to place an "alien entity" in its place, as if we remember a scene from the movie "Avatar", or even "The Substitutes" with Bruce Willis. On level 5 is the alien quarters, and the only sign in English is one that says "To Los Alamos" at the subway station. On level 6 is where the genetic laboratories are located, where experiments are carried out on animals and humans that are vastly altered from their original form. There are humans with multiple legs or arms and cages where bat-like humanoid beings are held captive.

Level 7 is undoubtedly the most chilling and guarded of the base. Thomas found caged humans on this level, and it was this fact that shook him and triggered his final decision to expose the harsh reality that was happening before his eyes. He was able to see hundreds of humans, hybrid remains, and humanoid embryos that were kept frozen for future experiments. « *I frequently found humans in cages, usually drugged, but sometimes they would cry and ask for help. We were told that they were hopelessly insane, and that they were involved in high-stakes drug trials to cure them. We were told never to speak to them. At first we believed the story, but finally in 1978 a group of workers discovered the truth. That started the war in Dulce*."

Thomas adds that the aliens are not interested in us or our planet's natural resources, what they want is the magnetic power that flows through the Earth. They are able to take advantage of it in a way unknown to us.

Philip Corso

Philip Corso, a man with an excellent resume: colonel, distinguished career military scientist, member of General McArthur's intelligence staff in the Korean War, member of the National Security Council in the Dwight Eisenhower administration, head of the investigative team and development of unknown (alien) technologies from the Pentagon in the 1960s, and other activities, writes a book upon retiring from the military, "The Day After Roswell." In this book, no longer committed to military institutions, he reports on the involuntary EBE (Extraterrestrial Biological Entities) intervention in the new discoveries and technological advances on this planet since the popular Roswell case.

The merit of Corso's confessions lies in the fact that, in addition to being supported by other uniformed officers with high-security credentials, also retired, and even active, it is he himself who is directly involved in the design, manufacture, and subsequent distribution by amid military industrial and related complexes, such as the transistor "discoverers" Bell Laboratories (Drs. Shockley, Bardeen & Brattain, at Bell Lab's Electronic Circuits Research Center, under the aegis of Vice President John "Jack" Morton of Maverick Bell Labs) of chips, fiber optics, microwave technology, laser night vision equipment, stealth technology, among others, and a series of its applications in household appliances, instrumentation, satellites, computers, and high-precision tools.

Alongside Corso, US Air Force Colonel Steve Wilson also maintains that the mysterious "black helicopters" possess anti-gravity technology such as the XH-75D or "XH Shark", manufactured by Teledyne Ryan Aeronautical Corporation of San Diego. The Colonel explains that several of these XH-75Ds were assigned to the Delta Force or "Delta Force" (Delta/National Reconnaissance Organization Division), which have the mission of recovering downed or crashed ships or VEDs.

The foregoing thanks to the study in laboratories of the remains of the alien silicon amplifier/switch", evaluated between October and December 1947 and of the remains recovered from the VED fallen in Roswell in that and subsequent years, being the common denominator in all these activities. and situations, Colonel Philip Corso From then on it was only a step to establish large industrial complexes in places away from undesirable eyes, with great security devices, the interested financing of the great economic conglomerates of the planet and with absolutely no obstacles. , which implies a "laissez faire" policy beyond the norm, in which the military, the political and the economic, the great powers throughout the history of the human being, were subservient to even greater powers.

These powers, unknown to the common people, are not unknown to the scholars or watchers of the behavior of hermetic philosophies and secret societies, a real gray eminence in the conductive threads of the destinies of the Earth, who always warned about the dangers of certain agreements behind the world's back.

Christa Tilton

Tilton is an abductee (July 1987) among millions but whose case represents a special element within Ebelogy (science that studies EBEs), along with a few others, since her abduction was characterized by elements that until then had been taken like simple hallucinations. His case is not particularly reminiscent of the mysterious events in Nome (Alaska) brought to light in the movie "The Fourth Phase", with the actress Milla Jovovich. Many other abductees tell the same story and whose emblematic cases we could summarize are those of Judy Doraty, Texas, May 1973 and Myrna Hansen, New Mexico, May 1980.

Tilton recounts that her abduction, like bedroom visitors by Grays, occurred in 1987, when she was taken in a small ship to the top of a hill, where she saw in the middle of the darkness how a light was emerging from the entrance to a tunnel. on the hill, where they took her, and inside which she saw armed guards. Inside the tunnel, he observed with special interest the large number of TV cameras, and small vehicles that took people, workers, and uniformed personnel inside; She also observed offices on the sides, understanding that she was on level one of an underground construction very close to where she was taken.

A blonde-skinned, light-eyed guide greeted her from the Grays and they entered through the tunnel. To the sides of the great construction, as they went, there were small ships or disks like the ones that had brought her here that were being treated by little Grays who paid no attention to anything around them, only their maintenance work. They entered an elevator with no doors and went down to level 5 of the building. He felt very afraid. The armed guards on that level were less friendly than those above, but they saluted their guide who wore no insignia, just his gray suit.

She was led through a room that smelled of formaldehyde, with many large tanks that had mechanical arms anchored to the floor and inserted into the tanks, producing a strange soft humming sound, all computerized. She tried to look out over the tanks, but her guide took her arm, saying that she didn't need to, as it could complicate things. They entered a large laboratory that caught her attention, since she was related to medical aspects and had never seen the machines and instruments that she saw there. She saw little Grays working backwards, heard the noise of metal against metal, the same as she heard when the doctors went to operate on someone. The noise was from surgical instrumentation.

The guide told him to lie down on a central table in the room and asked him to cooperate, that it would be easier that way. She was very scared and began to cry. She didn't want to be alone with the Grays in the room, so she calmed down. The guide moved away from there when a doctor entered who began to examine her, being one of the Grays who led the situation: Later she was intervened, subjecting her to internal operations. When everything was over, she had to put on her clothes and saw blood in her crotch, as if her period had arrived.

The guide talked with the doctor and then went to her telling her that all this had been necessary and to forget it. She saw more aliens, who were paying no attention to her. She asked her guide to explain that place to her and he only told her that it was a very sensitive area and possibly in a few years it would be taken there again, to which she asked where it was and he replied that for her own safety she shouldn't know. .

Walking towards the small vehicle, he saw people of other races who were in transparent containers standing against the wall, he got closer and saw that they were like strange figures, but he could not understand what he was seeing. He also saw live animals in strange huge boxes. Her abduction lasted around three hours, and she was later returned to her home in the same way. From then on he has dedicated himself to doing research on the Dulce base.

Excerpts from an interview with Christa Tilton:

Q.- Did you see any person who showed signs of being captive inside the building during your abductions?

CT.- Yes, I remember seeing some individuals, as if in suspended animation in large transparent tubes. I went over to some tubes and put my hands on them expecting some kind of response, but apparently I didn't get any; even so he couldn't tell if they were dead or alive or somewhere in between.

Q.- Do you know of any other bases that can be investigated?

CT.- There are many underground bases that have been used for different purposes, such as covert government projects, especially one in Los Alamos and another north of Tucson, Arizona, known by the code name of Evergreen Aviation, which is a the CIA. I have photographs of black helicopters parked there with no markings, also other types of rare craft. Now I am working with two very good researchers from Great Britain, who have written some research papers in this area, they are excellent researchers especially Tymothy Good, whose titles of his papers are "Above Top Secret" and "Alien Liason". They investigate underground bases in America and Great Britain.

Q.- What kind of reptilians, if you saw any, did you find inside?

CT.- I don't think I've seen any reptilians, the ones I saw and are related to my life have been little Greys, whom one, or those who know the subject, call "workers". These are beings that I believe have no soul or individuality, they are just workers for an established race of aliens. They are given certain roles, certain jobs, as if they worked for a big company. However I have seen some very tall, but without that reptilian look, but I know what you are talking about.

Q.- My belief is that the Grays operate with a basic animal instinct of predation in their agendas to increase their power base on Earth and exploit other cultures. That they will continue to do collectively until they are stopped by force, I believe that some of the Grays can be convinced by humans to speak and develop in them an emotional and individual degree, if they can be separated from that collective mind in which they work. What do you think of it?

CT.- I agree with you, to a large extent. Certainly the Grays think and act in a coordinated manner and subject to great energy or mental power working at a collective level, whose vital responsibility is to give orders and direct from a distance, since they act and think together. There is no longer any discussion about this, they do jobs or work on projects or certain things that are entrusted to them by high levels or alien beings with tremendous mental capacity and, perhaps, humans too, although the latter could not really confirm it for you. I have my doubts that humans have the ability to establish any control, natural at least, over some kind of ET here on Earth, and if humans and aliens are working together it is because there is a pact between the government and them. I believe that the aliens have come here for some powerful reason and certain individuals in the government have given orders to work together for a worldwide purpose.

Note: Christa Tilton has compiled hundreds of pages of information, documents and photos related to the base of Dulce and Paul Bennewitz, her investigations have been very thorough, her address to request more information is INTEL/Advocates, C/o Christa Tilton, 2163 South 78th East Avenue, Tulsa, Oklahoma 74129-2421.

PAUL BENNEWITZ

During the mid-1970s, a bizarre wave of cattle mutilations occurred in the United States, particularly concentrated in the New Mexico and Colorado area. It was a shocking, unusual phenomenon, whose characteristics immediately ruled out the intervention of rustlers. The actions, apparently without any sense, shocked the community, while in parallel many reports from civilians and researchers began to appear about strange and unusual lights crossing the sky at extraordinary speeds in very close areas, and even in the same place where mutilations occurred.

The bodies of the cattle presented externally small holes of two inches in diameter near their hindquarters, and sometimes the skin of the jaw area, including lips, had been severed and yet there was not a single drop of blood spilled. When analyzing them internally, the surprise was immense, since all the animals were missing their digestive system, their reproductive organs and their blood had been clearly drained, in addition to other characteristics. And all this very neatly done, with the expertise of a surgeon and with the medical or surgical technology that one would like to have today, and all in less than four hours.

In this context, Paul Bennewitz, physicist, scientific inventor, owner of Thunders Electronics, a small company-laboratory and ufological researcher of the APRO (Aerial Phenomena Research Organization) created by Jim and Coral Lorenzen, arrived in New Mexico worried like most about try to clarify the situation, taking many photographs, analyzing the versions and doing field work. He hooked up with Gabe Valdez, a local police officer, whose interest in cattle mutilations in the northern New Mexico area was evident, and they went on a few "raids" together night and day taking pictures and filming the unusual lights in heaven. He made many trips to New Mexico gathering more and more information to the point that his colleagues, the Lorenzens and others at APRO, had doubts about his objectivity.

Between 1979 and 1980 -the record of the date is not very clear- Bennewitz and an amateur psychologist named Leo Sprinkle, were investigating the story of a woman deeply affected by an abduction. This woman's name was Myrna Hansen, who stated that she and her son had seen a UFO while driving on a rural road near Cimarrón, in northeastern New Mexico. With the patient's permission, Dr. Leo Sprinkle subjected her to hypnotic regression, and after a while Bennewitz and Sprinkle heard a fantastic story from her. Under hypnosis, the patient said that she had not only seen several UFOs that day, but had also watched cattle being abducted by spacecraft. She also said that along with the animals, she and her little son were also abducted and taken to an underground base nearby, where they saw the mutilation process of the cattle, the drainage of their blood, and also metal vats where there were remains of unidentified meat.

They also saw human parts such as the torsos, arms and legs of people, floating in a thick orange liquid, while they heard a hum caused by a mechanical arm that gently stirred the vats. Finally, and after other strange and chilling details, she and her son were laid on a kind of stretcher and an implant "chip" was put in their heads to control their thoughts through these devices. Despite initial shock, being sent off to other tests, and Sprinkle's skepticism, Bennewitz believed Myrna's story for a very simple reason. Bennewitz lived at that time in Albuquerque, New Mexico, in a sector known as Cuatro Cerros, adjacent to the northeast to the military area of the Kirtland Air Force Base, which also serves as storage for nuclear weapons, being at the same time part of the complex of Watermelon laboratories next to a Phillips laboratory, where top-secret experiments and research are carried out for the US government and military.

His house was not more than half a mile from the entire military-scientific complex, therefore he had a privileged view of what was happening at said base, where in fact very strange things happened, which over time became a host of situations to be recorded on tape by Bennewitz. The area had electrified fencing and a concrete entrance to a bunker embedded in the base of the hill could be easily seen. The activity became very noticeable and he and his wife would observe and film the flashes of lights at times at night, recording the electrical activity, the underground noises, the night lights moving at incredible speeds or stopping in mid-flight, even the fall. of a circular ship near there and a lot of things out of order.

With all this background, Paul began to design and build more sophisticated recording devices, and thus directed his antennas to the nearby base with the capacity to record low-frequency waves, electromagnetic transmissions coming from the ships and the base where these were produced. situations. He also flew over the area many times taking infrared photos of the terrain, he began to intercept conversations, voice and video transmissions from the base and when developing the photographs he discovered landing piles of extraterrestrial ships —or perhaps terrestrial at this point—, hangars, entrances to the underground facility, underground connections to other sites, and limousines that came and went without license or from the CIA, NSA, or other such intelligence group. All this parallel to what he was investigating with Myrna Hansen, the mutilations in New Mexico and for some time in his house. All this information gathering Bennewitz called the "Beta Project".

The last straw came when he built a computer program based on a hexadecimal code that could translate the transmissions of the aliens who controlled the base and the ships that were seen outside. By intercepting and studying them, he came to the conclusion that, in addition to the fact that this base had a huge underground construction, connected to others, the intercepted video and tape recordings contained enough information to give him a chilling idea of what was happening there.

The Beta Project

The Beta project, an accumulation of graphic, written, and video information, carried out by Paul Bennewitz, was made with the intention of being delivered to the headquarters of the United States Air Force in order for them to know, based on the antecedents raised there, what was happening in Dulce and take action on the matter to avoid a planetary disaster. More than a report, it is also a detailed operational plan to stop, confront and combat the Grays that were inside and in control of the Dulce base.

According to some slightly more daring versions, but no less credible in view of the background, Project Beta is a proposal for a physical military attack on one of the largest bases or installations of the draconian forces of Orion and Zeta Reticuli, which it is the place where the Grays that were there (Branton) came from. And it is not the only testimony or statement or rumor that in Dulce there was an underground war between the US military forces (Delta Force) and aliens, whose results in light of the testimonies were disastrous for us.

Below are some summarized paragraphs of the information provided by the Bennewitz Beta Project about the intercepted transmissions from the Dulce base in New Mexico. This excerpt is part of a set sent in March 1986 to Clifford Stone, now director of UFO Contact International in Albuquerque, New Mexico. «*Dear Clifford there is a lot in this that has already happened, in these 7 years that I don't know where to start... I think it would probably be good to start with an approximation. The most terrible things are learned immediately and the beautiful things cost us our lives (Silvio Rodríguez) .»*

Once enough material had been compiled and with everything he knew, Paul went directly to the Kirtland Air Base on October 24, 1980, to report that there was an extraterrestrial threat against "El Manzano", the sector where they were located. They stockpiled nuclear weapons. First he contacted Major Ernst. E. Edwards, who referred him to Sergeant Richard C. Doty. Doty and Jerry Miller, a consulting scientist at the US Air Force Test and Evaluation Center at Kirtland AFB, interviewed Bennewitz at his home next door to the Manzano Air Force Base. They examined the films and photographs of Bennewitz and Miller and a Project Blue Book researcher at Wright Patterson AFB determined that the films definitely showed unidentified real objects. They also noticed Paul's electronic surveillance equipment and antenna designs pointed at the Apple Tree. The Bureau of Investigation and Intelligence declined to investigate the fact, but against all logic ordered a close surveillance of Paul Bennewitz, all his personal information, all his biography.

On November 10, 1980, Bennewitz presented his evidence again, this time to high-ranking Air Force chiefs, including Brigadier General William Brooksher. In the report or minutes of this meeting it was noted that Paul was warned to present all his evidence about the phenomenon. Again AFOSI declined to look into the case, but Bennewitz did not give up, and at the same time that he sent reports and whatever information he could to APRO, he contacted Senator Harrison Schmidt and US Senator Peter Dominici. ., a fact that most likely saved his life, as well as other ufologists such as Linda Moulton Hove and John Lear.

In 1982 APRO decided to investigate the Bennewitz case and they sent one of its directors, William More, a school teacher, writer and ufologist to talk with Paul —Moore wrote a book together with Charles Berlitz called "the Philadelphia experiment" and "the case Roswell"–, and Moore would later claim to have been recruited by an agent codenamed Falcon to help drive Bennewitz insane and discredit his investigations. His orders were given by the AFOSI agent Sergeant Richard Doty and for 4 years he was consulted for ways to misinform the rest of the investigators and the people in general about the Bennewitz case including his document "Aquarius", among whose topics he talks about of the existence of two races of aliens within the United States, the beneficial Whites and the nefarious Grays who have made a cooperation treaty with the US government to build underground bases and abduct a certain quota of beings humans in exchange for top-secret technology.

Paul Bennewitz, after his interviews at the airbase gradually became more and more paranoid, claiming to see gray aliens come out of the walls of his home at night, injecting him with chemicals. Likewise, he began to buy and keep firearms and knives throughout the house until he finally had to be hospitalized for "exhaustion." Over time he recovered and today he rejects any attempt to interview, quote, or make a statement about the events. occurred or any topic related to or that makes a simple reference to UFOs.

michael wolf

Dr. Michael Wolf served in the US Air Force as a pilot (Colonel rank), flight surgeon, and counterintelligence officer for the CIA and NSA, has an impressive MD degree in neurology, Ph. D. in theoretical physics, and a D. Sc. in computer science. As you can see, we are not talking about any subject, that is why his statements left many speechless. Unfortunately, Dr. Wolf is dying of cancer - which mysteriously appears to many of the people who face the veil of secrecy. It is not strange, cancer was created as a biological weapon in North American laboratories - and in such a painful situation he has decided to share with us what he knows about extraterrestrial civilizations.

In his book "The catchers of heaven" (1996), he makes incredible revelations based on his reports, as he has been adviser to the president on Homeland Security on extraterrestrial affairs since 1979 and a former member of MJ-12, as well as the Alphacom team. Dr. Wolf says that the most important mission of the Alphacom team is the resumption of negotiations with extraterrestrial visitors. According to him, in the 50's, the US administration entered into deals with the so-called "grey" extraterrestrials from a supposed fourth planet of the Zeta Reticuli star system, as confirmed by the naval intelligence officer Milton William Cooper.

These grays would have shared some of their technology with military and intelligence scientists, on a regular basis. While there were "guests" in underground military facilities in Nevada and New Mexico, the aliens reportedly gave the American government some anti-gravity technology, as well as a large amount of fuel known as Element 115. On May 1, 1975, during one of During these exchanges of technology in Nevada, in the demonstration of a small extraterrestrial antimatter reactor, the person in charge of the "greys" told the colonel of the Delta Force, in charge of the custody of the "guests", to remove all the rifles and ammunition from the room (so they wouldn't accidentally go off during energy emissions), to which the guards refused. In a misunderstanding, also in the midst of the commotion, a cash opened fire on the grays. The result was that a gray ET, two scientists and 41 military personnel died in the act.

One of the surviving guards stated that the aliens apparently used some form of mental energy in self-defense to kill attackers from the Delta group. Wolf comments that this incident ended the exchanges with the gray ETs, which parallels the testimony of Phil Shneider. Continuing with the statements of Dr. Michael Wolf, military and intelligence scientists would have learned extraterrestrial cloning techniques, after perfecting the technique in animals. Thus, Dr. Wolf and his team cloned a human being with artificial intelligence that they called "J-Type Omega", as part of the SENTINEL project, dedicated to creating the perfect soldier who follows orders without fear or doubt, as he argues. Chris Carter in his television series X-Files (Files X), referring to the "Super-soldiers".

The J-Type Omega clone had to be eliminated when it could not comply with the order to kill an innocent dog, since Wolf's team had programmed ethics into its artificial intelligence system. Another of the Alphacom team's purposes is to determine how alien technology can be used to return the planet to its pristine form and its state of natural balance. Aliens are also on the lookout for the proliferation of nuclear devices in many countries. Also the team is on a mission to determine the number and type of aliens on the globe, to learn about the interaction of humans with aliens in the past and present, the type of civilization of the visitors and how we can negotiate with them.

According to Wolf, many "confederations" of extraterrestrials are visiting us in a coordinated manner. They are known as: The Alliance, human-like in appearance and from the Altair Aquila system; The Corporate, the "Greys" of the Zeta Reticuli system; The Federation of Worlds, unspecified races from various systems; The United races of Orion, cultures of that system. The Alliance would be in affiliation with The Corporate and with The Federation of Worlds, The United Races of Orion would be in affiliation with The Corporate and through them with The Alliance and Federation of Worlds. Wolf says that the Vatican was lobbying regarding a possible announcement by Clinton about

UFO visitations, which only left in vain public comments by this former president on the Roswell case.

The objection is that "if it refers to extraterrestrial biological entities, the data would reveal in detail how and for what some religions were created." Wolf adds: "Well-organized religions feel threatened by such an announcement." Perhaps Wolf's most startling revelation is that within the UFO-themed cloak is a shadowy covert organization known as the "Cabal." Wolf describes it as a "well-organized cabal pack supported by the military and led by an Under Secretary of the Navy." The paranoid Cabal work against the goals of peaceful negotiations with the visitors. Apparently, the Cabal uses weaponry designed under Ronald Reagan's Star Wars project to shoot down alien vehicles and thus subjugate the visitors through military might. Wolf concludes by saying: "In all my training as a scientist I never prepared for such visitors, we must understand the complexity of the various forces at work on this planet, and on others as well."

Phillip Schneider

Philip Schneider (April 23, 1947 – January 1996) was a government structural engineer involved in the construction of deep underground military bases in the US. Most of the information regarding Phil Schneider has been quite controversial in nature. and it comes mainly from their own claims. These claims may or may not be true, have not been objectively proven, and have received little attention overall. However, it is clear that Schneider has made such claims, and thus has turned out to be a person of interest within UFO enthusiast circles.

During the last two years of his life, Phil Schneider gave more than 30 lectures to a variety of audiences around the world regarding conspiracy theories, in which he claimed to leak information about secret government covert operations. Schneider said he had a Level 3 security clearance ("Rhyolite 38") and was one of only three people to survive a violent incident that killed 66 people (44 of whom were Americans and the remaining 22 from other countries). This would have occurred in 1979 between the "grey aliens" and the US military at the Dulce Underground Base (New Mexico). Schneider himself showed part of one of his hands practically mutilated, seeing only two fingers, and this because of the firing of an alien weapon in said underground incident.

Schneider was found dead in his Wilsonville, Oregon apartment on January 17, 1996. He had apparently been dead for several days (perhaps even a week) and, according to sources, had a rubber hose attached to his chest. his neck. Regardless of such rumors, Tim Swartz wrote that the " *Clackamas County Coroner's Office attributed Phil Schneider's death to a stroke*." Some believe that Schneider was assassinated, evidently because he had vital information and data to expose him to public opinion. In fact, he claimed to have escaped at least 13 assassination attempts on him during the time he was giving the lectures on conspiracy theories. He suffered from various physical illnesses (osteoporosis, cancer, injuries). Officially, suicide is now listed as the cause of death.

9.

SPACE MISSIONS OR THEATER?

"Problems cannot be solved with the same level of intelligence that created them."
Albert Einstein.

THE FRAUD OF THE CENTURY

In 1879, the Royal British Astronomical Society issued an unusual circular to its members in which it expressed the wish to receive at its headquarters any report from its associates in which a good account of any anomalous observation on the surface of the Moon was given, the response It was not long in coming, since during the 2 years that followed his infrequent request, the offices of the British Royal Astronomical Society were literally flooded by an avalanche of stories in which they were described from the observation of lights that traveled inside from certain craters, to volcanic explosions of a certain magnitude. The large number of reports received - which exceeded 2 million - forced the company to cancel its analysis project and not issue any conclusive opinion on such an elusive matter.

In any case, what really revealed that unanimous reaction of British astronomers is that none of those stories was new or strange in the eyes of those experts. Not in vain in 1787 the prestigious Willian Herschel, discoverer of Uranus, had already spoken of his strange lunar observations, shamelessly denouncing having seen the eruption of three volcanoes on its surface... «I have detected them, Herschel wrote at that time in *different places of the dark part of the new Moon. Two of them are almost extinct or, in any case, in a state of near eruption that may occur in the next lunation. The third shows a current eruption of fire and luminous matter."* Two years after this "confession", another eminent selenographer, the German professor Schroeter, declared that he had seen, without any doubt, *« A brilliant burst of light, which was composed of many small and separated sparks [...] that moved all together in a straight line to the north of the Mare Imbrium and other places on the surface of the Moon."*

Both accounts are irreproachable. Not only because of the recognized scientific solvency of those who announced it, but because they rely on a vast casuistry of detections through light telescopes, domes, bridges and endless visual records of a similar degree of strangeness, for which science there is no convincing explanation. In general lines, this class of enigmatic lights have received, in the astronomical field, the name of Lunar Transient Phenomena (LTPs) -Lunar Transient Phenomena- clearly indicating the elusive and ephemeral nature of such apparitions on the lunar soil.

LTPs are commonly observed on the bright side of the visible face of our satellite and are almost always white lights the size of a star - although there are also records of red, yellowish and bluish lights - whose permanence on the surface varies between a few seconds and a few days. From the 6th century to today, the number of incidents of this type cataloged by private astronomers such as Winfried S. Cameron exceeds 2,000, including frequent sightings of intermittent flashes of light as if someone were trying to send a Morse signal to Earth. On the other hand, one of the last and most complete "official" lists of LTPs, prepared by NASA in July 1968, includes the not inconsiderable number of 579 profusely documented incidents between November 1540 and October 1967.

As the reader will no doubt have guessed, this issue has certain parallels with the familiar UFO mystery since, as in this one, testimonial, photographic and -more recently- filmic evidence show that "something" is flying over the Moon and moving occasionally along very specific areas of it (such as Plato or Aristarchus craters). And as if that were not enough, its activity seems to skyrocket when the planet Mars is closer to Earth.

Yuri gagarin

Gagarin died on March 27, 1968 when the MiG-15 he was flying on a routine flight crashed near Moscow. Let's remember that Gagarin was a Soviet hero for being officially the first man to leave Earth and make a cosmonaut flight in the stratosphere. What few stop to think is that the US would not allow the deep shame that it was a Soviet and not an American who was an international hero leaving Earth. That gives more reasons that the Americans were the real culprits in Gagarin's death and not by chance, less so for a pilot with as many flight hours as he had.

orbiter 2

On November 22, 1968, the Washington Post ran a front-page headline that read: *"Six Shadows of Mysterious Statues Photographed on the Moon by an Orbiting Capsule."* The Post story later picked up by the Los Angeles Time described a Lunar photo taken two days earlier by the US Orbiter 2 space capsule as it passed between 20 and 30 miles (32km and 48.3km) above the Moon's surface. The photograph appears to reveal six whorls arranged in a preconceived geometric pattern within a small portion of the Sea of Tranquility. The marking of the shadow of the Lunar objects indicates that they are all figures of either cones or pyramids. Although the official NASA press did not mention anything unusual about the photograph, other people found the photo remarkably interesting. Dr. William Blair of the Boeing Institute of Biotechnology stated:

« If the conical spirals really were the result of some geographic event it would be natural to see them distributed randomly. As a result, the triangulation would be scaled (three unequal sides) or irregular. Now, the one that concerns the Lunar object leads to a basic system with coordinates x, y, z for the right angle, six isosceles triangles and two axes consisting of three points each. » In Argosy magazine, space engineer Alexander Abromov went further, saying: " *The distribution of these Lunar objects is similar to the plane of the Egyptian pyramids, built by Cheops, Khaphren and Menkaure at Gizeh near Cairo. The center of the whorls of this Lunar "abaka" (arrangement of pyramids) is arranged in precisely the same way as the apices (peaks) of the three great pyramids.*"

Assuming that Drs. Blair and Abromov have not miscalculated, it appears that some of Earth's pyramids may be part of a permanent marking system that extends to more than one planet in our solar system. The system may extend to Mars. Objects such as pyramids have been photographed on the Martian surface. Photos taken by the US Viking mission in 1976 indicate that the Martian region of Sidonia contains pyramidal objects that appear to be enormous carved faces close to the starry sky. It is easy to deduce that the Martian pyramids and their faces are natural formations not unlike some found on Earth; however, one and possibly two more "faces" have been discovered elsewhere on Mars with strikingly similar shapes, such as the "helmet", cut face, and indentation above the right eye. Perhaps equally interesting is the fact that a pyramid at Sidonia has one side pointing to the North, the axis of rotation of Mars. Is this some sort of alignment or is there a connection to the Great Pyramid of Giza, which is also aligned according to precise compass directions?

Sure, it's possible that the objects on the Moon and Mars turned out to be rock formations after all. The available photographs seem inadequate to establish that they are artificial formations. If they are artificial, it can be seen in the photographs that they have suffered a clear degree of erosion. Only a closer look during future missions to the Moon and Mars will settle the controversy. The objects are certainly more rigorously investigated because the Moon has been a host to UFO phenomena for centuries, including around the sides of the Sea of Tranquility.

Orbiter 3 and Zond 3

It is clear that for some reason the aliens that were in that place did not want us to interfere in their affairs, and something similar was happening with the Moon, could this have been the reason that caused the confrontation at the Dulce base that withdrew relations? diplomatic relations with each other for almost 2 years? Lunar constructions are irrefutable and undeniable evidence of extraterrestrial existence. One of the tests stands out from July 1965, when the Russian probe Zond 3 obtained a photograph in which an image can be seen that has all the appearance of being a semi-transparent dome. When observing the photographs taken by the first Lunar probes sent at the beginning of the space race, including the photographs of Lunar Orbiter 3 (1966), there is one in which you can see what may be a kind of construction two kilometers long. highly eroded height, which is called a "shard", next to which is a huge glowing cube floating about seven miles from the lunar surface.

Surveyor 6

In 1967, the Surveyor 6 probe photographed in the lunar region of Sinus Medii a luminous haze on the semicircular surface that NASA was quick to say was due to a storm of sand particles caused by electrostatic charges. But to other observers it has all the appearance of a huge transparent dome-shaped structure. From the extensive catalog of NASA images, there are some of them in which strange formations can be seen.

Gemini Project

On April 8, 1964, those in charge of the control base of the Gemini capsule were stunned to see how 4 UFOs approached the Gemini at a speed of 40,000 km/h, the objects surrounded the capsule for an hour and 15 minutes. One of the radar operators commented: "It looked like it was being escorted. Two of those objects were placed on top of the capsule, one was placed below and the fourth was placed in front of it." Then the UFOs moved away with the same speed with which they appeared.

On June 4, 1965, the Gemini I capsule circled Earth with astronauts Edward White and James McDivitt on board. It was this one who observed a strange ovoid object, with a kind of arms, while they were flying over Hawaii. McDivitt, immediately began filming it. When the news spread, the Air Force quickly informed the press that it was simply the Pegasus II satellite, which according to official sources was only 15km from the Geminis orbit. Something totally false, the Pegasus II was really 2,000 km from the capsule. A NASA representative stated: "*After a study of the film taken by McDivitt from the capsule, nothing resembling a satellite has been found.*"

The Gemini 4

During 1965, the US Federal Bureau of Investigation (FBI) learned from a confidential source that a NASA informant was covertly "leaking" information about UFOs. The recipients were two people from Pittsburgh who, according to the FBI, had a personal interest in the UFOs. UFOs and they agreed with a NASA employee. In an FBI file, dated September 2, 1965, it is stated: "*The source believes that the information may be classified. For example, the source said that [redacted] had seen footage of a missile separating from a UFO appearing on the screen. Before the Gemini*

IV flight, [redacted] said he saw something interesting, because the spacecraft had UFO detection devices on board...»

The FBI documentation on this case highlights two important points: the reference to a film showing a UFO in flight confirms that NASA is in possession of data on UFOs that it hides from the public. Second, the mention of the Gemini IV mission. One of its pilots, James McDivitt, confirmed that, during the mission, he safely saw a form of unidentified object.

Although McDivitt does not believe the object was anomalous, he does not subscribe to skeptic James Oberg's theory that the object was simply the second stage of the Titan rocket that launched Gemini IV. As the researcher states in his 1996 book, Beyond Top Secret, "*If this was the case, the only puzzle that remains is McDivitt's apparent failure to recognize his own rocket.*"

Astronaut James Mcdivitt stated: "*My UFO sighting was way back in 1965 during the Gemini IV space mission. I was looking out the window when I saw a cylindrical object to which a tube or antenna was attached. The photo that was developed unfortunately did not correspond at all to the object that he had seen. It looked more like spots of light.*"

Gemini 7

In December 1965, astronauts Frank Borman and James Lowell, aboard the Gemini VII capsule, experienced a strange vision, for which they communicated to Houston:

Borman: « *Boys, we have a scarecrow over our heads, a little to the left. Please look again ...*"

Houston: "*Isn't that one of the stages of the Titan booster rocket you're looking at?*" »

Borman: « *Negative, this is an unidentified flying object. It is not a booster rocket... We know very well where the Titan is ...*"

Gemini 10

On July 19, 1966, astronauts John Young and Michael Collins aboard the Gemini X capsule broke the altitude record at that time, with 761km. Elated by the feat accomplished, they were stunned to find that they had company: two red lights in space ahead of them, moving at the same speed and in the same direction as the Gemini. The following communication occurred:

Young: «*We have two bright objects in our orbital path. I don't think they are stars. They are going at the same speed as us."*

Base: «*To which side are they? If you can give us an orientation maybe we can follow them.*»

As Young began to describe what he was seeing, the communication system was suspiciously muted for over a minute. When he was heard again, Young, seemed to have received instructions, it was then that he "assumed" that he had been seeing some satellite. This is what I communicated: «*They just disappeared...! I suppose they would be some kind of satellites.*» Later, it was officially said that the objects would have been pieces of the Saturn rocket that exploded days before. But since official explanations always turn out to be unfounded, this would be no exception. If they really were rocket pieces, why did these pieces decide to accompany Gemini X at the same speed? And if it were true that their orbits coincided with that of the space capsule, how is it possible that they abandon their journey and vanish so suddenly?

Gemini 11 and 12

In September 1966, an elongated UFO was photographed from the Gemini XI following the capsule as it flew over Madagascar. NASA affirmed that it was the Soviet rocket "Proton"... one more official lie to the long list, later it would be confirmed that the Proton was 550km away.

There is an impressive photograph that was taken during the Gemini 12 space mission on November 12, 1966. Analysis has shown that the UFO that appears in the upper right corner is a distant object, but NASA claims that it was actually it deals with waste that had been thrown from the Gemini capsule itself. During the Gemini 12 flight in 1966, with Edwin E. Aldrin, James A. Lovell declares that he has seen: «*Four objects in a line. I knew it wasn't about stars.*"

In November 1966, during the Gemini XII mission, astronaut James Novell managed to photograph an elongated moving object, perhaps a mother ship, which made an appearance while the astronaut was in full extra-vehicular activity. Here again the official version was given that it was space junk.

Gordon Cooper

In 1985, astronaut Gordon Cooper, one of the first to orbit the Moon, appeared before a panel of UN advisers chaired by then-Secretary General Kurt Waldheim, and issued an alarming warning: "I think [those] alien spacecraft *and their crews [who] visit Earth from other planets are obviously more technologically advanced than we are. I think we need a very high-level coordinated program to scientifically collect and analyze planet-wide data on various types of encounters in order to determine the best way to act friendly to our visitors. First it would be necessary to show them that we have learned to solve our problems peacefully and not by war, before being accepted as a full member of the universal team.»*

«Such an admission would offer our world fantastic possibilities for progress in all areas. So it would seem true that the United Nations has a vested right to deal with this issue in an appropriate and expeditious manner. For years, I have lived with a secret, the secret imposed on all specialists and astronauts. I can now reveal that every day in the United States our radar detects objects of unknown shape and nature. There are thousands of witness reports and many documents that prove it, but no one wants to publish them. Because? Because the authorities are afraid that people will imagine some kind

of horrible invaders. So the watchword remains: We must avoid panic at all costs."

Cooper's arguments for this statement were that he had been on the periphery of the large regions through which "they" move. He further said: "*In 1951, for two days I had the opportunity to observe many objects of different sizes flying in formation...at a height much higher than we could reach."*

Major Gordon Cooper formally denied seeing a UFO during space flight, however he did see UFOs in the 1950s while he was a fighter pilot in Germany. Gordon Cooper said: "*For several days in a row we watched metallic saucer-shaped vehicles at very high altitudes above the airbase and tried to get close to them, but they were able to change directions much faster than our fighter-bombers. I truly believe that UFOs exist and that the true unexplained cases emanate from another technologically advanced civilization. Given my aeronautical and space experience, I think I have a pretty good idea of what everyone on this planet thinks about the capabilities of their results, and I am convinced that at least some of these UFOs do not come from Earth."* (Omni, vol. 2, no. b, March 1980)

In another interview he stated: "*As far as I understand, there were many, many examples of unexplained UFO sightings in the world to eliminate the possibility of extraterrestrial life."* In May 1963, in orbital flight over Australia, astronaut Gordon Cooper was suddenly followed by a mysterious light, the strange object also being seen from the ground by several people. Gordon Cooper then declared: "*... I am convinced that they were of extraterrestrial origin."* On that same flight, communication between astronaut Gordon Cooper, aboard the Faith 7 spacecraft, and the control center in Houston was interrupted by mysterious interference from a strange, unintelligible voice. This intrusion was recorded in an exclusive transmission band for astronauts.

The X-15

Since NASA's creation in 1958, several of its pilots and astronauts have testified that they had seen flying devices of unknown origin. The first to announce a sighting was Joseph Walker, pilot of the X-15 test plane. According to a talk given in May 1962, in the preceding months Walker had an aerial encounter with two disc-shaped objects, which he filmed. In July of the same year, another X-15 pilot, Major Robert White, reported having found himself part of a UFO squadron while flying at an altitude of about 9,800 m.

NASA refused to support its pilots, and the photographs and films containing anomalies were never published. The official line was that the UFOs had been identified as ice. But, although NASA denied any interest in UFOs, this was soon shown to be false.

Project Mercury 7

Scott Carpenter, who participated in the Mercury program, stated: «*At no time during their stay in space were the astronauts alone: they were constantly watched by UFOs.*» Mercury program astronaut Donald "Deke" Slayton recounted in his book the encounter he had with a UFO during a test flight in 1951. Also recounted during an interview with the "National Enquirer" on October 23, 1979: «*I was conducting a test flight in a P-15 fighter-bomber in Minneapolis when I saw this object. I was at about 10,000 feet on that beautiful sunny afternoon. At first I thought it was a kite, then I realized that no kite could fly that high. As I got closer, it looked like a weather balloon, gray and with a diameter of approximately 1 meter. But as soon as I got behind that imposing thing, it didn't look like a balloon anymore. It resembled a saucer, a disk. At the same moment, I realized that he was suddenly moving away from me - and I was flying at more than 500 km/h. I chased it for a few moments and suddenly the damn thing just "took off". It went up at an angle of 45° turning and accelerating and disappeared. Two days later, I was having a beer with my commander, and I thought, "Of course, I'd have to talk to him." I did so and he replied that I had to report to the information service to report it. I did it and I have not heard anything since.»*

On May 24, 1962, astronaut Scott Carpenter manages to photograph a disc-shaped object while in space aboard the Aurora VII. Scout Carpenter, while orbiting the Earth at the height of Australia, communicated to the base: «*I am observing some luminous particles that are coming towards me. They are very fast! And they seem to have a brighter light than the stars... so they exist!... they are!... NASA gave an absurd explanation to the photographs, saying that they were "ice crystals attached to the windows. "*

When Carpenter was at an altitude of 275,000m, he saw "something" approaching the capsule, he immediately told Houston: «*It's metallic! and intensely reflects sunlight.*» The object continued moving in the opposite direction to the movement of Aurora 7, until it was out of sight. On his third return to Earth, Carpenter saw another object and told Houston: " *It is clear that this does not orbit the Earth... it comes from somewhere else."* Carpenter acknowledged having felt fear, he also said: " *It was cylindrical, huge... and it moved at great speed."* The object froze next to Aurora 7 and followed its same trajectory. Then 3 disc-shaped objects came out of that cylinder, which moved away. The instant the nurse disappeared towards the stars.

Russia landed on the moon first

In 1969, the Russian scientist Lev Mohilin escapes with his son from his country through Turkey and takes refuge in France. Now free from the danger of the KGB, he declares to the surprised press in Paris that on June 5, 1968, Russia had launched from a base in the Urals, the Marx I ship manned by astronauts Ilya and Eugini, who were heading to the dark side. of the moon. Having already landed on the moon, both discovered in the vicinity, artificial buildings. Eugini suddenly screamed in fright; when Ilya tries to pick it up, it was already dead. Being totally horrified, he receives the final order from the base to leave the Moon. Ilya, already on Earth, declares that a mechanical artifact was what killed his partner. After being thoroughly interrogated by the Russian authorities, Ilya was transferred to a sanatorium and officially declared "mentally ill", prey to recurring hallucinations.

Although many European stations intercepted the communications of the Marx I, this mission *"never existed"* for the Russians. Some names of astronauts who would have lost their lives in secret missions to the Moon, this was not disclosed by the government of the then USSR, they are: Terentity Shiborin, in 1959; Piort Dolgev, in 1960; Wassilievch Zavadovsky in 1961; Kennedy Mikhailov and Alexy Belokonev who saw an unidentified object in space in 1961.

apollo 8

According to some researchers, in 1962 NASA decided to create the code "Santa Claus" to refer to anomalous objects that its astronauts could see while in space. Thus, Walter Schirra, aboard the Sigma VII, was the first to use the code when a UFO approached his capsule. On Christmas Day 1968, Apollo VIII's communications were suddenly interrupted in an inexplicable way for 6 minutes. James Lowell exclaimed from the command module when he was behind the Moon the following: *"Please, they are *informed that Santa Claus is there."* As he spoke these words, Lowell's heart rate had risen to 120 per minute! Santa Claus may not have been a special code, but it was a way, in the middle of Christmas, to ironically refer to something they already knew about: the objects that pass everywhere between shuttles and space stations.

APOLLO 10

One of the most significant documents is the photograph 4822 of the Apollo 10 mission, the flight that preceded the arrival of man on the Moon. Despite the fact that Eugene Cernan and Thomas Stafford did not descend on our satellite, they flew over it in the Lunar module, and when they were just 24km from the surface they took that image, in which, by observing carefully, you can find a series of details that they do not fit with what is known about the Moon. In it you can see a series of rectilinear stone alignments or forming a square and above all, what seem like two strange reflections of something that is several kilometers high. With this and other evidence in hand, ufologists won't be satisfied until the space agency officially admits that its astronauts have had encounters. But NASA has been dead silent on this issue for thirty years, so an announcement like that probably won't be coming any time soon.

apollo 11

After the Gemini missions, the space race accelerated with the Apollo program. Following President Kennedy's promise to put a man on the Moon, interest grew in the mysteries of space and, in particular, in man's new frontier: the Moon. Thus, when the Apollo 11 astronauts took their first steps on the surface of the Moon on July 20, 1969, even the most recalcitrant of skeptics had to consider the possibility that the presence of life outside Earth was already a reality.

In July 1969, during the voyage of the Apollo XI spacecraft, with Aldrin, Collins and Armstrong on board, a solid cylindrical object made its appearance and accompanied the astronauts during part of their journey. The UFO was detected by the ground control base. During the Apollo XI mission, NASA received dozens of phone calls from amateur astronomers reporting that they were seeing a strange light phenomenon in the vicinity of the Aristarchus crater. Informed Neil Armstrong, he looked out the window of the Eagle module and said: "*Near the crater there is a considerably illuminated area. It seems to have some fluorescence.*" What could cause such an immense glow in the Aristarchus crater that it could even be seen from Earth? Surely what emitted the luminosity had to be something artificial and of non-terrestrial manufacture.

During the Apollo XI mission, NASA caused a 2-minute delay in the communication that occurred between the Lunar module and the control center in Houston, before transmitting the signal to television stations. These minutes gave NASA enough time to censor the original message received and broadcast only what they considered fit to be released to the entire world. Fortunately, many radio amateurs picked up the wave with which communications were transmitted between the base and Apollo, confirming what the astronauts really saw on our natural satellite: "someone" was there before them. The astronauts upon their return to Earth were informed that everything they had seen was classified as top secret and they were forced to lie to the press.

Vladimir Azhazha's doctor, who worked for NASA, stated: « *Neil Armstrong reported that two large and mysterious objects were watching them after he had jumped to the surface of the satellite, near the Lunar module. But this message was never made public. NASA censored it."* The transmission that, according to Otto Binder (ex-NASA employee), some radio amateurs picked up with their own VHF equipment, the day Apollo XI landed on the Moon:

Houston: What the hell, what is it? It is all I want to know!

Apollo XI: These little things are gigantic, they are huge... No, no, what happened now was an optical disfigurement of the terrain. Oh, God, no one is going to believe it!

Houston: What... what... what the hell is going on there? What's up guys?

Apollo XI: They are there, under the surface.

Houston: What's there? (interference occurs) Control calling Apollo XI.

Apollo XI: Roger (heard), the three of us are here, but we saw some visitors. They were here for a while, looking at the instruments.

Houston: Control Order: repeat last report!

Apollo XI: I say there were other spaceships. They are aligned on the other edge of the crater.

Houston: Repeat, repeat!

Apollo XI: Let us probe this orbit and home... On 625 to 5... Auto relay engaged... My hands are shaking so hard I can't do anything. To film? Heavens yes, those damn cameras have filmed.

Houston: Have you caught anything?

Apollo XI: I didn't have any film on hand, three shots from the saucers or whatever may have messed up the film.

Houston: Command Control; here, command control. Are you already on the way? What about that UFO commotion? Change.

Apollo XI: Yes, the mirrors are in place. But whoever made such spaceships can surely come and pull them out of the ground tomorrow. Over and out.

This communication was transmitted over a radio link and was "hacked by amateur radio", denied by NASA, of course:

Astronaut: *"What's that?"*

Houston: "*Don't worry, continue with your mission.*"

Astronaut: "*Guys! It's fantastic, you can't imagine it!*"

Houston: "*Roger, we know. Go to the other side, go back to the other side!*"

Astronaut: "*My God! What can it be? Now! there's light over there!*"

Houston: "*Hard communications!*"

In 1969, during the Apollo XI mission, a photograph was taken where the Lunar excursion module can be seen and on the background a ball of light that could not be identified by NASA engineers. But NASA, forced to give an explanation, however ridiculous and far-fetched it may be, I attribute the phenomenon to an error in the film. There are strong rumors that Neil Armstrong saw a tall and thin being near a UFO on the Lunar surface. Despite claims that the astronauts had seen nothing unusual, rumors circulated that the crew were never alone during their time on the Moon.

However, the evidence for this encounter on the Moon is very weak. Otto Binder, a former NASA employee, said this conversation was overheard by radio amateurs who can pick up a "reserved channel" for these messages. However, Neil Armstrong, the first man to set foot on the Moon, informed researcher Timothy Good that no object was recorded, found, or seen during the Apollo 11 mission, or on any other non-natural Apollo flight. The only corroboration of this story was obtained from Maurice Chatelain, a communications expert at NASA. In an interview carried out in 1979, Chatelian confirmed that a time delay in the transmission of the dialogue between the control center and Apollo 11 allowed NASA to censor the information regarding the visitors.

Ergo, there is no way to verify if this incident occurred on the Apollo XI mission. Many researchers doubt Binder's and

Chatelian's claims, and NASA denies that it censored broadcasts. However, a similar case concerning Discovery not only led to the cosmic Watergate in 1990, but also turned the statements of alien encounters by astronauts upside down. Neil Armstrong, reputedly the first man to walk on the Moon, informed researcher Timothy Good that no object was recorded, found, or seen during the Apollo XI mission, or on any other unnatural Apollo flight.

Only Maurice Chatelain (NASA communications expert) confirmed that a time delay in the transmission of the dialogue between the control center and Apollo XI allowed NASA to censor the information regarding the visitors. Also a certain professor, who wishes to remain anonymous, had a conversation with Neil Armstrong during a symposium:

- Professor: What really happened with Apollo XI?

- Armstrong: It was amazing; sure, but the fact is that they warned us that we had to leave. We were never told anything about a Lunar station...

- Teacher: What do you mean by "they warned us that we had to leave?".

Armstrong: I can't go into details, except to say that their ships were vastly superior to ours in size and technology. Armstrong confirmed this story but declined to go into details, admitting that the CIA was behind it by keeping the matter secret.

- Professor: But NASA sent other missions after Apollo XI!

Armstrong: Naturally, NASA was compromised at the time and couldn't risk a panic on Earth, but yeah, it was quick and back and forth.

The Apollo XI astronauts were ordered to change locations and land in another area, then return to Earth. This would not be a problem because Truman already had problems that could arise and ordered a whole "stage" (stage) to be set up by the director of the film "2001, A Space Odyssey." There was everything necessary for such assembly: cameras, spotlights, technical equipment and actors. In this fictitious scenario, they simulated an arrival on the Moon and recorded the whole deplorable spectacle that is seen in the supposed recording of Neil Armstrong stepping on the Moon and placing the American flag. Actually, Armstrong himself lasted a few minutes on Lunar soil and assured Houston that he would take off his helmet and breathe freely, shortly before having to return to the ship and take off for Earth.

A spectacular photograph was taken by Armstrong on the Apollo mission, in it, a strange light passes over the Lunar surface. During this mission, several similar photographs were taken.

apollo 12

During the flight of Apollo XII, strange events also occurred. On November 15, 1969, the crew reported to Houston:

Apollo XII: Since yesterday another flying object has been with us, we can see it through our windows when the angle of the ship is 35 degrees. What can be?

Hours later the following dialogue took place:

Apollo XII: OK, what can it be?

Houston: OK back to our drawing board.

Apollo XII: The object is very bright and rolls, without a doubt. Its rotation is 1.5 revolutions per second or, at least, it emits signals in that interval. Dick will tell you which star you are headed for.

Houston: As we look at these things from below, the SLA liner boards didn't get enough Delta V when separating. The SLA liners should be within 300 meters of you.

Apollo XII: One of the objects, whatever it is just came out of its orbit and is moving away from us at high speed... It could be, but my God, just as we turned around I saw one of those "tablets" at high altitude leave our proximity. I think that "board" moved away very quickly, more than a foot per second.

Houston: Since we have no idea how they disappeared or what their orbit might be like, it's awfully hard to say what the hell it was.

Apollo XII: OK Let's assume it was peaceful, as it seemed...

In November 1969, during the Apollo XII mission, in which astronauts Richard Gordon, Charles Conrad and Alan Bean participated, the following communication was recorded: «Houston, we are *seeing an object that remains rotating in the same place. Since yesterday it has been following us all the time ..."* Radio conference between Houston and astronaut Pete Conrad during the Apollo XII mission in 1969:

« There is an object behind us, it rotates on itself... it is always at the same distance, it seems that it is following us.»

Houston: Roger, Pete, this object you've seen near the window, we think it might be one of the license plates.

Conrad: It could be that, but when we turned around, I saw one of those objects jump at a very high speed.

apollo 13

During the Apollo XIII mission, a photograph is taken where the shape and luminosity of a ship in the shape of a cigar or cigar can be clearly seen, you can even notice what appear to be its windows. This photograph is from the NASA archives. What the Apollo VIII crew actually saw was a disc-shaped UFO that was circumnavigating the Moon. Lowell would later say: "We were told that Santa Claus did not exist." This would show that NASA does not reveal the truth about the UFO presence even to its astronauts, exposing them to suffer strong shocks while in space, and thus putting their lives at risk. It should also be mentioned that at a certain point in this mission, the communication systems detected unknown voices that spoke in a strange language.

apollo 14

A photograph of this flight has been known, taken by the crew of Apollo XIV, it constitutes one of the best proofs of the close presence of UFOs to the astronauts sent into space, in this one you can see even the details of the object in the form of disk that was moving near the Lansberg crater, on the Lunar surface. In another image you can see that one of the rocks found on the Moon has the whimsical shape of a human face. Is it a coincidence? Astronaut Edgar D. Mitchell, who, among others, piloted the Lunar Module of Apollo XIV, declared in 1971: « *We all know that UFOs are real. The question is: where do they come from?* »

On the other hand, he stated that he believed that military devices used technology derived from a captured and dismantled alien spacecraft. This supposed secret was kept for decades under the rule of a parallel government independent of the president and the highest authorities of the Pentagon. During a public lecture, he declared: « *When I was on the Moon, 26 years ago, believing that we were the biological center of the universe was part of popular, religious and philosophical wisdom. Few, if any, educated and cultivated people remain, still accept such a theory [...] I am convinced that there are other forms of life in the universe. The question is to know what is its degree of development, how many thousands of years ahead of us. Based on what I know today, what I have seen and experienced, I think the tests are safe and many of them are classified top secret by the government.*"

Then, on December 4, 1991, during a conference organized by the Institute of Noetic Sciences, in New York: "*In the last two or three years I have changed my opinion - in the last two years to be more precise - to suggest that we now have enough evidence, that we really need a serious and open debate and a declassification of the information, which, there is no doubt, the government and other governments possess, and that this forms part of our official knowledge... Now, Whether true or not, that warrants serious investigation. There's too much smoke for there to be no fire...If that's real, let's deal with it openly; Let's break the bolts that that bureaucracy has imposed on the whole thing. There is enough evidence that clearly demonstrates that this information is hidden. How far could we go with all that? I don't know.»*

Edgar Mitchell has also assured that extraterrestrial beings visited planet Earth during the last 60 years, as he pointed out in an interview on Radio Kerrang on July 23, 2008. He is currently 77 years old and assures that NASA hides information and that he is aware of it. many UFO visits to our planet but they have been covert, but that some have been leaking and have been known. He is the author of the books Psychic Exploration: a challenge for Science, The Way of the Explorer Putnam 1996 and El Camino del Explorador. He also usually gives lectures at different universities around the world.

Apollo 15, 16 and 17

A strange luminous object is seen by the crew of Apollo XV on the Moon. In another photograph of Apollo XVI, you can see another kind of tower, which thanks to the shadow you can see that it has a considerable height. There is also a spectacular photograph taken from Apollo XVI of a disc-shaped UFO moving on the Lunar surface.

Eugene Cernan, commander of Apollo XVII, who was also part of the crew of Apollo X, declared in the "Los Angeles Times" of January 1973: «I am one *of those who have never seen a UFO. When questioned, I have publicly said that I thought they came from another world, from another civilization.* » Words collected by Chriss, Nicolas, "Cernan Says Other Earths Exist ". « *I have been asked many times about UFOs and I have said in public that I think they are someone else, from another civilization .*»

John Glenn

Senator Colonel John Glenn, the first American astronaut declared: " *Certain reports about UFOs are justified."* And several years later during a televised show on the American network BC, on Tuesday, March 6, 2001: « *In those glorious days, I was uncomfortable when we were asked to declare things we didn't want and deny others. Some asked us, you know, were you alone up there? We have never answered the truth, and yet we have seen things there, strange things, but we know what we have seen up there. And we couldn't really say anything. Our superiors were very afraid of this, they were afraid of something similar to the war of the worlds, and of the general panic in the streets. Therefore, we had to shut up. And now we only see these things in our nightmares or perhaps in movies, and some of them are very close to the truth.*"

"*We'll never know the real answer,*" said former astronaut and United States Senator John Glenn on a sitcom: " *Still, we saw things out there, strange things ...*" The large audience for a show that occupies the Prime time on American television was able to see Glenn in a fictitious situation in which he bared his soul before the microphones of a radio program without knowing that it was being recorded: "We know perfectly well what we *saw out there, but we can't tell anything.*" Glenn referred to another well-known radio broadcast, the 1938 dramatization of HG Wells' novel "The War of the Worlds," which caused a veritable panic attack in the United States when thousands of listeners actually believed that the Earth was under alien attack. Public reaction to the magnificent Orson Welles Mercury Theater broadcast is all too often cited as the reason why the alien presence on our planet cannot be publicly disclosed. Depending on the statistics cited at any given time, 50% or more of the American public believes in the possibility of UFOs or extraterrestrial intelligence acting on our planet.

The positions of former astronauts on UFOs could not be more contradictory. While some defend that there is an official cover-up by the agency, others refrain from declaring about it or believe that it is mere paranoia: « *During the decade that I served in the NASA astronaut corps, neither Neither I nor any of my companions were indoctrinated as to what we would have to do or say in the event of a UFO sighting during a mission,"* Gordon Cooper wrote in his autobiography, entitled "Leap of Faith."

The Soyuz and Salyut

The cosmonaut, Russian pilot of the Soyouz-5, Yevgeni Khrunov declared in the magazine "Spoutnik" of December 1980: *«Is the presence of extraterrestrial civilizations conceivable? Of course! While the uniqueness of the Earth has not been proven, such a hypothesis must be considered as completely acceptable. As for UFOs, their presence cannot be denied. Thousands of people have seen them. Perhaps it could be due to optical effects, but some of its features, for example its ability to change direction by 90° at high speed, are simply beyond our imagination."*

The Russian cosmonaut, Georgiy M. Grechko, who participated in several Soyuz and Salyut missions, declared: *"If I were free to tell what I saw in space, the world would be shocked."* For their part, cosmonauts Vladimir Kovalyonok and Alexander Ivanchenkov recount that they saw a UFO during their Soyouz 29 mission in June 1978: *« The object moves at 20-30 degrees, passes under our ship. It looks like a ball, it gets bigger and bigger. It's dark orange, it's getting too close to us."*

In 1993, in his village of Kosnikov, near Moscow, Aviation Major General Vladimir Kovalyonok declared, during a video interview with Giorgio Bongiovanni: *«On May 5, 1981 we were in orbit on the Salyut-6 space station. I saw an object that did not resemble any cosmic thing with which I could familiarize her. It was a round object similar to a melon, round and a bit elongated. In front of this object was something resembling a rotating flattened cone. I can draw it, and it is difficult to describe. The object resembled a barbell. I saw it become transparent and as if it had a "body" inside. Towards the other side I saw something as if discharging gas, like a reactive object. Then something happened, which is hard for me to describe from a physics point of view. Last year in the magazine "Nature" I read about a physicist... we tried together to explain this phenomenon and decided that it was a "form of plasma". I had to admit that this did not have an artificial origin. It was not artificial because an artificial object could not have this shape. I don't know of anything that can do this movement... shrinking, then extending, pulsing. Then as I watched, something happened, two explosions. An explosion, and then 0.5 seconds later, the second part went off. I called my colleague Viktor Savinykh, but he did not arrive in time to see anything.»*

What are the particles? First conclusion: the object moved in a suborbital trajectory, otherwise I would not have been able to see it. There were two clouds, like smoke, that made a curious formation. It came close to me and I could see it. So we went into a curtain (cloudiness) for two or three minutes after that. When we came out of the curtain we no longer saw anything. But for some time we and the ship were moving together.

General Pavel Popovich

During the MUFON International Symposium in 1992, Russian Major General Pavel Popovitch, one of the first cosmonauts, "Hero of the Soviet Union" - invited as president of the CIS Unified Ufological Association - gave a lecture on the topic: "Ufology in the Commonwealth of Independent States: Organization Problems". He said: " *Today it can be stated with a high level of confidence that UFO manifestations are no longer confined to the modern picture of the world, or to mere refutations of the orthodox paradigm of natural science. The historical evidence of the phenomenon, of the uniqueness of its kinematic, energetic, and psychophysical characteristics once again allow us to presume that since then humanity has been coexisting with this extraordinary substance, which has manifested itself at a high level of intelligence and consciousness. technology. UFO sightings have become the constant component of human activity and require serious global study. In order to realize the position of man with respect to the Earth and in the universe, ufology, the scientific study of the UFO phenomenon, must occur in the midst of other sciences that deal with man and the world ..."*

« The influence that UFOs have on people, as well as the effects it produces, should become the elements of a special investigation. The interaction between UFOs with the environment, the behavior it motivates, and its genesis also present interesting areas for concentrated study. Today, many specialists are of the opinion that the investigation of the UFO phenomenon should be taken together with the comprehension and understanding of other unexplained phenomena... The development of new approaches for the identification and study of energy and information processes will allow an enthusiastic move towards understanding the phenomenon. The results of these studies should help the survival of people on Earth..."

« It is necessary to carry out the popular ufological clarification, since there is a probability of a personal meeting with the UFO crew members, and this person must be ready for this event. Preventive measures are especially important. It is necessary to tell the truth, which has been previously distorted by the sciences dedicated to politics and which has recently been exposed by ufologists. The main purpose of the primary local groups, that of controlling the UFO situation, must be forgotten. Ufologists should know all the UFO landing sites and contact in their regions. They must relate to local authorities, and particularly, with the police, civil defense forces, as well as informational, scientific, and medical organizations."

The Discovery

In November 1984, during the sts-51 mission of the space shuttle Discovery, which would consist of dismantling the Westar VI satellite that was in poor condition, there was an encounter with an unidentified flying object. During the approach process, from the shuttle to the satellite, the filming camera was able to capture a strange sphere with a metallic appearance, which seemed to come from the heights. The artificial object would perform surprising evolutions until it disappeared to the right of the satellite after a few seconds.

At around 6:30 a.m. on March 14, 1990, Donald Ratsh, a radio amateur from Baltimore, Maryland, was following transmissions from Shuttle Discovery when he heard the following communication: "Houston, this is Discovery, we have a problem. We have a fire." Shortly after, Ratsh says, an additional transmission was heard: Houston, this is Discovery. We still have the spacecraft under observation. This revelation encouraged many people, including Bob Oeschler, a former NASA mission specialist, to do their own research. After an intense period of investigation. Oeschler concluded that the message was not transmitted from the shuttle. Instead, he ventured that the signal may have come from an area around Fort Meade, Maryland, the headquarters of the US National Security Agency, which has long been involved in investigating UFO reports. Oeschler could only conclude that the broadcast was an institutionally orchestrated fraud for some subtle intelligence purpose.

However, a NASA source informed Oeschler that, at the same time, the shuttle was involved in a UFO incident. Oeschler reports that the encounter lasted eight hours and caused problems with Discovery's electrical systems. Needless to say, the questions have not been answered and the case is still under investigation. It also seems that ufologists will not be satisfied until NASA officially admits that its astronauts have had encounters. But the space agency has been dead silent on the subject of UFOs for thirty years, so an announcement like that probably won't be coming anytime soon.

In 1991, the SPS 48 Discovery spacecraft filmed a UFO that was coming in a certain direction and then abruptly changed its path making a 90° turn, immediately noticeable as lightning appearing near where the UFO disappeared. The official explanation was that it had been nothing more than space junk and the lightning had been produced by elements that the shuttle ejected towards its surroundings.

On April 14, 1992, cameras aboard the space shuttle Discovery capture a sequence during the sts-48 mission with 70 orbits to Earth, in which it is observed how Discovery was followed by strange lights.

the atlantis

It is very likely that it is an invisible UFO (those that are captured only by technological devices and not by the human eye) filmed from the Atlantis shuttle in 1989. In September 1989, a radio amateur captured the communication signal between one of the astronauts of the Atlantis shuttle with the control base, startled, one of the cosmonauts mentions the presence of a UFO that they had near their ship.

In April 1991, during the sts-37 mission of the Atlantis space taxi, a spherical and metallic-looking UFO made an appearance, which was seen and filmed by the astronauts. The object appeared at the top of the scene, and made oscillating movements that defied all physical laws.

On September 10, 2000, during the sts-106 mission of the space shuttle Atlantis, a photograph was taken showing a strange unidentified flying object with a cylindrical or cigar shape, which made an appearance in full activity of the astronauts.

the columbia

In October 1993, two luminous spheres of different sizes, which appear and intersect making strange movements, are photographed and filmed from the space shuttle Columbia.

In another shot, the astronaut in charge of the camera is taking a panoramic view of the Earth, when he notices the presence of a strange organic-looking object, which looks like a kind of worm, which floats in the upper Earth's atmosphere, the cameraman begins to follow the strange object, which makes sudden back-and-forth movements and rotates on an apparent luminous central filament. It should be noted that these organic objects have been seen and filmed many times from the ground, flying over different areas of the planet.

Orbits later, through filming, the astronauts witnessed a spectacular episode: Some objects were moving in a strange way through the Earth's atmosphere, suddenly in the lower left part of the screen, another object appears that rises slowly and in rhythmic form. Other objects start moving at the same instant in different parts of the scene. The most spectacular part is when another object suddenly appears almost in the center of the screen, the UFO begins to ascend diagonally towards the left of the image, until a flash seems to drastically change the trajectory of all the objects that appear in the images, another object begins to follow the first UFO, unleashing an attack.

It is impossible that they were airplanes since the objects do not seem to have the shape of these, besides that they were in the upper zone of the Earth's atmosphere, where airplanes cannot reach. The space junk explanation is downright ridiculous. Could space junk get together to "play war" by making smart moves? NASA, using its international prestige, comes to tell us "anything" as an official scientific explanation, and the most unfortunate thing is that most end up believing their stories.

In 1996, from the space shuttle Columbia, a film was made showing a group of luminous objects circling the Earth over Asia, making a series of trajectories very different from those of space debris or terrestrial satellites. For a change, the UFOs made perfectly defined triangles, that is, they were in formation.

the sputnik

An object appeared in front of Sputnik II and was describing its same orbit, Moscow immediately suspended information about the satellite. The day after the launch of Sputnik IV, a flashing light appeared following it, then Sputnik radioed a human voice with a strange, metallic timbre. Subsequently 4 unknown objects follow the same satellite. Moscow announces that the ship is going aimlessly. Subsequently both Sputnik II and Sputnik IV return to their original orbits.

the vodstock

In 1961 the Russian cosmonaut, German Titov, aboard the Vodstok 2 capsule, observed and photographed several unidentified flying objects while orbiting the Earth, which were even very close to his capsule. Then, in June 1963, Valeri Bikovski aboard the Vodstok V space capsule, communicated with base control in a state of tremendous agitation:

"A luminous body seems to fly in the direction of the capsule!

Something accompanies me through space! It seems to be flying very close to my capsule! At this moment he rushes towards me!

The car has passed me at enormous speed! It has almost skimmed the capsule...

Shortly after, the unidentified device headed towards the capsule of Valentina Tereskova, who was aboard the Vodstok VI, she communicated to the base:

"I see an unknown vehicle dangerously close to the capsule...! Give me instructions...! It's too close..."

In July 1969, the Russians sent the Lunik 15 as a spy, aware of a possible encounter between American astronauts and extraterrestrial beings. Astronauts Yury Romanenko and Georgui Grechko witnessed how several UFOs came close to their Salyut-6 space station in 1977. The objects followed them for 3 complete orbits, they were also photographed.

VICTOR AFANASYEV

In April 1979, cosmonaut Victor Afanasyev took off from the base known as "Star City" to begin a mission aboard the Solyut 6 space station. But something happened along the way that was not foreseen in the flight plans. Afanasyev saw how an unidentified object suddenly appeared in his field of vision and began to follow his ship closely: «It *followed us for half an orbit. We could see it when there was light, but when we entered the shadow zone of the Earth it disappeared completely. Without a doubt, it was an artificial, metallic object about 40 meters long. It was spindle-shaped and had hatch-like openings. In some parts it presented structures similar to ailerons. The object remained very close to us. We were able to photograph it perfectly when it was about 25m from us.*"

In addition to photographing the UFO, Afanasyev was continually in contact with mission control reporting what was happening. Upon returning to Earth, he was ordered not to tell anyone what he had seen, and both cameras and film were confiscated. Officially, neither the photos nor the recordings of the aforementioned mission exist.

Russian probe Phobos 2

A Soviet scientist, Victor Borishov, claimed that the Phobos II space probe photographed a warning inscribed on solid rock on the surface of Mars, reading "Stay Away," allegedly addressed to humanity. Coincidentally that same day the Phobos II probe stopped transmitting signals and was declared lost by the Soviets on March 28, 1989. At a time when the Russian Phobos II probe was taking a series of images of the Martian surface in its extension, a strange shadow appears from an elongated object that was behind the ship, then the aforementioned photograph.

The last photograph that the Phobos II probe sent after it received the order, from the base, to turn around to see what the object behind it was, has caused a lot of controversy. After being hidden by the Russian authorities, it was finally disclosed by the former military and now a Russian researcher Marina Popovic. The image shows an elongated cylindrical object about 20 km in length. The object at the top corresponds to Phobos, the satellite of Mars.

Phobos II, before its strange disappearance, sent amazing images of the planet Mars, where some of them show objects that do not match what scientists officially tell us. In the following photographs you can see: in the first an artificial pyramid-shaped construction, in the second what appears to be a monolith on the Martian satellite Phobos, and in the third a semi-buried triangular UFO! which seems to have had an emergency landing, from the trail left behind.

On the Mir space station

In May 1997 the MIR space station was engulfed by hundreds of UFOs moving in different directions found above, behind and in front of the Russian shuttle. Then an astronaut who was filming the event is forced to lower the camera and stop filming, because they knew that there were people watching the mission, since the signal could be captured by amateurs with satellite dishes; but it was all too late, because the filming from the ground had already been achieved.

Important official statements

The Nobel Prize in Chemistry in 1951, Glenn Seaborg, and president of the United States Atomic Energy Commission wrote in 1969, in his article "The strangers of the Moon" the following: «Various perceptions of the astronauts of Apollo XI and XII indicate *that at a time that cannot be determined exactly, other non-terrestrial beings landed. Some photos that have not been published to date, taken by Apollo XI, show very clear traces in various places on the Moon, the contours of which are extraordinarily precise. Possibly other ships that used the Moon as a link station landed there.* NASA has always said that what was found on the Moon by the expeditions has no secret, however, Dr. Farduk Elbaz, one of NASA's most prominent scientists admitted: "Not *everything discovered has been announced.*" He also added that a "secret code" was used in the conversations between the astronauts and the control base on Earth.

Scientist Maurice Chatelain, who was in charge of the Apollo communications team, stated that: "*All the Apollo and Gemini spacecraft were followed by spacecraft that do not belong to this planet. Whenever this happens, the astronauts inform the control center and from there absolute silence is ordered.*» He further added that: "*The Apollo XI astronauts not only heard strange noises on the radio as they approached the Moon, but they were met with a welcoming committee: two UFOs contemplating the moon landing.* " Chatelain thinks that some UFOs are in our solar system, specifically on Titan.

Fred Bell, another scientist who worked for NASA says: "*Astronauts have kept quiet about their UFO encounters because they are trained to believe it is a matter of national security.*" In addition, Dr. Bell claimed to have seen photographs of UFOs taken by astronauts. He assured that the Apollo Project was abruptly interrupted because "*too many things were found out there*", surely fearing that everything would come to light and become public knowledge.

NASA astronaut Guion Bluford, PhD in Aerospace Engineering and 700 hours in space, participating in 4 space missions, stated in an interview that his explorations in space have contributed to his belief in extraterrestrial life in the Universe. On his third trip in 1991, he says that he had an experience that he would never forget. Of his fourth mission in 1992, he says that it remains classified and that "I *could talk to them about it, but then I would have to shoot them all.*"

Washington Press Club

Scholars cannot explain this wide strip on the Moon, which looks like a landing strip. Dismissed senior NASA officials offered a press conference on October 30, in which they revealed a secret kept by the US government for nearly 40 years: There are traces of human construction on the Moon.

As revealed by the Russian newspaper "Komsomolskaya Pravda", a conference was held at the National Press Club in Washington on the 30th, convened by Ken Johnston, director of the Photo Conservation Section of the NASA Laboratory on the Moon suddenly fired on October 23, and former NASA adviser Richard Hoagland; both had participated in the "Apollo" project and the latter presided over the broadcast of the Apollo moon landing on live television.

Johnston confirmed the following: «*In the 70s of the last century, American astronauts saw and recorded with cameras "remnants of human constructions of remote antiquity" on the Moon and photographed some technological remnants. Upon bringing the photos back to Earth, they handed them over to Johnston, who is responsible for photo preservation; NASA leaders ordered him to destroy them, and yet those photos were secretly kept by him. Almost 40 years later, Johnston decided to post these photos that would rock the world. At the same time, he accused NASA of falsifying, since all the officially released photos went through special treatment and, in particular, the photos of the moon landing were modified.*»

Hoagland said: "*The astronauts also brought back some artificial products, the technologies of which have already been used by the United States, Russia, China, India and Japan. These countries are carrying out a new wheel of contention for the Moon. As far as I know, the Americans brought back to Earth an amazing secret discovered during the astronauts' stay on the Moon and kept this secret confidential for many years. The new wheel of contention will have a denouement and, unlike the political contest with Russia 50 years ago, this denouement will decide the fate of each and every human being on Earth."*

These two people definitely ended the calm situation, because if what they have said is believed, the history written by NASA is full of lies. However, NASA does indeed have the right not to disclose scientific, technological and information related to humanity and is free from congressional surveillance, which constitutes a protection provided by the United States Department of Defense. Hoagland made it clear that in addition to the hidden truth about the Moon, the fact that the 1976 "Pirate" drone discovered microbes on the surface of Mars was also covered up.

Due to the fact that it received the news very late, the aforementioned newspaper did not report in greater detail about the concrete evidence, but the two published photos can verify some things. According to other information, Edwin E. Aldrin, one of the "Apollo XI" pilots, recently said that he had seen UFOs on the Moon. And, not long ago, the suitcases 698, 699 and 700 in which the records of the "Apollo XI" moon landing of 1969 were kept disappeared. There is also a version in the sense that this North American decision to "make known" has something to do with the "Chang'EI" satellite launched on October 24 by China. (Source: People Online. November 2, 2007)

life on the moon

There are regions on the Moon where plant life develops and changes color with the different seasons. This seasonality effect is due to the fact that the Moon does not always present, contrary to what is stated, the same side towards the sun or towards the Earth.

There is a region that comes out of darkness at certain seasons, and on the fringes of this region plant life exists. On the Moon there are artificial lakes and ponds, and you can see clouds that have also been filmed. There is a certain gravity and man can move freely on its surface without having to wear a space suit, although after having undergone a decompression analogous to that of scuba diving. Photographs have been seen, and some of them have been published in the book "We discovered Alien Bases on the Moon", by Fred Steckling.

According to former US Naval Intelligence officer William Cooper, in the early days of space travel and Lunar landings, each expedition was accompanied by extraterrestrial spacecraft. Apollo astronauts observed and filmed the Lunar base "LUNA". In the photographs you can recognize domes, large ball-shaped constructions similar to silos. You can also see huge T-shaped vehicles for paving land, which leave deep tracks on the Lunar surface; as well as large and small alien ships.

The official space program is a huge farce and exposes a monstrous waste of money. The third alternative is a reality and is not science fiction at all. Most of the Apollo astronauts have been tremendously impressed by what they have seen. Upon his return, his life, as well as some rumors about them, irrefutably demonstrate the pressures to which he has been subjected in order to obtain his silence. They have been ordered to remain silent on pain of death, a threat that was deemed necessary. Despite everything, an astronaut spoke to the English producers of a television program about "Alternative 3", in which he confirmed the accuracy of these accusations.

GEORGE H LEONARD

George H. Leonard, who, in his book "Some one else in on our Moon" (1976) convincedly showed some NASA photographs of our visit to the Moon where - in his opinion - samples of alien technology were clearly visible. Their arguments were based on poor quality images in which traces of wheels seem to be visible on the Lunar dust, presumed gigantic excavators or entrances to underground bases. However, contrary to what can be deduced from the delusional plot line followed by Leonard in his book, this work contains some interesting data, which in themselves constitute a genuine astronomical problem.

I refer to the relatively frequent observations of domes, bridges and presumably architectural structures seen on our satellite that Leonard echoes. The best documented references to this kind of observation date back to the middle of the last century and, more specifically, to 1848, when the notable German astronomer Gruithuisen from Munich claimed to have discovered traces of cities in the southern part of the visible hemisphere of the Moon. Selenites. And what's more, I claim to have seen greenish spots inside some craters that moved irregularly and that the astronomer did not hesitate to identify as vegetation or, in the worst case, with huge plagues of insects. Peo Gruithuisen was not the only one to defend such "heresies".

thouvelot

In 1885 another astronomer, this time Thouvelot, thought he had located another group of ruins near the Petico crater. The arrival of the space missions that meticulously recognized our satellite from its comfortable orbits did not dispel the rumors that referred to the existence of ruins of ancient cities on the Moon. In fact, one of those most responsible for spreading this "rumor" was the American professor Willian Blair who, after gaining access to some of the secret photos of the Orbiter-2 mission in April 1966, discovered in one of them several monuments of more than 200m high geometrically distributed on the Lunar soil. For Richard W. Shorthill, nothing suggests that they are artificial formations, but rather the product of a complex "geophysical phenomenon" that has given rise to the false impression that they are buildings or cusps. The most orthodox astronomy tends to apply this solution to the "Blair cusps" to as many similar accounts written by astronomers from all over the world, and from all historical periods they find in their path. In this sense, special attention deserves the astronomical observations of domes and bridges in some sectors of our satellite made by astronomers of all credibility. About the first - as noted by Joseph Goodovage in his article for the American magazine SAGA in 1974 *«in recent years more than 200 whitish, circular and dome-shaped structures have been observed on the Moon and cataloged but, for some strange reason, they often disappear from their place to reappear in another.»* Astronomers don't know what kind of phenomenon these elusive visions are due to, or whether they are simply a gas bubble that occasionally forms on the Moon's surface. And it is true that the evanescent nature of this phenomenon prevents its careful examination and analysis.

The same is not the case with the bridge that has been seen with relative frequency over the Sea of Crises and which, according to some reports, could reach 18km in length. For the most daring astronomers, such as the British HP Wilkins, such a structure, even though it does not always seem to be in the same place - it must necessarily be artificial - but... built by whom?

Lunar Channels

In short, the more data we collect on our satellite and the closer we get to it to explore it, the more or more mysteries it presents to us. One of these is the one that refers to the existence on its surface of regions that seem to have been occupied by water currents for hundreds of years, or to have been huge beaches in the remote past of this planetary body. Without going any further, at the beginning of this century Professor WH Pickering cataloged, from his observatory in Arequipa (Peru), thirty-five narrow zones on the Moon that were virtually identical to the beds of dry rivers on Earth. These are irregular courses that end up flowing into craters and which, in the past, gave rise to the idea that, as on Mars, there were channels on the Moon. Or at least, that's what the astronomer and eminent Italian "Martianologist" Cerulli defended in 1896.

Another enigmatic aspect is the recurring observations of light rays that cross the surface of the satellite in perfect straight lines and that overcome obstacles of all kinds, from mountains to craters, without this deviating one iota from their rectilinear orientation. They tend to appear in strong sunlight and can be seen from Earth even with a small telescope, as long as it is pointed toward places where these rays traditionally appear, such as Copernicus, Tycho, and Kepler craters. Although there is no systematic study of this phenomenon, it is known, for example, that they usually occur in the vicinity of "new" craters, with pronounced edges, and that they are capable of traveling hundreds of kilometers without deviating a single degree in their trajectory.

However, contrary to what one might think, these lines are not uniform, but often break, giving the impression that they are discontinuous lines and suggesting their merely optical origin. In a certain way, the revolutionary Polish astronomer Nicolás Copernicus already warned us when he wisely stated "that no one expect anything certain from astronomy, since it offers us nothing certain". His words, almost prophetic, fit like a glove to the challenge that, multiplied since we arrived at it, our enigma poses to us daily.

Lunar and Martian Base of the Third Reich

There have been many authors who maintain that the Germans of the Reich for many years (about sixty years) have had a base on the Moon (if not a real country). Having such spaceships, it is not a problem for them to reach the Moon or Mars. Reich UFOs don't have to worry about carrying thousands of tons of liquid fuel, nor about the cost, like NASA or ESA space programs.

During the Apollo XI mission to the Moon, the crew of Apollo XI had a conversation with the control center in Houston, coincidentally captured by some radio amateurs who were listening to a "reserved channel", which reveals that they had an encounter with aircraft "far superior *in size and technology to ours.*" According to some, the entire Moon would be in the hands of the Germans of the Reich, which is why the Americans have not returned to it: they have "Hausverbot", that is, the Germans of the Reich have forbidden them to set foot on the Moon. That is why NASA now says with a certain tone of contempt that " *the Moon is no longer an interesting target for the Space Agency.*" NASA declares that it is more interested in Mars, where according to authors such as Jan Udo Holey or Hans Altmann, the Germans have also been established in underground constructions for decades. The repeated failures of NASA on Mars would be explained by the actions of the Germans in the Reich.

For their part, the missions to Mars are another waste of money since the true purpose is hidden as well as the missions that are carried out both on the Moon base and on the Mars base. In 1877 the Italian astronomer Giovanni Shiaparelli announced that he had observed a network of intertwined lines on the surface of Mars, he called them "canali" which in Italian means "groove" but the translation given was channels. In his time these "channels" were proof of the presence of intelligent life on Mars. Percival Lowell was greatly attracted to this discovery as well as the works of Camille Flammarion and dedicated himself to building an observatory in Arizona. Lowell died in 1916 without having made any definitive discoveries but he managed to capture the imagination of Martian life for many decades. Lowell claimed that the function of the canals was to supply water from the polar caps to the inhabited tropical and equatorial zone. The belief that Mars was inhabited or at least could be habitable was common among scientists and the general public until the second half of the 20th century, but this idea was diluted by the bleak images offered by the probes that began to reach Mars. about the mid 60's.

No channels were found, but a more detailed view of certain structures present in some images of the Martian region of Sidonia caught the attention of certain open-minded scientists who developed one of the most fascinating and transcendent hypotheses that humanity still has to deal with. to face... the OAC hypothesis, that is, the hypothesis of the Artificial Origin of Sidonia. Today Laura Eisenhower, the great-granddaughter of former US President Dwight Eisenhower has confirmed many facts of life on Mars, along with lawyer Mr. Basiago and Alfred Webre. In an exclusive interview released by ExopoliticsTV on January 17, 2011, Laura M. Eisenhower revealed that in 2006 and 2007, she was invited to come to the secret US colony on Mars. At the time, she wrote: " *My great-grandfather, the President, who was also the general of the army that led the Allied forces to victory over Hitler, fought against the corrupting powers of evil on Earth and took part in some of the most challenging scenarios." of history. As I grew up, I could sense that this battle that has ancient roots was ending. When Hitler died and the Nazis lost power, the entities - including those that were extraterrestrials - did not. They continued to find hosts and create deals with people who were a part of...the Global Elite, who want to function through scare tactics, control, and suppression of Sophia or divine feminine essence.*"

Ms Eisenhower goes on to state: "*We must face the fact that much of what has been going on in secret has created inevitable future drama, because it has spent trillions of dollars of our tax dollars on projects that serve only their elitist mentality. These include a secret space program with colonies off planet Earth reached via teleportation, targeting and capturing individuals, those perceived to be a threat, HAARP, psychotronic weapons, deep underground military bases, and false flag events. like 9/11 to further embody us within a police state. Behind the scenes, occult practices - including dark rituals, gruesome pedophilia, and the creation of agents and slaves to serve them - are used to infect the planetary body with negative frequencies that are nourishment to them. This is the way they hold power and influence behind the curtain. This spawns the fear, pain, and negative feelings that are the life force in which they live. As dire as all this sounds, there is actually a way out. This is why it is crucial that we understand the Christ-Sophia concept of consciousness and how lower forces have affected our DNA, and a DNA produced from unused and unactivated waste, and how, in turn, that connects with the planetary body and its veils, as well as the suppression of the goddess. It's not a New Age thing. This is old. This does not need to be labeled. It's not even about the physical, or being a female. It is about Creation and what we are rising against and how much the scales have been tipping towards the warmongers, abusers and control freaks. We must strive and soften everything, restore our world, and return power to Gaia."*

«His lust for our powerlessness and hidden faith is further exacerbated by his use of mind control and microchips that do not allow individuals to access their inner voice and connection to Source. Some, of course, are directly involved in the programs, while others languish in a kind of trance-like state, such as ELF microwave frequencies (Extremely Low Frequencies, that is, radiation frequencies from 3 to 30 Hz) that are broadcast on our televisions, which keep us locked in a lower mode of thinking, obsessed with the lives of others and consumerism. The nervous toxins of the chemtrails keep us in a state of permanent disorder of the nervous system, as they are

delusional sensations, together with a deep emotional and psychic longing that also infects us, and thus we are very far from being free, because things are barely correct. The lower alien races and their technologies chose Earth allies to create programs with. They exist on Earth and in the underground bases (particularly the greys) for the intended breeding programs to destroy the will of Nature, the Soul and the Highest Consciousness of All - so that they can run the Universe and have maximum domination, and lie in wait in their off-planet colonies, until perhaps they can return to Earth and reign, or take it beyond the stars and leave Earth just to its own destruction. There are also many benevolent races, and our challenge is to know the difference. In the past, treaties have been broken, deceptions have happened, and what may seem friendly doesn't always mean they are.»

Andrew D. Basiago, a lawyer in Washington state, has publicly revealed the existence of a secret US Department of Defense time travel program that began in the late 1960s and in which he was a child participant, which included identifying future American leaders using various forms of "quantum access." In a Cost-to-Cost AM radio chat with George Noory on November 11, 2009, Mr. Basiago described how this secret program involving time travel identified future persons of interest, including those destined to serve as President and Vice President of the United States, and then informing such persons of their fates.

His interactive historical exposé, of what he calls "Marsgate", on Exopolitics radio was based on his direct personal experience. For Mr. Basiago, this consisted of the two trips he made to Mars in 1981, when, at the age of 19, he walked on the surface of the Martian terrain after being teleported there in a "jump room" located in a facility Hughes Aircraft (underground base) in El Segundo, California. Mr. Basiago believes he was tapped to go to Mars because he was already teleported as a child participant in

Project Pegasus. Other names cited by Basiago and Eisenhower about the secret US human colonies on Mars include Michael Relfe, who in two books documents his 20-year service (1976-1996) as a member of the US military. staffing the secret Mars colony, and US Department of Defense scientist Arthur Neumann, who has publicly claimed that he was teleported to the secret Mars colony for project meetings.

Ruins found by the Mars Pathfinder

Researcher Richard Hoagland appears to have discovered archaeological remains in some of the photographs taken by the Mars Pathfinder probe. In the enlargements to the images of the "Twin Peaks" hills are what appear to be terraces similar in shape to the stepped pyramids of Central America. In addition to a formation in vertical and horizontal arrangement of the rocks, similar to terrestrial constructions. Hoagland explains that the hill would really be an artificial pyramid, highly eroded, due to a flood that affected that area. Other photographs show suspicious geometrically shaped rocks, as if they were eroded blocks torn from some kind of artificial construction.

The following photographs taken by space probes spark controversy. Who built that strange dome that can be seen in the first image? In the second photograph you can see a hemispherical construction that without a doubt cannot be something natural. Next, some photographs taken by the probes sent to Mars, where artificial structures can be seen that show that scientists hide too much information from us that humanity should know... The face of Mars, pyramids, buildings, machinery, canals, vegetation, are Some examples.

Structures on Mars before human colonization

Apart from the formations you already mentioned, in Sidonia there are other presumably artificial structures. In another region of Mars, in Elisha we also find other pyramidal formations and it is very possible that new formations will be discovered in the future. In fact, a group of British researchers from Glasgow have recently identified what appears to be a large quadrangular pyramid, called the NK pyramid located 40km west of the Face and at the same latitude as the D&M pyramid, which we will study later.

On February 8, 1972, the Mariner IX photographed some strange formations in the area known as the Elysium Quadrangle. The MTVS 4205 image showed a set of four tetrahedral pyramidal formations, in a second photo of the region the same formation was appreciated. These photos were not taken into account and only a small article was published in Icarus magazine in 1974 by Mack Gipson and Victor K. Ablordeppy under the title "Pyramidal Structures of Mars" in which they effectively pointed out the existence of formations pyramidal and triangular structures on the surface of Mars. These structures cast triangular and polygonal shadows and set the average diameter of the pyramids at around 3km and rise up to 1km above the plain, it is estimated that the volume of the largest was 1,000 times that of the Great Pyramid of Egypt and the height, 10 times greater. These four pyramids seemed to be in alignment relationships with each other.

On July 25, 1976, Dr. Tobias Owen, a member of the Jet Propulsion Laboratories imaging team and Professor of Astronomy, was looking at Viking I images of the Sidonia region in search of possible landing sites for the module of the Viking II when it ran into an immense structure with the shape of a face that looked lost towards the stars and some strange pyramidal formations. It was photo 35A72 obtained at an approximate altitude of 1,500 km.

The DiPietro-Molenaar pyramid is named after its discoverers. It is a pentagonal structure found 16km from La Cara and has an almost perfect NS alignment with the planet's axis of rotation. Its smallest side measures 1.5km, its longest axis almost reaches 3km, it is almost 800m high and it has some strange buttresses at the base of each of its five angles. Their faces have different lengths and their angles are different. In 1988, Erol Torum, a cartographer and systems analyst for the United States Department of Defense Mapping, wrote to Hoagland stating and detailing that there was no natural mechanism to explain the pentagonal formation of the D&M Pyramid. Torum carried out a deeper analysis and came to the following conclusions: (some of them were already known)

Another important investigation was that of "The mounds", which was carried out by Stanley McDaniel, professor and director of the Department of Philosophy at Sonoma State University, and Dr. Horace Crater, specialist in theoretical particle physics. These mounds are between 90m and 210m in diameter and 30m high. They are aligned with respect to the Face and the D&M Pyramid. Crater identified the 16 mounds with a letter, "A" through "P." Firstly, he studied the EAD formation (see diagram) that formed a perfect isosceles triangle. Crater then studied the tetrad GADE which contains two identical right triangles, AEG and GAD. The next closest mound, B, was then included, forming the pentad GABDE. The triangles ADB and EAB are the exact reflection of the triangles AEG and GAD. The next mound was P. Triangle PE is a reflection of GEA and EAB. The most surprising thing is not this wonderful gear but the fact that the angles of this gear are related to the constants "t" and "pi" as well as the angle of 19.5°.

PILOTS

Some interesting testimonials from pilots that we can highlight, despite the exorbitant number of cases, are:

M. Gabriel Voisin, aircraft builder, forerunner of aviation: "*A more insurmountable barrier than the Himalayas separates us from those extraterrestrial explorers: our technical backwardness and our greatest ignorance."*

M. Louis Bréguet, aeronautical constructor: *"Flying discs use a means of propulsion different from ours. There is only one explanation left: flying saucers come from another world."*

M. Pierre Clostermann, World War II axeman: *"Flying saucers are of extraterrestrial origin. Neither the Russians nor the Americans are capable of building machines of this category.*

The characteristics of these vehicles are far superior to the current possibilities of science."

Cdt J. Howard, observed an immense flying cigar and 10 "saucers": "*They must be species of airships from another world."*

Cdt WB Nash, observed 6 large discs: *"I think Extraterrestrial Intelligence guides those vehicles."*

Cdt R. Adikes, whose apparatus was accompanied by a luminous object: *"Before this observation, I was not convinced of the existence of UFOs, now I believe in them!"*

Both pilots and astronauts are obliged not to reveal any type of event related to the "UFO" phenomenon, it literally appears in a section of the air regulations and regulations that "every experience with some type of unidentified flying object that can be seen in *the air is strictly prohibited from revealing it to the public.»* This coincides with the book Introduction to Space Science, where it is stated that *"UFOs are either manned or remotely controlled extraterrestrial spacecraft."*

10.

THE SECRET GOVERNMENT

"Knowledge makes good men better, and bad men worse."
(Anonymous)

THE REAL MJ-12

Behind the powerful web of deception is a titanic global control organization: MJ-12. MJ-12 is made up of 6 members belonging to the government and 6 director members of the CFR and/or the Trilateral Commission (TC). The Majority for Joint Intelligence Agency is officially called the Senior Interagency Group (SIG). It is very important to understand that the CFR and its affiliate, the TC, not only maintain control over everything, they own the entire country. Before World War II, they were already the true guides of the politics of the United States. The CFR, LA TC and their counterparts abroad are dependent on the "Bilderberg" group. Since World War II almost all of the highest military and government leaders are members of the CFR or TC. And all US members of the TC were or are also members of the CFR.

Each major foreign nation has its own branch of the CFR and the national members work together internationally, under the supervision of the "Bildergergs", for the achievement of their common goals. The foreign members of the TC each belong to their own national organization. A simple cursory examination would show that CFR and TC members dominate the major institutions, all the major media and publishers, the largest banking groups, and all relevant industries; they also occupy the upper echelons of governments and control most vital branches of the economy. Its members are picked and chosen for their financial power and other specific interests. Only the common people have nothing to say.

They are undemocratic and in no way representative of the vast majority of Americans. However, they will be the ones who will decide who will survive the Holocaust. The "Bilderbergers", the CFR and the TC are the secret government, and they run the nations through MJ-12, and secret societies like the "Jason Society" and "Jason Scholars". The higher levels of government are made up of its members.

Alternatives 1, 2 and 3

Something fundamental within the purpose of the Majestic 12 (MJ-12) is based on the knowledge of the end of time and its intervention to avoid events or at least find solutions to the inevitable extinction of planet earth. A secret order from President Eisenhower entrusted the Jason Scholars with examining the scenario and devising alternatives to the warnings resulting from the Events of Fatima between 1915 and shortly after 1917. The Jason Scholars confirmed the results of the scientists' study and raised three propositions: alternatives 1, 2 and 3.

In the alternative 1 box, nuclear warheads were to open holes in the stratosphere through which accumulated heat and pollution were to escape into space. Next, civilization had to carry out a total conversion and transform the current exploitation of the Earth into operations to protect the planet. However, of the three, this was the solution that was considered the least convenient, in view of the unwillingness of people to transform quickly and the additional damage that the atomic explosion would cause.

Alternative 2 proposed the construction of a vast network of underground cities linked by tunnels, in which a cross section of all cultures and all professions could survive and allow the survival of the human race. The rest of humanity would be left to fend for themselves on the planet's surface.

Alternative 3 was to, using both extraterrestrial and conventional technologies, allow a small sample of humans to leave Earth and found colonies in the universe. In this regard, see the book "Alternative 3" by Leslie Watkins. I cannot ratify or deny the existence of the supposed deliveries of groups of humans that had to constitute the slaves to work towards the achievement of said plan. The Moon, called Adam, would be the first medium-term goal, followed by Mars, called Eve.

Underground bases for survival

The measures that had to be taken to control overpopulation were the same in the three alternatives: birth control, sterilization of people, and contamination by deadly microbes. AIDS is the result of these plans. (Since population decline was considered paramount, it was decided, in the interest of the human race, to make the undesirable elements of society disappear.) The United States and the Soviet Union jointly rejected Alternative 1 and ordered the immediate start of Alternatives 2 and 3. In 1959, the Rand Corp. organized a symposium on underground construction. The final report shows machines capable of building a 15m diameter tunnel at a speed of 1.5m/h. It also shows plans for tunnels and huge underground rooms that, apparently, could accommodate huge complexes and even cities.

It therefore appears that the five years that followed the development of the alternatives were used to improve underground construction methods. It is then that those who held power thought that one of the possibilities of financing extraterrestrial projects or other secret projects was to organize an illegal drug market. An ambitious young CFR member was contacted. It was about who at the time was president-general director of a Texas oil pipeline company. This company was experiencing a new technology at that time. It was thought that the drug, transported by fishing boats from South America to Bohr Island, might then be brought ashore by Navy supply ships, whose cargo was not inspected by customs or the Coast Guard, thus so he did not raise suspicions or was subjected to any control. This person accepted and organized the collaboration with the CIA. The plan worked better than expected and is still in force throughout the world today.

There are obviously other methods of getting drugs into the country. But, despite everything, we should remember that it was this character who began to sell drugs to our children. And also that the CIA controls all the drug markets in the world. John F. Kennedy wanted to denounce these black manipulations and the exaltation of the extraterrestrial truth, for this reason, and like many others, he was assassinated, keeping the secret that will soon be revealed before any human force that wants to prevent it.

ALTERNATIVE 3

In the book The Third Alternative, the real identity of the astronaut has been supplanted by the pseudonym Bob Grodin. It was led to believe that he had committed suicide in 1978. This cannot be confirmed, and I believe that numerous assumptions in the book are, in fact, reported to misinform. « *I remain convinced that this is the result of the pressure that has been exerted on the authors, in order to neutralize the effects that the broadcast on English television of the program "Alternative 3" caused on the general public.* » Cooper confessed. The headquarters of the great conspiracy described in the book is located in Geneva. The steering committee is made up of members of the aforementioned governments, as well as leading members of the "Bilderbergers". Meetings of the Master Plan Committee even take place inside an atomic submarine under the icy layers of the Pole. The need for secrecy is so pressing that it is the only sure method against eventual eavesdropping.

From William Cooper's own experience and from other sources, I can assume that the book reflects 70% truth. I suppose that the misinformation contained in the book was nevertheless an attempt to discredit the program broadcast on British television by means of information that could easily be doubted, in the same way as the "Eisenhower briefing" document, published in the USA as a plan of help under the name of "Majestic 12", whose veracity can also be doubted.

The official space program of the United States was notably increased by President JF Kennedy, who, in the speech at the beginning of his term, declared to the world that before the end of the 60's a man would walk on the Moon. His plan allowed those responsible to divert fantastic sums from the budgets for their plans and to have the American public misled about the real space plan. A parallel program served the same purposes in the Soviet Union. In fact, when Kennedy offered this speech, a base for joint use between the Americans, the Russians and the extraterrestrials already existed on the Moon.

On May 22, 1962, an unmanned spacecraft landed on Mars and confirmed the existence of an environment conducive to human life. A short time later, the construction of a base on Mars began. Cities inhabited by selected people from various cultures, professions, and countries can currently be found on the surface of Mars. This, evidently, has not been revealed to public doctors and its existence and functions are hidden. Despite the fact that the United States and the Soviet Union are actually very close, there is officially a strong enmity between them to get money under the pretext of National Defense, but in reality to dedicate it to secret projects. Space mission fraud is spearheaded by Apollo 11 and subsequent missions to the Moon, as well as probes sent to Mars.

Elimination of evidence

Due to public pressure and reports accusing NASA of hiding information, the Information Service intervened destroying an old Luna base and some constructions of Sidonia such as the "Face", so that when better pixelated images arrived from the probes that photographed Mars in 1998 it seemed that everything had been a visual deception. NASA's intention has not always been to hide the truth, it is rather the FBI who currently prevails in the dissolution of reports and is in charge of discrediting the revealers of extraterrestrial or related reports, who pressures NASA not to reveal reports.

This is how in 2001 a large group of scientists and senior officials from the US presented to the English media many irrefutable reports that the US government was hiding the truth about extraterrestrials, and its intentions not to revealing the truth depended on the interests of oil control. The constant recordings from space show formations of ships that constantly cross the Earth, in and out, as well as constant dogfights outside the Earth and in front of the Moon. All this is becoming more noticeable and for decades it has been common for NASA and the astronauts who continuously live with these experiences.

END OF MILTON WILLIAM Cooper's will to Congress

The former naval intelligence officer Milton W. Cooper wrote in 1989 to the Senate and the House of Representatives of Congress the whole truth about what was happening around the extraterrestrials (3 years before they killed him): «... *The leaders of the all-powerful and secret organization start from the basis that the planet Earth is going to destroy itself because of our stupidity or because of the Divine Will. These men are honestly convinced that they are doing the right thing in trying to save the human race. It is a tragic irony of fate that they have been forced to choose as their mates an extraterrestrial race, which must face a severe test for its own survival. In this attempt, many compromises have been made to the detriment of law and morality. These compromises are big mistakes that need to be rectified and those responsible to be held accountable for them. I understand that fear and urgency were determining factors in the decision not to inform the public. However, I cannot accept this decision* ."

« Throughout history, small groups of powerful men have believed that they were the only ones capable of deciding the fate of millions of human beings. And time and time again, they have been wrong. Our country owes its existence to the principles of freedom and democracy. I strongly believe that the United States will never achieve anything by ignoring these principles. The public has a right to all the information about what is happening and all of us together must try to save the human race. We are governed by a powerful organization made up of humans and aliens that intend to enslave part of the human race. We must do everything in our power to prevent this. The alien power has manipulated and abused the government in order to enslave or destroy the human race. We must prevent it from coming to this."

« In short: something is happening to us that defies our imagination. We must strive to know the facts and the truth to act accordingly. Whatever the truth, we must know it and know what is happening today, we have the right to do so. The situation we find ourselves in is the result of our own actions and our neglect over the past 44 years. The fault is only ours, and only we can change things. Through ignorance or overconfidence, we the people have abandoned our role as watchdog of our government. The government is based on the following saying: "the people, by the people, for the people." »

« It has never been taken for granted that we should give up our role and place all our trust in the hands of some strange men who meet in secret and decide our fate. In fact, the structure of our government was set up to prevent this very thing. If we had assumed our true role as citizens, all this would not have happened. Most of us are ignorant of the most elementary functions of our government. We have become a nation of sheep, and in the end, the sheep are herded to slaughter. The time has come to face the situation and behave like real men. I remind you that the European Jews meekly headed towards the crematory ovens, despite the warnings they received, they could not imagine *that the events were real. When the holocaust caused by Hitler was announced, he could not believe that it had happened (I affirm here and now that Hitler was manipulated by extraterrestrials).* »

I have exposed the truth as I see it. I don't care what they think of me. I have only done my duty. My destiny is totally indifferent to me: now I can present myself before God with a clear conscience. I believe in God. I believe in Jesus Christ, my savior. I also believe in the Constitution of the United States of America as it was thought and written. I made a promise to protect and defend her against any enemy within or without. I am firmly determined to keep my promise." (By: Milton William Cooper (1943-2001) who worked for many years in US naval intelligence under prominent admirals, was involved in "black" operations at the highest level, and was discharged due to the ethical problems that his job was giving him)

For 15 years, Cooper denounced the enormous cover-ups that were being carried out by his government, as well as its lack of scruples when it came to making cruel decisions against even the American population itself. President Bill Clinton described him as "*... the most dangerous radio announcer in North America...* ", since he had a radio space, where he publicly denounced the terrible and secret actions that his government was carrying out worldwide. .

The Disclosure Project

Currently the US, Spain and England are working together on secret missions with a view to occupying the Megiddo area near Jerusalem to the Euphrates in the near future, knowing that a war like never before has been unleashed. On the other hand, this is the report of the EFE of Washington that revealed that the agencies of the United States and the United Kingdom hide what they know of the encounters with extraterrestrials, and have seized the technology copied from the ships that they have shot down, as stated by a group of military, scientists and former government officials.

" *Aliens from advanced civilizations have been visiting us for decades, but this has remained within the most compartmentalized and secret program of the United States and other countries* ," said Steven Greer, director of the Disclosure Project group. Greer and twenty former government officials, military personnel, scientists, former members of intelligence agencies and businessmen presented in 2001 at the Press Club what they described as irrefutable testimonies of the existence of extraterrestrials, their visits to our planet, and the cover-up of that experience. " *There are some agencies within the US and UK governments that control this information and resist disclosing it because it threatens the interests of the big oil companies, of those who hold power,*" *Alfred Webre told EFE, who during* the administration of President Jimmy Carter was part of a White House study group on extraterrestrials. Experts and witnesses presented by the Disclosure Project argue that aliens made their presence more apparent after World War II and due to humans' development of nuclear weapons.

Greer stated that "*since at least the 1940s, and perhaps the 1930s, space vehicles of extraterrestrial origin have been shot down, occupied, and studied by government agencies. Testimony, corroborated by multiple military witnesses, shows that the United States and other countries have militarily attacked these alien vehicles and, in some cases, shot them down,*" he added. Greer and other participants in the Disclosure project called for an immediate halt to all efforts to militarize space and called for US congressional hearings to release information about aliens. Project Disclosure maintains that, through the process of "reverse engineering", the technologies that operated the alien spacecraft have been unraveled, and that the agencies involved in this conspiracy have known for decades "a new physics" and "uses of energy" that they would change the entire economic structure of the Earth.

" *I want to be clear on this: The entity that controls the issue of unidentified flying objects and related technologies has more power than any government in the world, or any ruler in the world,"* Greer said. Webre also said that " *aliens are concerned about nuclear weapons because of the ecological impact, and we have testimonies from former members of the intelligence services who tell how UFOs have followed planes carrying from Spain, for example, the components of nuclear weapons that had to be replaced periodically [...] We also have evidence that there is a law and an order in the universe, and in that order we terrestrials occupy a very low step among the species that have not yet evolved beyond use of war for conflict resolution.* » Webre, adviser in the White House under the mandate of Jimmy Carter, added in that presentation: « *The Anglo-Saxon countries are the greatest exponents of armaments, and of the entire socioeconomic system that depends on the use of hydrocarbon energy -what before it was called the 'big seven' oil companies - that's why they keep all this hidden."*

Greer said that " *no one has claimed that there is a real threat to humanity from these UFOs [...] Obviously, any civilization capable of routine interstellar travel could wipe out our civilization in a nanosecond, if that were their intention,"* adding that " *the fact that we continue to breathe on this Earth is abundant testimony to the non-hostile nature of these extraterrestrial civilizations."* Greer spoke further, stating that " *the national missile defense system - now supported by the George Bush administration - is actually a cover for the secret deployment of a weapons system to track, target and destroy alien vehicles."* when they approach Earth or enter the atmosphere *."*

Why was Kennedy killed?

Clearly Kennedy was against the conspiracy. He and Abraham Lincoln were among the only US Presidents who were not associated with Secret Societies or Freemasonry. His opposition was clear: « *The very word "secret" is repugnant in a free and open society; and we are, as people, inherently and historically opposed to secret societies, secret oaths, and secret procedures. We decided long ago that the dangers of excessive and unjustifiable concealment of relevant facts outweighed the dangers, which are cited to justify them .*" (John F. Kennedy, addressing newspaper editors, April 27, 1961).

The assassination of John F. Kennedy, his son John Kennedy Jr., and his brother Robert "Bob" appears to be one of the most intricate conspiracies ever carried out by MJ-12. Precisely when George HW Bush was director of the CIA in 1963, it was when the CIA agents in Dallas received the order to assassinate the then president of the United States, and when the son of HW Bush was competing for the presidency of the USA in 2001 against Kennedy's son, he died strangely in the middle of the ocean with his pregnant wife, while taking a plane ride, with good weather conditions and many hours of flight behind him. Although the discovery of some amazing facts that John F. Kennedy planned to communicate to the American people, about the existence of contacts at the highest level, were the major cause of his assassination, as well as issues related to drug trafficking and the Secret Government.

Professor Lawrence Merrick, famous American historian, who had worked for years on the case of the assassination of the president, author of the book "Killing the Messenger: The Death of JFK", in which he makes these impressive revelations.

On November 22, 1963, the then President of the United States, John Fitzgerald Kennedy, traveled to Dallas (Texas). He was traveling in an open limousine, along with his wife and accompanied by the governor of Texas Conally, at 12:30 am, the vehicle enters Dealey Plaza, it was a dry day, suddenly, a guy opens a black umbrella, and various sounds are heard. gunshots, the president had been assassinated and Conally wounded.

The response of whoever murdered him and the real reason for his murder could cause worldwide chaos. In a document delivered by former secret projects military officer Milton William Cooper to Congress in 1989, he wrote: "... *At one point, President Kennedy partially discovered the truth regarding drugs and aliens. In 1963, he issued an ultimatum to MJ-12. He threatened the committee to end the drug problem if they didn't. He informed MJ-12 of his intention to make the American people aware of the existence of aliens and prepared a plan to carry out this decision. President Kennedy was not a member of the CFR (Council on Foreign Relations) and knew nothing of Alternatives 2 or 3. These operations were controlled and directed at the international level by a committee called the Master Plan Committee. President Kennedy's decision disturbed those responsible. His assassination was decided by this committee and carried out by MJ-12 agents in Dallas, at the time when W. Bush Sr. was CIA director and gave the order to assassinate him.* »

« *President Kennedy was assassinated by the secret agent who was driving the car in Dallas. This is clearly evident in the film. If you see her, look carefully at the driver and not at Kennedy. In addition, all eyewitnesses close enough to the car to have seen William Greer shoot Kennedy were also killed over the next two years. The Warren commission was a sham: the majority of the commission of inquiry was made up of members of the CFR – founded by the Rockefeller Freemasons. His efforts to confuse the American public were successful, and in the years since, many other Americans who have tried to make the secret of the aliens public have themselves been assassinated.*"

« *The meetings of the Master Plan Committee even take place inside an atomic submarine under the icy layers of the Pole. The need for secrecy is so pressing that it is the only sure method against eventual eavesdropping. From my own experience and from other sources, I can assume, for example, that the book Third Alternative reflects 70% truth. I suppose that the misinformation contained in the book was nevertheless an attempt to discredit the program broadcast on British television by means of information that could easily be doubted, in the same way as the "Eisenhower briefing" document, published in the USA as a plan of help under the name of "MAJESTIC 12", whose veracity can also be doubted.»*

What was the drug-related factor?

The CIA controlled and controls drug trafficking "intentionally" for decades to subsidize military bases and the facilities of the Ministry of the Navy and Federal institutions that study technological advances with these funds. Due to this, it was decided in 2001 to invade Afghanistan, since it was the number 1 exporter of opium that moves around the globe. Keep in mind that Afghanistan currently produces 80% of the world's opium. From 20% to 40% was produced before the Taliban invasion, after their invasion it only produced less than 10%. It was necessary to take control of this drug market and this was done.

Kennedy, as he said in several previous speeches, was against the attitude of secrecy that was maintained in high military circles, claiming "national security" as an alibi to keep certain events succinct. Weeks before the attack, JF Kennedy had become aware of a series of events that had occurred since 1947, and which made reference to the relationships maintained by important figures in political, military and economic life, with beings foreign to planet Earth, that is, about the Roswell case. Days before the attack, John F. Kennedy had had an interview with the former president of the United States, Dwight D. Eisenhower, and Professor Merrick comments that it is possible that Kennedy was seeking advice to deal with this incredible secret.

After the attack, the documents that Kennedy was carrying that day, including a series of handwritten cards with which the assassinated president helped himself during speeches, were recovered by Governor Conally's men. Subsequently, the governor hid the cards in a safe deposit box, keeping secret the events that the president planned to communicate to the public in Dallas. Years passed, and in 1993, after Conally's death, Professor Merrick discovered the existence of the aforementioned cards. After intense efforts, the Governor's secretary opened the safe in which the manuscripts were hidden. Thus, Prof. Merrick, put the aforementioned cards in the hands of several graphologists who came to the following conclusion: - We give a 95% chance to the fact that these cards were written by the president of the United States JF Kennedy-

John F. Kennedy's last speech

The message that JF Kennedy intended to communicate, and that appears in the manuscript, is the following:

"Dear fellow Americans and inhabitants of the World, today we are leaving for a new era, the childhood of this humanity is ending, and another stage is about to begin. The new stage of which I speak is full of many challenges, but I believe that yesterday, and the discords of the past, have singularly prepared this generation to reach the goal.

Citizens of the world. We are not alone. God, in his infinite wisdom, has populated the Universe with other intelligent beings and creatures like us. With what authority do I allow myself to pronounce these words? In the year 1947, our military forces recovered from the dry desert of New Mexico, the remains of a ship of unknown origin, science determined that this vehicle came from far outer space, since then, our government has had contact with the creators of that spaceship.

Although my news may seem fantastic, and in fact, even terrifying, I urge you not to receive it with fear and pessimism. I assure you as your President, that these beings do not want to do us any harm. In fact, they have promised to help our nation overcome Humanity's most common enemies. - Tyranny, poverty, disease, war

-. We are convinced that they are not only enemies, in fact, they are friends.

Together with them, we can create a good World. I cannot assure you that on the path that we are going to undertake, we will not encounter setbacks and slip-ups. But I believe, that we have found the true destiny of the people of this great Earth, to lead the World towards a glorious future. Over the next few days, weeks and months, you will learn more about these visitors, for they are here and our leaders have kept their presence secret for a long time.

I ask you not to be shy about the future and to face it with courage. Because we can achieve that ancient vision of Peace on Earth and Prosperity for all humanity." (John F. Kennedy, November 22, 1963)

Steven Greer, founder of the Disclosure Project, in the early 1990s informed the first Director of the CIA –R. James Woolsey, Jr.- of President Clinton on the UFO issue, and *"it was made very clear to me that the executive branch of the US government did not want to go public because, and I quote: 'the president was concerned about ending like John Fitzgerald Kennedy.' And I'm not kidding. That's what President Clinton's closest friend told me."* (Steven Greer, FastWalkers)

Positive and Negative Aliens

Even if Kennedy did not know the details about the specific group (grays) with which the US was related, he was at least aware that there was no threat of invasion, or that other entities were in favor of helping us. According to existing information, these "positive" extraterrestrial entities have the following fundamental objectives: Bring humanity knowledge of truth and growth based on the LAW OF LIGHT UNIVERSES, unmask their extraterrestrial-terrestrial leaders, their clones, their estates , practices, cults and religions implanted by them and their organizations; guide man to his true development in his essence of light creation, with the wisdom, strength, truth, knowledge and Law that govern man in the universe, given by the Eternal Father and by all the light forces of Creation.

The fundamental objective for which so many light forces of creation have moved in the galaxy and the universe is the preparation for the coming of Jesus to Earth, where the conscience and works of each human being will be read, where each one will present before Him, the fruits of all that was given to grow in the light; it will be the beginning of a new time, of a new life for humanity; evil will never exist again in any of its forms on Earth; where the teachings that Jesus framed in: "I AM THE WAY, THE TRUTH AND THE LIFE" are understood and practiced. The one who was in the times of Enoch, Ancient of Days, the one who came, Jesus and the one who will come.

These reports say that the total number of positive and negative races in this galaxy is 76, with 136 different types of ships, ranging from 30cm to 10km in diameter, classified as observation ships, manned ships, mother ships and colonies, which They move between solar systems and planets, being able to live in space, under the Earth, in the air and under water.

The positive civilizations of the galaxy would come to be, among others: the Pleiadins or Pleiadians, located in the constellation of the Pleiades, 410 light years from Earth in our way of counting, similar in appearance to humans, white skin, light eyes , blonde hair, height between 2m and 3m, spiritual and luminous bodies, knowledgeable and acting in the LAW, with wisdom, knowledge and consciousness, techno-spiritual technology, union of the energy of mind, spirit and matter; They travel through time and space at speeds greater than light. Other positive civilizations are located in places like the Iades, Gal, Venus, Jupiter, Proxión, Vega among others, being positive, they form a unit and stellar organization for their mutual growth, defense and guidance for themselves and for worlds in the process of development and consciousness in compliance with the LAWS OF CREATION.

In itself, man in his original genetic and light structure of creation called "ADAN" is universal, who has developed in galaxies, solar systems and viable worlds for his existence. Some of the pre-existing civilizations that grew in different solar systems and worlds in the galaxy became negative, destructive and dark due to their violation of the Creational Law and acts against life and Man. These forces were located in the Riguel, Ophiquius, Draco, Orion, Barnaris, Z. Reticuli, Z. Zilón, Z. Tucane, Sirio, Can Mayor, Eridane, Betelgueus, Marcabianos, M-42 System systems, among others. It is also said that they have colonized and subjugated 36 worlds in the galaxy, some in their awakening, have been forced to face them for survival. Both positive and negative forces have arrived on Earth for more than 4,300 million years, each bringing their respective essences and teachings.

Since ancient times men, still primitive in knowledge and technology, saw ships and their crews as gods, said dark negative forces and extraterrestrial beings took advantage of man's condition and supplanted the name of GOD CREATOR, calling themselves gods and angels of God, who from that moment were located on Earth, establishing their bases in different parts of the planet, giving their main base by name, according to some, Agarta, Eden 5, or Shambhala. From there they would have implanted a whole program of death, subjugation, deceit and destruction towards man. Said beings reached different parts of the planet and established religions, in which, supposedly, humans would worship the true Creator God; Said dark program is currently on the planet, at its maximum level, irradiated in all the institutions of the world.

Hardly the true angels of God managed to restore things in a specific point of our geography and began a project of renewal and salvation for humanity through two young people born in the midst of an unprecedented rebellion, who were educated with all wisdom and they were trained and formed to be immortal in the midst of the world in destruction and deterioration. Their offspring fought for survival among hostile peoples and influenced by the Dragon System, and after forming their offspring as a nation they were banished and mixed among the world, so that it would receive its culture, genetic mix, and education, mainly brought by the mouth of disciples. of the king of this nation: Jesus. All this would be necessary to prepare an outcome of the entire rebellion that originated millions of years ago by a general administrator, today known in fables as Satan, his 7 kings and 10 princes who revolted from the General Assembly that rules the universe. All these rebels are believed to have created races from genetic engineering, such as gray aliens, reptilians and so on, while they are hiding vagabonds in other planetary systems waiting to come and destroy the Earth, or, at their discretion, leave. victors and take Creation by force.

The Great Cover Up

The powerful of the world have some notion of this information, but the contact is veiled to them, because the dark ETs have told them their false and disguised version of the facts, so that the elite of this globe can be their useful lackeys. Many people have known part of this for decades - some more than others, although all limited by a small portion of revealed truth -, mostly senior military officials: « *Incidents occurred in the Soviet Union before it collapsed. They also occurred all over North America. At intercontinental missile bases. Where "they" went down, staying on the warehouses and interfering with electronic equipment. Photographs were taken. Hundreds of witnesses watched them. [...] It's top secret, you'll never hear about it, except from snitches and loudmouths like me!*» (Robert O. Dean, retired Master Sergeant)

«*We have more than one witness who has been involved in tracking these objects on radar. And many people say: Well, look if these things are real, why are there no records on the radar? I said, we've got them! We really have the radar tapes! From the FAA (Federal Aviation Administration)!"* (Dr. Steven Greer, The Disclosure Project)

« They are not simply UFOs, nor that we are being visited by guys from other planets. I later learned this; our security, our intelligence people, our military people, concluded and learned, we are not simply dealing with an interplanetary visit. We are being visited by beings from other star systems. Which, technically, we know what he means. They are not just from another analogous planet like Venus or Mars or somewhere...! These guys are from other stars." (Robert O. Dean, Retired Master Sergeant. Served in Field Intelligence Operations while with SHAPE or Supreme Headquarters Allied Power Europe, the NATO arm)

«I am convinced, after studying it since 1958, that the evidence is overwhelming, and the planet Earth is being visited by intelligently controlled extraterrestrial spacecraft. In other words, some UFOs are alien spacecraft." (Stanton T. Friedman, nuclear physicist)

"... They had about 18 scientists, and they've all been working on various stages of the project, gathered around a large oval table at the Los Alamos headquarters with Edward Teller, the head of the Nuclear Energy Commission, sitting at the head of the table, [later] one of the aliens, on the opposite side of my engineer friend's table, wearing a white sweater and pants to look less alien, but of course, he still had his big head and big eyes black aliens, and he was sitting in a conference and could understand each one because he handled telepathy, and it was the only way he could communicate, although he could also communicate by signs that he had developed with my engineer friend to respond to the questions. But the fact is, there was a man, an alien from another planet sitting at a conference, in 1968 at the Los Alamos headquarters, on the progress of the project about

bridging the gap, between alien technology and our own.» (Retired Colonel Wendelle C. Stevens, USAF Fighter Pilot)

"What 10-206 of the Air Force Manual says is: A US Air Force pilot who sees a UFO, has to disclose it [to the institution] in a particular way and manner. They outline in this document exactly how they have to report it. They say: list the size, shape, direction of travel, how big the object was, what were the weather conditions like? And you go through this protocol, and in the end you know, your sighting was a UFO. Then the manual calls for the pilot to take this to NORAD. This is an Air Force base that claims: oh no, we haven't collected this stuff since 1969. The problem is, this form was last updated in October 2004.» (John Greenwald Jr, The Black Vault)

«In 1977 I proposed and became Director of an advanced study on extraterrestrial communications, done together with President Jimmy Carter of the White House. Jimmy Carter, of course, had had a close encounter with a UFO, in the company of 10 members of the Learly Georgia Lions Club in 1969, as he was running for Governor of the state of Georgia. While he was Governor of Georgia in 1973, he had delivered an official UFO report, which is now visible to the entire world on the Internet . In 1976 the American presidential campaign was extraordinary, because Jimmy Carter's proposal was being debated, because on the one hand, he had had a close encounter, and in the campaign, held on a platform, the disclosure of the UFO issue was proposed. Absurd. Jim my Carter was asked about this on several occasions, and it is documented." (Alfred L. Webre, JD, M.Ed.)

«...Well, I am involved in the Political Resolution of... what is usually called... well, what I prefer to call 'The Embargo of the Truth', which the government has imposed, in fact, with respect to the extraterrestrial presence. That presence is established, I think, a long time ago, for the investigations of citizens that have been carried out

since the 1940s. The government did studies, but they were primarily as a show to look good. And the censorship of the matter from the government's point of view has been run, very intensively, since 1947 at the earliest! Managing this censorship. The government took care of this, but divided the powers with the National Security cabinet, and they will never recognize that this phenomenon exists.» (Stephen Basset, founder of Paradigma Research Group)

«In one night I saw between 200 and 300 different individuals, white and tall, they were so many that I could not count them, lined up along the mountains to the east, where the ammunition bunker [of the Nellis Air Force Base] was. On the night the tall white lady known as Pamela, who was supposed to finish her exam to be head of the technology transfer team, was supposed to go to Livermore. Among those 200 to 300 tall whites [...] there were also US Air Force personnel, no one below the rank of Colonel. There were others like a 4-star General rank, a 3-star one. There were many of them. In addition, there were many people from the American government, in civilian clothes there." (Charles Hall, author and nuclear physicist)

«How can we know exactly how many extraterrestrial races are visiting us or interacting with humanity? Well, there are different sources spreading this information. I find one of the most credible 'snitchers', people who have worked on various secret projects, who have somehow been given information that gives them an idea of exactly how many races there are. One such source is Air Force Staff Sgt. Clifford Stone. And he has been participating in these secret projects, which involve the recovery of crashed UFOs. In the process he was able to obtain some information about how many extraterrestrial races are visiting us, and he proposed the figure of 57. Others have gone so far as to suggest that there are more. Another important whistleblower, a CIA employee, is John Lear. And he talks about 60 races, who are visiting Earth." (Dr. Michael E. Salla, Ph.D.)

«*There are various groups, individuals, species, that from time to time come and visit this planet, and I think that trying to attribute any particular motive to them is equivalent to us looking in the air for a Boeing 767 plane and saying: are those good people? or bad? You know, you just can't ask that. They are just a group of intelligent beings, some of them are good and some of them are not. But I must say that I don't think there is any reason for great fear and anxiety."* (Jim Marrs, author and journalist)

«*My life changed and I was never the same again. So the study itself was as comprehensive as it could have been. They concluded what they wanted to conclude: 1. There was no threat involved; 2. It wasn't the Soviets; 3. The evidence was overwhelming, they were aliens; 4. There were 4 groups involved. Four different groups. And all of them were humanoid. But they were not human. Only one of the 4 groups was what we consider to be human beings. One of the four groups looks a lot like us. Almost identical to us, I mean."* (Robert O. Dean)

« *These aliens have a body like ours, and these UFOs... I am using this in a broad sense, or the people inside the ship, it is very difficult to think how they could have crossed such enormous distances? They must come from a planet thousands of kilometers away, huge. So it is likely and logical that they are inside a ship, instead of coming from somewhere without a transport vehicle. So they must be made up of a spiritual part, like the soul, they must be people like us. They must have a body, otherwise they would be angels."* (Corrado Balducci, Monsenior)

«*There is this 'ridicule curtain' that is drawn around the UFO phenomenon, and as long as that smear curtain is strong, scientists will be afraid to contribute to anything, or investigate UFOs directly. And part of this curtain of ridicule involves the fact that no major newspaper has published the scientific information on the subject. So the curtain of ridicule can be pulled back slightly now that they have the papers they can refer to, if they feel like writing their own UFO papers."* (Dr. James W. Deardorff, Ph. D. author and researcher)

« Secrecy has invaded, like a cancer, many institutions, including the media, the government and corporations. "The only institution that is more corrupt than what I describe as 'Transnational Cleoptocracy' is the mass media. Worse than Congress, worse than the White House, worse than the Pentagon and its enormous levels of command, is the big media. The mainstream media do not report the truth about these things, because they are not free to do so [...] This is the biggest secret in the history of the human race. In the modern history of government. And they have cooperated to keep it a secret." (Steven Greer)

«As this cover-up continues, it is maintained, beyond international borders, and if it is, are their motivations the same? The most likely guess is that since America (US) has so much economic power, even worse than America hating you, America ignoring you. So many economies are dependent on the US that I think they take orders from America in some way. When you talk about the UFO cover-up, then the US dictates what to do." (Rob Simone, researcher and radio director)

« There is an overwhelming mass of evidence, real, government documents that have been released in large part, through the 'free access to information law', showing decades of, for example, airline violations. Very protected places, where objects are seen doing what seemed to be the impossible. We have these documents from the '40s. We have them from the '50s, we have them from the '60s, '70s, '80s, and beyond. So these air violations continue. They're provocative... they're occasionally, seemingly contentious. We have the pilots who have been going to meet [them], who have been denounced for chasing these phenomena, and they have described it from time to time, saying: 'yes, it seems to be a metallic disc shape, there it goes.' »

(Richard Dolan, author and researcher. National Press Club of Washington press conference - Exopolitics)

«I started in this matter trying to reverse engineer anti-gravity devices in 1968, but now I am looking for official secret documents. And some of the documents tell an impressive story. One of the discovered documents started with Franklin Delano Roosevelt, and FDR (D. Roosevelt) had the system, by Vannevar Bush, called the 'non-terrestrial science and engineering' committee. These were the scientists, after the recovery of a crashed flying saucer in 1942, who had been given the parts and charged with figuring out how they worked. They went back to FDR in 1944 and asked for the money. And he said, 'No. First we have to win the war and defeat the Nazis. And then in 1947, Vannevar Bush went to see President Truman, who didn't know about all this, and he said, 'By the way, we have these abilities, we could do some reverse engineering so that we can improve our country, improve our culture, improve our standard of living. And that's when the money started flowing." (Dr. Robert M. Wood Ph.D., physicist)

«Surely there are rules and regulations that govern everything. And the [Galactic] 'Councils' have the history books of all the planets and all the records. Thus, when a planet reaches the point where it can support life, it is a pivotal moment in that planet's history. At that moment, the planet is given its statutes of Life." (Dolores Cannon, author and researcher)

"Everything has been covered up. The toxicity of pharmaceuticals, you don't know the truth about vaccinations, you don't know the truth about many medications. The pharmaceutical industrialists, which I prefer to call the 'Military Pharmaceutical Medical Petrochemical Cartel', basically have control over the mass media, and therefore have control over the minds of the masses. And as a result of those imposing powers, people are not given factual information by which they can make informed decisions. They receive propaganda. And as a result,

the decisions that people make are genocidal, and I mean genocidal in the strict sense, that is, the mass murder of people for economic, political and/or ideological reasons. And those pharmaceutical industrialists are intimately connected with those people who want to control the population. They have written about what their intent is, not just about how to control it, why their control is necessary, but ultimately to influence current technologies to do just that. As of today, a 50% reduction of the planet's population has been set as the goal to be achieved.» (Dr. Len Horowitz, author and researcher)

"Humanity was developed as a species, as a spiritual being. And I think that we have strayed so far from who we really are that it is very difficult for us to go back and digest that perhaps we have cosmic brothers and sisters. We fight each other over our differences, I mean, if someone comes along and they're completely different, we fight each other. So I think, oh my gosh! What are the ETs involved thinking about our way of behaving with people different from us...? They're probably terrified of showing up because of what we might do to them. We haven't handled diversity very well." (Paola Harris)

«One day I hope that the people of Earth rise up and extend their hand as friends to those peoples, we have never done that on this planet. You know, we've shot them. We have done everything: we have shot with radar, we have shot lasers, [with] everything. We have to say... 'Hello!'." (Alan G. Tolman, aerospace engineer)

Let 's think about it. You can't say, 'Good! Star Children! These wonderful advanced children have been transformed by contact with star people, while at the same time you say that there are no such things as UFOs ." (Dr. Richard Boylan Ph. D. writer)

CONCLUSION

The extraterrestrial, intraterrestrial and ultraterrestrial existence is an undeniable fact and is capable of changing the lives of people who investigate and delve into learning more about this entire subject. Thinking and knowing more about extraterrestrial civilizations opens the way to a new world of possibilities, theories, existential approaches, changes in consciousness and universal understanding.

All our historical records are very clear about the visit of "space brothers", also about wars and political divisions in our galaxy. The ancestral visits were made in order to improve the conditions of our world for the development and sustainability of multiple forms of life, but the insurrection in armed forces that were destined for Earth -and elsewhere- changed all the plans of the high command of those who administer the existing worlds. Later, the visits were longer and more periodic, all for the purpose of establishing colonies on our world. About all these facts, our world is plagued with clear evidence, both of these visits and of the astronauts that appeared in prehistory.

The most significant changes to our world would have come hundreds of thousands of years, perhaps even millions, to genetically create "intelligent" life forms and to modify the life forms that had been brought here to adapt to the varied ecosystems of Earth. our globe. Later, as prehistoric civilizations flourished, other beings from space came and caused a quantum leap in human culture, changing a world in caves for a civilized society, knowledgeable in agriculture, mathematics, astronomy, medicine, metallurgy. , pyramid builder, and promoter of civil laws and orders. Not enough, this was not as favorable as it seemed at first sight, and it provoked a revolution in all social areas, including bloody wars that prevailed for centuries.

But where did all these visitors come from? Who created them? Why have they not helped us out of tyranny and poverty? The records speak of an unprecedented war that took place in our galaxy billions of years ago when the physical world that came from the mental universe materialized: « The universe was made by the word *of God, so that what is seen it was made of what was not seen.* » (Hebrews 11:3. New Testament) Not in a way as creationism believes that the universe was created, but in a quantum way complicated to describe, more like a thought explosion; thus was created what exists. Although we will deal with all this in detail in "The Sakla Rebellion", we must clarify the fact that some of the first collaborators in the life projects, with their way of being intransigent, led to a rebellion. It was supposed that everything was being shaped from the invisible universe to the visible one to deliver it to the one who should reign over all: The Son. For this reason it was written: «... *because in him all things were created, those that are in heaven and those that are on Earth, visible and invisible; be thrones, be dominions, be principalities, be powers; everything was created through him and for him.*" (Colossians 1:16)

As the order in the universe drastically changed, opposing factions appeared in the galaxy, and this is recorded in the historical annals of Contact groups, mythologies, and religions. At the time of this, genetic engineering and strife increased, leading to the manipulation of entire human and animal races, as well as causing political splits and warfare of all kinds. Humanity as we know it, would come to emerge in the midst of these events, which is recorded in the legends and mythologies of our world.

The ultimate goal of all those regressive institutions (SAS – Service To Themselves) would be to consolidate their great legendary sedition, and in the present, on our planet, found an empire of slavery, subjection and social manipulation. The counterpart, the positive classes (SAO – Service To Others) would be collaborating with humans from Venus and the Pleiades, in favor of the spiritual liberation of human beings, the regeneration and improvement of their bodies, and their integration into the universal concert. This second group would have been called in the Old Testament as "malachim" and in the New Testament as "aggelous", which, in both cases, are protective entities, ministers of the Universal Father, officials of the "Kingdom of Heavens" come from to help and minister to us.

When will they return?

At the end of 2010, astrophysicist Craig Kasnov of the SETI project confirmed what had been said from different sources: "*three gigantic objects are approaching Earth*." It is also known that more than one giant object circles Saturn, another one approaches 18° RA from the orbit of Neptune, another is stationed long ago 1.5 million miles from our south pole, in the middle of outer space. There are also ships with the Hale-Bopp comet. Everything is at the gates. It is expected that in a few years a first contact with people from Mars will begin, including that the United Nations will receive a first extraterrestrial group sometime between the end of 2011 or the end of 2012, according to Alfred Webre (Adviser to the then President of the USA), Jimmy Carter). Professor Wang Sichao, a planetary astronomer at the Purple Hills Observatory of the Chinese Academy of Sciences, publicly declared on August 6, 2010, that between 2011 and 2012 the Earth would be visited by a massive arrival of interplanetary spacecraft -although that hasn't happened yet. Later, on the 23rd of that same month, he declared to the media that some of the ships that visit us work with antigravity devices and that a large percentage of UFOs filmed and photographed to date are really of extraterrestrial origin.

Furthermore, in contrast to the prestigious professor Stephen Hawking, who also recently stated that intelligent extraterrestrial life is probably predatory in nature, Wang dismissed that theory as "alarmist and premature" and stated that "a species of aliens are visiting Earth *with research and development purposes only, and therefore are friendly and capable enough to initiate cooperation and mutual exchange with our species.*" A summary of Wang's remarks was published by a number of Chinese newspapers, including the influential "People Online." Word has since begun that the Chinese authorities are tacitly fomenting an exopolitical debate about the motivations of advanced extraterrestrial life in order to prepare the Chinese and the world public for the inevitable official disclosure of the existence of extraterrestrials, while that the most "conspiracy theorists" are also disseminating through the streets of China the theory that all these recent scientific statements about extraterrestrial life are just cover-ups to justify the existence of "military UFOs".

However, some suggest that this is all part of the Blue Beam project, a future holographic setup that NASA wants to develop by UN opinion -according to some at the London Olympics and/ or, later- to develop an alien invasion. artificial in space. In this way they would force all the nations of the planet to drop their nuclear weapons to defend themselves and only the UN, the connoisseur of fraud, would be left with weapons, to then establish a Single Global Army for a Single Global Government. Likewise, this would be part of a three-dimensional montage game to expose a false Rapture where God would come to take away the Christians of the world. One more trap of the world government.

God bless you!